Prologue

Donald R. Brown and Joseph Veroff

University of Michigan

The present volume consists of original contributions prepared for presentation in October 1985, at the colloquium honoring John W. Atkinson on his retirement from active teaching at The University of Michigan. Each chapter was revised for publication and represents the current perspective of the authors all of whom were doctoral or postdoctoral students of Atkinson.

As a psychologist who devoted himself to trying to unravel the theoretical bases of human strivings, Atkinson has had a profound impact on motivational psychology. He taught many, collaborated with many, and through his writings affected countless others. On the occasion of his retirement, this series of papers was thus a partial payback for these many sources of inspiration. Some of his co-researchers and former students were invited to speak of their current interests in motivational research. This book is a testimony to the rippling effect that Jack's work has had on the science of human motivation in general.

Some of the papers were directly derivative of Atkinsonian thinking; others were more their own visions of human strivings with only a subtle lineage to an Atkinsonian perspective. Nonetheless, they all shared Atkinson's enthusiastic analysis of theory, but theory that lends itself to framing specific research procedures and to collecting data that can inform not only about original ideas, but also about ideas not yet considered.

What is the Atkinsonian perspective? We cannot tersely sum up an answer to that question; we cannot come up with a summary sentence that represents the essential Atkinson except for his continuing stress on expectancy, activation, and individual differences. Perhaps that is so because Jack Atkinson's career covers at least three different theoretical periods. While they built on each other, these different periods focused on distinctive problems. The first period reflected his own fascination with Lewinian thinking about the dynamic interaction of personality with the environment. Beginning with his own doctoral dissertation, he explored human motives not as traits willy nilly evident in behavior, but as dispositions that interacted with various specific life situations to affect ongoing behavior. Murray's newfound method of coding motives from stories told in response to pictures, the TAT, inspired many people's wish to see how these assessments predicted behavior in real life contexts. Atkinson was no exception. He quickly realized that motives affected the intensity of a person's striving and the kinds of alternatives selected out of an array of choices. The way he went about demonstrating these effects was in a Lewinian perspective. The particular settings where achievement behaviors and choices occurred were carefully noted. The method of assessment of motives, derived in collaboration with David McClelland, became an intriguing avenue for thinking about the dynamic model that Lewin offered. No clearer unraveling of the Zeigarnik phenomenon has occurred than in

Atkinson's work on this problem many decades ago (Atkinson, 1953). His research showed that need for achievement affected recall of successes and failures differently under different conditions of ego-involvement. Both person and environment must be attended to simultaneously.

He found this Lewinian position vague and so he became much more preoccupied about honing in on the nature of both the structure of personality and the dynamics of situations. With this set, he developed his own version, an expectancy-value model, a theoretical perspective that became his second career position. His theory of achievement motivation, derived from this more explicit look at the concepts that were involved in situational analysis, had far reaching consequences for thinking about human strivings.

These were very seminal years. Many of his students began to elaborate and articulate the general framework of expectancy value interactions with new concepts—such as, increasing the time perspectives on goals, thinking about new avoidant motives that describe motive structures, adding to the number of motivations that underlay both expectancies and values for particular tendencies, considering the meaning of persistence as a reflection of a variety of tendencies, and refining the combining rules that make up the multiplicative functions of this theory.

Not content with the specification of the thinking during the second period, he and David Birch moved on to still another period and developed a very new perspective about motivation that looked simultaneously at all behavioral tendencies that occurred over time. He graduated to a general theory of human action specifying formally all the parameters thought to govern change in activity. This was a totally new way of looking at human action, not as discrete discontinuous actions but as a stream of behavior. The dynamics of action was born. The complexity of the parameters was too great for ordinary human processing, and thus his excitement about computer simulation. This was a far cry from his early dissertation work on the Zeigarnik phenomenon. The future of motivational psychology began to come into perspective.

The trouble with many of us who were connected with Jack's thinking from each of the stages is that we were unable to move as quickly as he was into new orbits of motivational analysis. There were those who were stuck in the first period—wishing to explain the variety of factors that explain personality x situation interaction. There were those of us who started working on the details of the more specific expectancy-value position and came to be devotees of Atkinson's thinking about that issue. Many of us have remained there. Nevertheless, there are those of us who started with or did become involved with the more sophisticated and formal dynamics of action involved in the thinking.

The papers in this series sample from each of these stages. Some represent a bit from each of these stages. Some represent only one of them. While the differentiation of his thinking clearly evolved over his career such that his interest in the first stage waned as he moved on to the second and incorporated his thinking from the first, and his interest in the second stage waned as he moved on to the third and incorporated the thinking from the second, the impact of any one of these stages by themselves remained fresh and long in much of our own thinking. So let us go through each of the stages to see how the various ideas and researches that are examined in the papers for this volume carry on the essential theoretical issues highlighting each stage.

There are a number of examples in this volume that reflect the first stage in Atkinson's thinking (the dynamic theory of personality summarized by the personality x situation formulation). A major question asked in this theory is, how do you assess personality to begin with? How do you assess a motive as a dispositional aspect of a person which can be seen as something transacted in a variety of settings? In this volume are a number of psychologists who began with his original formulation but are now suggesting new ways. Raynor and Nochajski's paper has given us a research program for looking at the motive orientation to a specific type of goal. They are convinced that assessment has to be done with regard to specific activities and not to general categories of activities like achievement. Once they generate a technique for assessing motivational constructs for any given behavior, like sports, they feel the technique can be generalized to any other specific behavior. Feather, long a devotee of the motive assessment for personality, introduces in his paper a new way to gauge motives—through conscious values. Values were once thought to be only a small part of motivational life. Feather presents evidence to make us take values more seriously in the delineation of personality. Veroff's paper points also to conscious values as important assessments of personality, but it does not make motives and values functionally equivalent as Feather does. Furthermore, Veroff suggests that one should look at a variety of motives as the pattern of personality, and not just one at a time. He also notes that we should examine how a given motive differs at different points of life stage development.

In Blankenship's compilation of the many uses of the computer in motivation research, there is yet another suggestion for how we should assess the achievement motive. An intriguing computer technique is suggested. While Brody did not address the assessment of motives directly in his paper, implicit in his argument about unconscious motivation lies a justification for assessing motives through procedures that would permit unconscious processes to come through. He gives us some exciting reinterpretations of new and old data to show that unconscious processes of motivation are not simply summarized by what people can verbalize directly about their experience. Affect may play key roles in our behavior quite separately from what we can consciously verbalize about our feelings. Brody does not point this out, but this conclusion was an old assumption of the TAT assessment of motives. Thus, with its careful documentation of unconscious processes, Brody's paper could be used as a rationale for the procedures that Atkinson first adopted to measure motives and persisted with through all stages of his career.

There are also many ideas in the papers presented in the volume that pertain to the second level of development of Atkinson's thinking. The expectancy value position that he formulated in this second stage posited that tendencies to act a given way are an interactive function of motives, expectancies and values. This was a deceptively simple formulation, first applied to level of aspiration choice but then applied to other phenomena, such as persistence under conditions of failure. Many researchers both in this country and abroad used it as a basis for experimental studies, especially in educational settings. They gradually elaborated its simplicity, and we still have those who are attempting to articulate and refine its theoretical implications. Let us list some of the ideas reflecting their position found in papers in this volume.

In a scholarly paper about research on people's perception of future time, an offshoot of an expectancy concept, Lens suggests that we look at the future time perspective that persons have as part and parcel of their motivation. A person expresses values or goals within a future time frame, and how persons localize these goals within that future, Lens feels, will be diagnostic of the quality of their motivation. New vs. distant goals are new ways of thinking about risk-taking originally considered in the expectancy-value formulation.

Feather has linked the motive and value formulation as being possibly more related than Atkinson originally considered. In the original position they are seen as separate concepts. Feather sees values as functionally equivalent to motives. The implications of that assumption are very far reaching for the simple expectancy-value position both Atkinson and Feather started with.

Weiner's paper suggests that the basis of value may be in the implicit affects that are associated with people's attributions to their own behavior and the behavior of others. Weiner thus sees attributions about our past specific behaviors as emotional proscriptions for future action. The attributional scheme for emotions that Weiner proposes is a new way of looking at both values and expectancies. Brody's paper implies that we look more closely at the unconscious as a generator of motives, expectancies and values. Raynor and Nochajski's paper focuses in more closely on the whole notion of competence as a basis of expectancy and also systematically sees that it is important to distinguish positive from negative orientations to values.

Finally, there are ideas in the papers presented in this volume that reflect the most mature level of differentiation in Atkinson's thinking; the dynamics of action point of view. Revelle's paper brings into sharp focus the fact that it is the rate of change in the stream of behavior that a motivational theorist wants to predict and understand, rather than a specific change itself. This is a general principle of the dynamics of action position. Revelle suggests a pair of principles that may give us some leverage in making such predictions.

In a series of elegant studies, Blankenship employs the concept of consummatory value and she postulates that consummatory values for success and failure are different. She finds these postulates useful in predicting that her subjects will react differently and based many of her predictions on computer simulation of dynamics of action outcomes.

Kuhl, in a very exciting paper, suggests that the ongoing processes of change that are implied by the Atkinson and Birch position in the dynamics of action, should lead to predictions of indeterminacy. Kuhl argues that while theory building generally leads to more and more elaborated concepts and principles to handle changes in the stream of behavior that occur over time that are not simply predicted, the dynamics of action position should predict chaos at certain points. Kuhl's position says that if you take the dynamics of action position seriously, that in fact there would be specific predictions of multiple possibilities in behavior tendencies rather than the activation of a single behavior tendency.

And Birch, who worked with Atkinson in the original statement of the dynamics of action model, expands it even further. He speaks of the problem of understanding how much time it takes to activate a particular behavior given the strength of various tendencies to act that people have. He raises a very important question for motivation: What is meant by a tendency in the first place? What unit of action should one use in describing a tendency, the basic building block of the dynamics of action? He carefully outlines the implications of taking one or another unit of action in making predictions.

Thus we have ideas in the papers in this volume which reflect basic issues raised at each of the stages of Atkinson's thinking. On the one hand, these are all new ideas. On the other hand, they reflect some of the basic notions that Atkinson had proposed at different points in his career. While these papers echo the voices prescribed by an Atkinson orchestration, they also lead us into very new sounds. There is a considerable diversity in the ideas that are suggested by these papers and there are distinctively new developments emerging from his devotees. Atkinson never got caught up in the desire to make motivational theory cognitive. Although he maintained that motivation involves cognitive determinants, for him affective dispositions and reactions ruled the day. It would be hard to label Atkinson as a cognitive motivational psychologist. While cognitive processes are always evident in his thinking, they were downplayed. Motives are real forces for selecting and accentuating human strivings. And so it is perhaps within the cognitive realm that many of the papers presented in this volume expand beyond the concepts articulated by Atkinson. Lens on time perspective, Weiner on affective attribution, Raynor on the specification of feedback, Feather on relationship of attitudes to values, all are scientists pursuing new cognitive views of motivation.

Another distinctive feature of some of these papers that is different from an Atkinsonian perspective is that many of them focus on the specific context for behaving as critical to the analysis of motivation. For Raynor this requires a complete overhaul in methods of assessment. For Veroff this means enumerating a variety of ways of thinking about changes in the motive as people go into or emerge from different contexts in their lives. For Weiner this means interpreting affective experiences less unidimensionally. Achievement affects are not merely achievement affects according to Weiner. They can be described as shame or guilt depending on the situation surrounding the experience of a failure. Atkinson always had a flair for the more abstract way of thinking about motivation, the theory that perhaps generically underlay the way people operate. He was less distracted by the mundane, the specific settings that people find themselves in when they are achievement motivated or concerned about failure, or the like. He did not ignore them but he did not give his full attention to these issues. So, by savoring the contexts in which people's motivations exist, many of the papers establish new directions from an Atkinsonian view.

While the diversity of these papers does speak to theorists and researchers being their own persons, the diversity also speaks to the versatility of the scientific mind of the person in whose honor they were written. Jack Atkinson looked down many avenues, found many fellow travellers along the way, and now has a legion of motivation psychologists who are willing and interested in following whatever path it requires to create a systematic understanding of the dynamics of human action. These diverse papers expand his remarkable contribution into the next decades.

REFERENCE

Atkinson, J. W. (1953). The achievement motive and recall of interrupted and completed tasks. *Journal of Experimental Psychology, 46*, 381–390.

ACKNOWLEDGEMENTS

This volume owes its existence to many. First of all to Jack Atkinson whom it honors. His stature as a scholar, his role as mentor, friend and colleague made easy the task of enticing such a stellar group of his students to assemble and to contribute to this volume. The support of the Department of Psychology and its Chairman, Albert Cain, a grant from the President's Fund of the University of Michigan, and the resources of the Center for Research on Learning and Teaching provided the wherewithal to proceed. Most important was the work of Susan Nelson, Shirley Silverman and Nancy Bates of the Department of Psychology with the arrangements for the affair itself. The greatest debt is owed to Maria Huntley whose skill, patience and goodwill shepherded this volume through the technology of electronic composition. She was assisted in these tasks by Lynda Ward-Stevenson, June Brown, and Maureen Lopez.

We gratefully acknowledge all of these contributors as well as the chapter authors.

Donald R. Brown

Joseph Veroff

CONTRIBUTORS

David Birch
Department of Psychology
University of Illinois at Urbana-Champaign
603 E. Daniel
Champaign, Illinois 61820

Virginia Blankenship
Department of Psychology
Oakland University
Rochester, Michigan 48063

Nathan Brody
Department of Psychology
Wesleyan University
Middletown, Connecticut 06457

Donald Brown
Department of Psychology
580 Union Drive
University of Michigan
Ann Arbor, Michigan 48109

Norman Feather
Discipline of Psychology
Flinders University of South Australia
Bedford Park
South Australia 5042
Australia

Julius Kuhl
University of Osnabrück
Department of Psychology
Postfach 4469
D-4500 Osnabrück
West Germany

Willy Lens
Department of Psychology
University of Leuven
Tiensestraat 102
3000 Leuven
Belgium

David McClelland
Department of Psychology and Social Relations
William James Hall
33 Kirkland Street
Harvard University
Cambridge, Massachusetts 02138

Thomas Nochajski
State University of New York at Buffalo (SUNY)
Department of Psychology
4230 Ridge Lea Road
Amherst, New York 14226

Joel Raynor
State University of New York at Buffalo (SUNY)
Department of Psychology
4230 Ridge Lea Road
Amherst, New York 14226

William Revelle
Department of Psychology
Northwestern University
Evanston, Illinois 60201

Joseph Veroff
Department of Psychology
University of Michigan
580 Union Drive
Ann Arbor, Michigan 48109

Bernard Weiner
Department of Psychology
University of California at Los Angeles
405 Hilgard Avenue
Los Angeles, California 90024

TABLE OF CONTENTS

Chapter Seven

MOTIVATION AND EFFICIENCY OF COGNITIVE
PERFORMANCE 107

William Revelle

Northwestern University

Chapter Eight

CONTEXTUALISM AND HUMAN MOTIVES 132

Joseph Veroff

University of Michigan

Chapter One

DEVELOPMENT OF THE MOTIVATION FOR

PARTICULAR ACTIVITY SCALE

Joel O. Raynor and Thomas H. Nochajski

State University of New York at Buffalo

The senior author began research on achievement motivation over 20 years ago (Raynor & Smith, 1965) when the concept of subjective-expected value was entirely defined in terms of perceived difficulty of a particular activity—that is, as the inverse of expectancy of success in theory of achievement motivation (Atkinson, 1957). This research has evolved from the study of future orientation as a determinant of aroused motivation (Raynor, 1969, 1974), to interest in the role of self-importance and the self-system (Raynor, 1982a; Raynor & McFarlin, 1986), to concern over perceived competence (Raynor & Brown, 1985) and past importance (Nochajski, 1986). Now, almost full circle, we are interested in the study of motivation for particular activity.

During this time there has developed an increasingly more complex and elaborated conceptual scheme for specifying the determinants of achievement motivation for a particular activity in a particular situation (Raynor & Entin, 1982). However, it has become apparent that concern with conceptual issues has come to dominate over concern about discovering new empirical relationships. The enterprise seemed to be primarily theory-driven rather than data-driven. While this is a laudable long-term goal, the limitations of existing empirical relationships (their lack of robustness and replicability) made me increasingly feel a premature commitment to explanation in great detail of data that could not completely support such a complex conception. Whether that feeling is/was justified, it was strong enough to direct a "return to basics," as it were, to confront the issue of stable and replicable findings in research on human motivation.

The study of human motivation must be relevant to the understanding of life activity. The prediction and explanation of that activity is the primary goal of scientific study. A concern for empiricism, measurement, and stable relationships between variables should play as important a role as the development of theory. Initial research on achievement motivation is an excellent example of how theory building was guided by data collection. But the preoccupation with theoretical issues has lead researchers to use the implications of their equations as the primary source of inspiration. This need not be the case. I decided to use those empirical relationships that I thought were robust, replicable and directly relevant to motivation of life activity to guide a return to empiricism. The first step in such a return seemed to require addressing the issue of measurement of human motivation for life activity.

The primary goal in work on the Motivation for Particular Activity Scale (MPAS) was to develop and begin to validate a self-report measure of motivation for particular life activity. While traditional measures of achievement motivation (n Achievement and Test Anxiety) have generated a substantial amount of construct validity (Atkinson & Feather, 1966; Atkinson & Raynor, 1974; Raynor & Entin 1982), they suffer from two apparent inadequacies. First, they are unable to account for substantial amounts of variance in criterion variables despite the increasingly greater number of variables with which they are seen as interacting to determine resultant motivation. While measurés of achievement-related motives are not alone in this regard (intelligence tests apparently do no better), continued extension into increasingly greater conceptual complexity does not seem to have increased the robustness of their predictive efficiency. One strategy has been to accept this lack of robustness and build theory to explain the variability in behavior (Atkinson & Birch, 1978). There can be an alternative approach. Use of a simple measure of perceived importance has led to substantial and replicable relationships with variables involved in career striving (Raynor & Entin, 1982; Raynor & Brown, 1985). This measure accounts for far greater variance with much less conceptual complexity needed to explain its functioning. Second, an important pragmatic issue has arisen. Particularly for the n Achievement score, inability to meet criteria for internal consistency has become a serious handicap. No amount of debating the validity of a new theory of testing that might underpin the logic of the n Achievement score without internal consistency (Atkinson & Birch, 1978) seems to make its use more acceptable to a generation of psychologists recognizing factor analysis, convergent and discriminant validity, and multiple regression as means of validating a test and accounting for variance in a criterion.

Evidence that conceptually relevant, self-report measures might be developed that are relatively homogeneous and able to account for substantial variance in life activity comes from previous studies in my research program on career striving as well as the recent work of Spence and Helmrich (1983). Recent work suggests that high intercorrelations are obtainable between various measures of perceived competence, perceived importance, affective reactions, and reports of time spent in activity, in the range of .5 to .7. This makes use of self-report measures of human motivation a worthwhile and promising enterprise. If previous attempts with self-report methodology were relatively unsuccessful, perhaps their content rather than their structural properties precluded obtaining meaningful relationships. Work reported by Spence and Helmrich (1983) suggests that use of self-report methodology is worthwhile. After all, use of the Test Anxiety Questionnaire for almost 30 years suggests that individuals can make meaningful self-reports about motivational variables. The accumulation of research findings suggested some clear notions about changes in the contents of self-reports that might lead to robust, replicable findings as well as further conceptual understanding.

To anticipate the coverage of this chapter, we have developed a new assessment device that can be targeted to any activity, that has high internal consistency and temporally-short (6 to 8 weeks) test-retest reliability (both are .9 for a 24-item scale). Relationships between conceptually-derived component scales are meaningful and show expected gender differences. Results make intuitive sense concerning the predominance of doing well versus finding out about ability in activity where competition rather than assessment of ability appears to be more important. Initial data bearing on the relationship between the MPAS and traditional measures of n Achievement and Test Anxiety suggest they are unrelated. Relationships of the MPAS or its component scales to various laboratory behaviors and assessments of career striving serve as a starting point for interpreting the meaning of scores and building a conceptual framework. Validation has just begun, however, and the primary purpose of this report is to present properties of the instrument and an indication of relationships among its component scales.

Conceptual Scales of the MPAS

Perceived competence was included because of its importance in a number of conceptual approaches, including Bandura's (1977) views of self-efficacy, research on self-esteem, Nicholl's (1984) emphasis on demonstration of ability in ego-involving achievement situations, and Trope's (1986) continued concern with self-assessment in achievement activity. Most importantly, degree of possession of self-relevant attributes had been shown to correlate substantially with ratings of the future- and self-importance of possession of such attributes (Raynor & English, 1982) in a number of different studies (Raynor, 1982b). Perceived importance was included based on its critical role in arousal of achievement motivation as evidenced in many laboratory and field studies, including its predictive efficiency in several studies of career striving (Raynor & Entin, 1982; Raynor & Brown, 1985) and its relationship to affective reactions in test-taking situations (Raynor & English, 1982). Both future-importance and self-importance were included because they are substantially correlated in all but one of many studies. Measures of positive and negative affect were included based on their successful use as indicators of arousal of positive and negative achievement tendencies, respectively, in research on achievement motivation (Raynor, Atkinson, & Brown, 1974; Pearlson, 1982; Raynor & Entin, 1983) and their meaningful relationships to importance and perceived competence (Raynor & English, 1982; Raynor & Brown, 1985).

The distinction between doing well and finding out/demonstrating competence was included because recent conceptual emphasis in theory of achievement motivation has shifted from affective value (doing well to experience positive affect) to information value (finding out to be clear about how much competence is possessed). This distinction was addressed because most of recent research on achievement motivation emphasizes information value, while earlier research emphasizes affective value. Conceptual issues dictated attempts to assess both kind of motivation (Raynor & McFarlin, 1986).

Note that concepts concerning stable dispositions were explicitly excluded from consideration in the development of the MPAS on the assumption that evidence for such stability was an empirical question to be answered by research rather than a conceptual property to be assessed. Preliminary work suggests that replicable and stable (over a brief period of two months) patterns of relationships between variables comprising the scale can be obtained.

Specificity of Motivation for Particular Activity

The commitment to a strategy of measuring motivation for particular activity was empirical rather than conceptual. That is, two unpublished studies[1] strongly suggested that relationships among perceived possession of attributes, self-importance and future-importance, and positive and negative affective reactions were similar across different activities, but correlations between each measure when obtained for different activities were much smaller and often not statistically reliable. The overwhelming impression was that correlations among conceptually relevant dimensions were substantial for a particular target activity, similar for other target activities, and substantially higher within a particular activity than between activities.

In the first study, subjects were asked to rate the extent they perceived themselves as being each of eight person-descriptors, each thought to represent a different kind of activity; domestic worker, sports analyst, financially self-supporting person, company director, typist-stenographer, intelligent person, foreign correspondent, and a person highly respected in the community. Subjects then indicated to what extent seeing themselves as each was important for their own positive self-evaluation, for attaining their own future goals, how desirable was seeing themselves as each, and how eager they were to participate in activity related to each. A separate sample of subjects rated each person-description (i.e., activity) as masculine, feminine, and along a combined masculine-feminine dimension. The intercorrelation matrix showed rs among assessed variables within person-descriptors that ranged from .61 to .87 ($N = 222$) versus rs between activities that ranged from $-.10$ to .50. Medians for within-activity rs were .79 for males ($N = 71$) and .81 for females ($N = 151$), while median between-activity rs were .20 for males and .17 for females. The average within-activity r was .78 for males and .80 for females while the average between-activity rs were .34 for males and .17 for females.

Factor analysis using the principle components method of factor extraction and varimax orthogonal rotation supports the conclusion that the person-descriptors as target activities represented specific dimensions. The analysis yielded 9 factors, with the first 5 corresponding to 5 of the 8 descriptors. Each of the first four factors show that the 5 questions for that activity load highly on that specific dimension, and low on other dimensions. For example, the first factor represents "sports analyst" with factor loadings for items from .82 to .91, with loadings across other factors from $-.09$ to .12. The second factor, domestic worker, shows loadings for items from .84 to .92, with off-factor loadings for these items from $-.07$ to .22. The third factor, foreign correspondent, shows within-factor loadings from .82 to .92, and off-factor loadings from .12 to .24. The fourth factor, typist-stenographer, shows within-factor loadings from .84 to .89, with off-factor loadings from −.17 to .16. The fifth factor of company director contains only 4 items (extent of possession drops out), with within-factor loadings from .82 to .87 and off-factor loadings from −.11 to .25. These five factors account for 50.25% of the total variance, with each of these factors showing eigenvalues around 4. Given that there were only 5 items per occupational description, this suggests that around 80% of the total variability for these occupations is accounted for by its specific factor. Since care was taken to have each question that was rated for all activities appear on the same page, it is unlikely that methods variance in the form of a halo effect produced these relationships. If such an effect were operative, the factor structure should have yielded 5 factors corresponding to each content question, rather than factors corresponding to specific target activities.

These findings suggest strong, positive relationships between desirability, future-importance, self-importance, and eagerness, but only within the specific person-descriptor that indicates a particular kind of life activity. Inspection of correlations between variables within each factor suggested similar patterns. Additional analyses suggested that sex-typing of the occupation descriptions did not add to the predictability of its desirability or degree of motivational arousal (eagerness) for it, and that males and females perceived the occupations in a similar fashion.

A second study was conducted in which there was a balance of masculine, feminine, and neutral job descriptions that were intended to range from high, moderate, and low status within each. Thus 9 activities were included. Independent ratings for sex-type and prestige indicated that the selections were generally perceived as intended except for a restricted range of feminine prestige around moderate values. Ratings of desirability-undesirability of seeing oneself as this kind of person, eagerness-reluctance to engage in that occupation, and the likelihood of engaging in that occupation at some time in the future were also obtained. The median r among desirability and likelihood to engage in the activity within occupations was .55 for males (ranging from .71 to .20, $N = 47$) and .52 for females (ranging from .83 to .14, $N = 37$) while the median between-occupation r was .09 for males (ranging from −.34 to .59) and .04 for females (ranging from −.55 to .56). A corresponding analysis using sex-type and prestige ratings intercorrelated with ratings of likelihood of undertaking the activity suggests that the specific desirability of the activity was a better predictor than either sex-type or prestige of occupation.

Factor analysis used the principle components method of factor extraction and varimax orthogonal rotation to derive factor loadings. The analysis yielded 13 factors with eigenvalues greater than 1, which accounted for 79.7% of the variance. Seven factors involving desirability and eagerness ratings accounted for 51.3% of the total variance and 64.55% of the explained variance. This was almost twice as much as was accounted for by factors representing prestige and sex-typing items (accounting for 28.3% of the total variance and 35.55% of the explained variance). These data suggest that sex-type and prestige are not accounting for relationships between desirability, eagerness, and likelihood of engaging in specific activities. Motivation for specific activity, as assessed by eagerness and likelihood of engagement, are influenced by factors that determine the specific desirability-undesirability of that activity to the individual.

While the second study showed greater variability in factor structure than the first, the implication of the above two studies seemed unequivocal and straight-forward. Motivation as assessed in this manner does not appear to be a general factor influencing eagerness for life activity, while the pattern of relationships between variables across activities is stable and meaningful. The evidence suggests that different activity arouses motivation differently for different individuals, but motivation for each activity is influenced similarly by such variables as perceived desirability, perceived importance, and perceived competence in it. The conclusion from this data seemed inescapable that there was little point in trying to develop a general measure of motivation across different activities, as had been the strategy in previous research on achievement motivation. The data clearly suggested that items be targeted toward specific activity. Transsituational generality could be addressed as an empirical question after the development of scales to be applied to a particular activity and after demonstration of similar relationships among variables across those activities. Whether a general measure of motivation emerges or not will determine the utility of the concept of individual differences in general motivation for life activity. Whether scale scores for a person remain stable or change over time will determine the utility of the concept of stable motivation for a particular life activity and/or for general motivation for life activity.

Development of the MPAS

The MPAS consists of a series of items that elicit reactions to and attitudes toward a particular activity; thus far, individual sports competition or leadership activity. For sports, subjects received the first third of the Test Anxiety Questionnaire (TAQ; Mandler & Sarason, 1952) along with the MPAS. The MPAS consists of conceptually defined scales to measure four components; perceived competence, perceived importance, positive affect, and negative affect, each targeted for the goals of finding out about ability and doing well. The format was based on Alpert and Haber's (1960) Anxiety Scale and Brown's (1982) earlier version for the domain of parenting activity.

Subjects. Subjects were drawn from three separate introductory psychology classes at the State University of New York at Buffalo. In Study 1, 158 subjects participated, with incomplete data from 3 males and 1 female leaving 97 males and 57 females. Study 2 used 157 subjects, with incomplete data from 6 males and 1 female, leaving 76 males and 75 females. Study 3 used 417 subjects with incomplete data from 18 males and 17 females leaving 190 females and 192 females. Assessment of test-retest reliability used 15 females and 25 males, with no missing data.

Procedure. In Studies 1 (sports) and 3 (leadership) the MPAS was administered in a mass testing session. In Study 2 (sports) the MPAS was administered after subjects participated in a complex study of risk-taking in which they first rated various choices for a basket-throw game and then played two games that were most preferred. In the assessment of test-retest reliability (sports), subjects were given the first administration in a large group session. The second testing occurred 6 to 8 weeks later in groups of 4 to 20 individuals.

Factor structure. Responses to the MPAS from each study were subjected to factor analysis using the principal components method of factor extraction and varimax orthogonal procedure of rotation. Oblique rotation was also used but yielded similar results; only the orthogonal findings are reported. The factor structure and item loadings are shown in Table 1. For sports, 3 factors of similar structure emerged: positive affect-resultant competence, positive affect-perceived importance, and negative affect, accounting for 100% of the explained variance for Study 1 and 81% for Study 2, and 61.58% and 51.19% of the total variance, respectively. For leadership (Study 3), four factors emerged: positive affect, resultant competence, importance, and negative affect, accounting for 100% of the explained variance and 59.16% of the total variance. Note that items for finding out about ability and doing well do not load on separate factors, indicating that items for both goals are substantially correlated for each of the 4 factors that emerged in the three studies. Generally, the conceptually defined scales emerged as expected, with the notable exception that positive affect is so highly correlated with resultant competence and importance for sports that positive affect items are found in these other factors.

Internal consistency. Cronback alpha coefficents are shown in Table 2 for four conceptual scales (competence, importance, positive affect, and negative affect) and the total MPAS score[2]. We chose to use conceptual scales rather than factorially derived scales to simplify interpretation of results. Reliability coefficients for the total score were .92, .89, and .91 for the three studies. Reliabilities for conceptual scales ranged from .71 to .91 over the three studies (see Table 2). These data reflect high internal consistency for the total MPAS score and acceptable internal consistency for the conceptual scales. Results for sports (Studies 1 and 2) are similar, despite the fact that in the latter the MPAS was administered after an actual sports competition in a laboratory setting.

The means, standard deviations, and correlations of each conceptual scale with the total MPAS score for the three studies are presented in Tables 3 and 4. Only 2 items for Study 1, 4 items for Study 2, and 1 item from Study 3 are not significantly correlated with the total MPAS score. These are mostly negative affect items. Intercorrelations among the four conceptual scales indicate that competence, importance, and positive affect are positively related, while negative affect tends to be relatively independent of importance and negatively related to the other scales.

Test-retest reliabilities. Table 5 shows means, standard deviations, and correlations for the test-retest administration ($N = 40$) over 6 to 8 weeks for the total MPAS (.92) score and for the four subscales (ranging from .73 to .91).

Gender differences. Means for men and women for the conceptual scales (see Table 6) show men have higher ratings than women on competence,

Table 1

Items and Factor Loadings for the MPAS[a]

Item	Item Number	Study 1: Sports	Study 2: Sports	Study 3: Leadership
Positive Affect—Resultant Competence				
How eager are you to participate in ___ when you anticipate doing well?	4 P*	.73	.47	.22**
The more important to me is the ___ the more excited I seem to get.	11 P	.72	.61	.71
How enthusiastic are you about doing well in ___?	17 P	.71	.71	.60
The more important to me is the ___ the more excited I seem to get about finding out how good I am.	14 P	.71	.46	.83
How good a ___ do you see yourself as being?	10 C	.68	.79	.44**
How enthusiastic are you about having your competence demonstrated in ___?	15 P	.67	.60	.74
How important is doing well in ___ for feeling good about yourself?	2 I	.66	.67	.27**
The prospect of ___ seems to turn me off.	20 N	−.65	−.70	−.50
How poor a ___ do you see yourself as being?	18 C	−.64	−.75	−.28**
How competent do you see yourself as being in ___?	1 C	.63	.69	.37**
How eager are you to have your ability evaluated in ___?	7 P	.62	.42	.73
The prospect of evaluation of my skills and talents in ___ seems to give me a good feeling.	8 P	.51	.45	.69
The prospect of ___ seems to turn me on.	13 P	.51	.20	.70
How incompetent do you see yourself as being in ___?	12 C	−.49	−.65	−.14**
Eigen values		6.89	5.76	5.03
Percentage of explained variance		46.32	37.99	35.47
Percentage of total variance		28.42	24.01	20.99

Table 1 (continued)

Item	Item Number	Study 1	Study 2	Study 3
Negative Affect				
The more important to me the ___ the more worried I seem to get.	22 N	.71	.50	.73
How apprehensive are you about having your incompetence demonstrated in ___?	23 N	.70	.10***	.73
The prospect of evaluation of my weaknesses and inadequacies in ___ gives me a bad feeling.	16 N	.69	.77	.68
How worried are you about doing poorly in ___?	5 N	.66	.69	.66
How afraid are you to have your ability evaluated in ___?	19 N	.57	.66	.65
How apprehensive are you about participating in ___ when you anticipate doing poorly?	9 N	.56	.07***	.51
The more important to me is the ___ the more nervous I seem to get.	6 N	.56	.65	.68
Eigen values		3.92	2.82	3.91
Percentage of explained variance		26.92	18.60	27.57
Percentage of total variance		16.52	11.76	16.29
Importance—Positive Affect				
How necessary is doing well in ___ for achieving your own future goals?	3 I	.84	.85	.64
How necessary is finding out how much ability you have in ___ for achieving your own future goals?	21 I	.78	.81	.57
How important is finding out how much ability you have in ___ for feeling good about yourself?	24 I	.62	.65	.65
The prospect of evaluation of my skills and talents in ___ seems to give me a good feeling.	8 P	.59	.62	.11
How eager are you to have your ability evaluated in ___?	7 P	.50	.56	.00
Eigen values		4.04	3.70	1.95
Percentage of explained variance		26.76	24.40	13.73
Percentage of total variance		16.42	15.42	8.11

Table 1 (continued)

Item	Item Number	Study 3
Competence (Study 3 only)		
How competent do you see yourself as being in ___?	1 C	.67
How eager are you to participate in ___ when you anticipate doing well?	4 P	.64
How poor a ___ do you see yourself as being in ___?	18 C	−.60
How good a ___do you see yourself as being in ___?	10 C	.57
How important is doing well in ___ for feeling good about yourself?	2 I	.55
How incompetent do you see yourself as being in ___?	12 C	−.52
Eigen value		3.30
Percentage of explained variance		23.23
Percentage of total variance		13.73

[a] Factor loadings of .5 and above determined that an item belonged in a particular factor. Items 7 and 8 appear twice to indicate their loadings on more than one factor.

*Capital letters denote conceptual scale: C = Competence, I = Importance, P = Positive affect, N = Negative affect.

**These items loaded on the competence factor of Study 3.

***These two items formed a separate factor with loadings of .61 and .75 respectively. The factor accounted for 10.35% of the explained variance and 6.54% of the total variance.

importance, and positive affect while women have lower ratings than men on negative affect. Men, therefore, score substantially higher than women on the total MPAS score for both individual sports competition and leadership activity.

Interrelationships Among MPAS Conceptual Scales and Items

A series of analyses of variance were carried out to view the various relationships between conceptual scales and items of the MPAS.

Importance ratings. A 2 x 2 x 2 ANOVA was performed for each study separately, with gender (males vs. females) as the between-subjects factor, and goal of activity (doing well, items 2 and 3 vs. finding out, items 21 and 24) and type of importance (self, items 2 and 24 vs. future, items 3 and 21) as within-subjects factors. Each study yields similar, significant effects for gender ($ps < .05$). Each effect shows higher ratings of importance by males than females (see Table 6). Each study yields similar, significant effects for goal of activity ($ps < .0001$). Each effect shows higher ratings for the importance of doing well than for the importance of finding out about ability. Each study yields similar, significant effects for type of importance ($ps < .0001$ for sports; $p < .02$ for leadership). Each effect shows higher ratings for self-importance than for future-importance. Each study also yields a similar, significant Goal of activity x Type of importance

Table 2

Internal Consistency Coefficients

for Conceptual Scales of the MPAS

Scale	Study 1	Study 2	Study 3
Total	.92	.89	.91
Competence*	.85	.86	.78
Importance	.83	.78	.74
Positive affect	.91	.84	.89
Negative affect	.77	.71	.82
N	154	151	392

*Items contained in each of the scales were as follows:

Competence: 1, 10, 12, and 18; the latter two were never keyed.

Importance: 2, 3, 21, and 24.

Positive Affect: 4, 7, 8, 11, 13, 14, 15, and 17.

Negative Affect: 5, 6, 9, 16, 19, 20, 22, and 23.

interaction (Studies 1 and 3, $ps < .001$; Study 2, $p < .05$). Each interaction effect shows that doing well is more important than finding out about ability when self-importance is considered by the respondent, while the goals of doing well and finding out are more equally important when future-importance is considered. No other interaction effects were statistically reliable for any of the studies.

Importance ratings also varied as a function of type of activity (sports vs. leadership). A 3 x 2 ANOVA was carried out using Study as the between-subjects factor and Type of importance as the within-subjects factor. There was a significant Study x Type of importance interaction ($p < .0001$). While self-importance is higher than future-importance, the difference was substantial for sports, and negligible for leadership.

In summary, these data indicate that males placed greater importance on both sports and leadership activity than did females, that self-importance was rated higher than future-importance for sports, while self-importance and future-importance were equal for leadership, and doing well was more important than finding out for both sexes in both activities.

Affective reactions. ANOVA was applied to affective reactions using gender

Table 3

Means and Standard Deviations for Conceptual

Scales and Total MPAS Score

Scale	Study 1		Study 2		Study 3	
	Means	SD	Means	SD	Means	SD
Competence	14.01	4.06	14.89	3.89	14.96	3.57
Importance	11.50	4.09	12.64	3.79	13.86	3.70
Positive affect	26.47	7.73	28.04	6.01	27.22	7.08
Negative affect	14.96	6.01	15.15	5.38	14.95	6.92
Total	77.04	17.69	80.42	14.88	81.10	16.86
N	154		151		392	

Table 4

Intercorrelations for Conceptual Scales

and Total MPAS Score

Scale	Competence	Importance	Pos-affect	Neg-affect
Study 1				
Importance	.62			
Pos-affect	.75	.77		
Neg-affect	−.58	−.16	−.32	
Total	.89	.76	.89	−.65
Study 2				
Importance	.45			
Pos-affect	.67	.68		
Neg-affect	−.59	−.14	−.30	
Total	.86	.70	.86	−.67
Study 3				
Importance	.49			
Pos-affect	.65	.63		
Neg-affect	−.68	−.19	−.37	
Total	.87	.67	.85	−.75

Table 5

Test-Retest Correlations and Means

for Individual Sports Competition*

Scale	Pretest		Posttest		Correlation
	Mean	SD	Mean	SD	
Total MPAS	77.80	18.10	80.08	17.51	.92
Competence	14.13	2.51	14.78	3.98	.91
Importance	11.15	3.86	11.20	3.98	.80
Positive affect	26.83	7.32	27.83	7.25	.90
Negative affect	14.30	6.63	13.72	6.42	.72

*N = 40

as a between-subjects factor, with Goal of activity, Type of anticipated affective reaction (positive vs. negative), and specific affect (eager, enthusiastic, excited, feel good vs. worried, apprehensive, nervous, feel bad) as within-subjects factors. Each study yields similar, significant effects for Goal of activity ($ps < .0001$). Each effect shows higher affective ratings for doing well than finding out. Each study yields a similar, significant interaction between Gender and Type of affective reaction ($ps < .001$). Each interaction effect shows higher positive affect for males than females and higher negative affect for females than males (see Table 6).

Correlational Analyses for Eagerness to Evaluate Competence

For each study, eagerness to evaluate competence is positively correlated with the competence conceptual scale ($rs = .70, .53,$ and $.45, ps < .001$), and the importance conceptual scale ($rs = .66, .57,$ and $.39, ps < .001$). These findings will be discussed later.

Multiple Regression

Multiple regression analysis was performed to determine which conceptual MPAS scale would better predict anticipated affective reactions, taken as a traditional (dependent) measure of motivational arousal as in previous research on achievement motivation. Nicholls (1984) suggests that perceived competence is the critical element in determining motivation arousal, while Raynor (1982a) and Eccles, Adler, and Meese (1984) would suggest that importance as a measure of subjective value is the critical factor. Subjects in Studies 1 and 2 (MPAS for sports) were administered the TAQ. For these two studies, gender, TAQ, and competence and importance conceptual scales were used as the independent variables in a multiple regression analysis, with resultant anticipated affect (the

Table 6

Means for Males and Females for the Total MPAS Score and

Each of the Component Scales Along with F Values for Gender Differences

Scale	Gender	Study 1		Study 2		Study 3	
		Means	F-Value	Means	F-Value	Means	F-Value
Competence[a]	Males	15.13	22.84**	16.73	48.69**	15.60	12.99**
	Females	12.05		12.93		14.31	
Importance	Males	12.38	13.04**	13.36	6.12*	14.27	4.79*
	Females	9.95		11.88		13.43	
Positive	Males	28.69	25.48**	30.09	21.86**	28.32	10.02**
affect	Females	22.55		25.87		26.08	
Negative	Males	14.19	4.87*	13.02	31.42**	14.15	5.30*
affect	Females	16.33		17.43		15.77	
Total MPAS[b]	Males	82.03	24.45**	87.15	43.47**	84.05	12.52**
	Females	68.23		73.25		78.05	

* $p < .05$

** $p < .005$

[a]Items for negative competence (12 and 18) are reverse keyed to obtain the competence scale score.

[b]Items for negative affect are reverse keyed to obtain the total MPAS score.

positive affect conceptual scale minus the negative affect conceptual scale) as the dependent variable. For Study 3, TAQ scores were not available. Variables were entered in a stepwise, first-in, last-in fashion such that at some point each independent variable was entered last to determine its ability to account for unique variance in the criterion measure. Results (see Table 7) indicate that standardized beta weights for competence are far greater than those for importance and TAQ. Increments in R^2 when competence is entered last are far greater than when importance, TAQ, or gender are each in turn entered last. These data suggest that perceived competence is a far better predictor of anticipated affective reactions than perceived importance, gender, or TAQ in individual sports competition and leadership activity as assessed in these studies.

Table 7

Results for Multiple Regression

With Resultant Affect as the Dependent Measure

Variable Entered	Study	Standardized Regression Coefficient	F Ratio	Increment in R[+]	Simple Correlation
Gender[++]	1	−.051	1.22	.0023	−.36
	2	−.094	3.30	.0066	−.47
	3	−.037	1.14	.0013	−.23
TAQ	1	−.099	5.02 *	.0094	−.20
	2	−.167	12.30 **	.0108	−.28
	3	—	—	—	—
Resultant competence	1	.694	141.86 ***	.2664	.84
	2	.582	101.55 ***	.2041	.79
	3	.685	348.59 ***	.3838	.75
Total importance	1	.174	9.51 **	.0179	.62
	2	.271	27.57 ***	˙.0554	.53
	3	.147	16.70 ***	.0184	.42

Full Equation Study 1 $R^2 = .7258$ $F(4,146) = 96.63$ ***

Full Equation Study 2 $R^2 = .6945$ $F(4,152) = 86.40$ ***

Full Equation Study 3 $R^2 = .5827$ $F(3,379) = 176.41$ ***

* denotes $p < .05$

** denotes $p < .01$

*** denotes $p < .001$

[+] When entered last

[++] Male coded = 1, Female coded = 2

Relationships Between the MPAS and Traditional Measures

Study 2 referred to above included both traditional measures (n Achievement and TAQ) and the MPAS. n Achievement was assessed prior to a study of risk-taking behavior using a basket-throw game to assess risk-taking. The TAQ and MPAS were administered after measurement of risk-taking and performance in the most preferred games. Since the factor structure of the MPAS and relations between its conceptual scales are similar to that found for Study 1, it is unlikely that its relation to n Achievement was affected by its administration after rather than before performance of the laboratory task. For this study, n Achievement and MPAS are essentially unrelated ($r = .10$, $N = 157$, n.s.), and n Achievement is not significantly related to any of the conceptual scales. MPAS and TAQ are slightly, negatively related ($r = -.18$, $N = 157$, $p < .05$), primarily due to the relationships between TAQ and both the negative affect ($r = -.36$, $N = 157$, $p < .01$) and negative competence ($r = -.19$, $N = 157$, $p < .05$) conceptual components of the MPAS. In a second study, n Achievement, TAQ, and MPAS were administered under neutral conditions prior to the study of risk-taking behavior in a laboratory setting. MPAS and n Achievement are not significantly related ($r = .16$), nor are MPAS and TAQ ($r = .07$, $Ns = 41$). However, there is a significant relationship between n Achievement and the difference between positive and negative affect conceptual scales of the MPAS ($r = .37$, $p < .05$). Generally, total MPAS versus n Achievement and Test Anxiety are assessing different aspects of motivation.

Relationships Between MPAS and Laboratory Behavior

In the risk-taking task of Study 2, subjects played a basket-throw game consisting of their most preferred sequence of tasks consisting of up to 5 throws in a row. Points were known to be awarded for a hit and taken away for a miss, depending upon how close or far away the throw was from the basket, according to the rule $Is = 1 - Ps$, as specified in achievement theory. Consistent with achievement theory, n Achievement scores were significantly related to preference for sequences of distances having an average probability of success between .8 and .4 ($ps < .05$ for each). That is, the higher the n Achievement score, the greater the preference for moderate risk. TAQ scores were significantly but negatively related to preference for sequences of distances having an average probability of success between 1.00 and .3 ($ps < .01$ for each). That is, the higher the TAQ score, the greater the preference for both easy options (as predicted by achievement theory) and moderately difficult options (contrary to achievement theory). A combined n Achievement-Test Anxiety score would, therefore, show no relationship to moderate risk. MPAS scores were significantly related to preference for distances having an average probability of success between .3 and .1 ($ps < .01$ for each). That is, the higher the MPAS score, the greater the preference for difficult but attainable goals. According to these data, n Achievement and MPAS are differentially related to risk-taking; n Achievement to preference for moderate risk as achievement theory predicts, and MPAS to preference for difficult risk options.

Neither n Achievement nor TAQ were related to points won in the most preferred game ($rs = .14$ and .02, n.s., respectively), while the MPAS score was significantly related to points won ($r = .20$, $p < .05$). Thus those high on the MPAS preferred relatively difficult options but won relatively more points than those low on the MPAS.

A second risk-taking study investigated choice among risk options involving picking up differently sized poker chips within a time limit. Options could involve up to 5 differently sized chips in any order, where probabilities of success in picking up the chip were induced to decrease as the chip size decreased. n Achievement, TAQ, and the MPAS were administered prior to task selections and performance (see above). Results showed no significant relationships between either n Achievement or TAQ for any preference ratings of the risk options. Total MPAS scores were positively correlated with preference for only one of many possible options—that involving one chip with $Ps = .5$ ($r = .34$, $N = 44$, ; $p < .05$). Corresponding rs between n Achievement and TAQ for this option were .02 and –.10, respectively, both nonsignificant.

The results of these laboratory studies suggest that MPAS scores obtained from individual sports competition are positively related to either moderate or difficult risk. However, relationships are relatively small and do not offer great promise for empirical validation based on robust findings that are consistently replicable.

Possible Relationships Between MPAS and Other Criterion Measures

At this point there are no theoretically-derived expectations concerning possible behavioral correlates of standing on the MPAS. We wish to discover such relationships, then build theory to explain them. However, previous research on career striving indicates that there are strong relationships between importance ratings and the following variables obtained from the assessment of the future plans of college men, $N = 186$ (Raynor & Entin, 1982, Ch. 2): high importance was positively associated with attractiveness of achieving their future goal ($p < .0001$), repulsiveness of failure to achieve their future goal ($p < .0001$), willingness to work hard to achieve their future goal ($p < .0001$), and certainty of their future goal selection $p < .0001$). The total MPAS score may be related to these variables in a similar manner since importance ratings form a conceptual scale of the MPAS and are positively associated with both competence and positive affect. In addition, there are substantial positive correlations between total importance ratings and both ratings of positive affective reactions to and time spent in parenting activity by women of grade and high school students (Raynor & Brown, 1985). We may obtain similar relationship using the total MPAS score; importance and positive affect are conceptual scales of the MPAS that are positively correlated. Reports of time spent in parenting activity approximate a behavioral measure of motivation for the parenting career. The magnitude of relationship (rs between .5 and .7, $N = 151$) has the robustness required for building conceptual interpretation. If behavioral measures of time spent in a structured parent-child interaction yielded similar findings for the total MPAS, we would claim that distribution of time in career-related activity (i.e., here, parenting) is an important correlate of standing on the MPAS.

Discussion

The results reported here are consistent with some of the ideas that lead to the development of the MPAS, while they challenge others. We first treat results consistent with expectations.

Internal consistency and test-retest reliability for the total MPAS score and for its conceptual components are high—extremely high for measures of motivation—and approach the level found for traditional measures of ability. The total scale yields 3 (or 4) distinct factors rather than a unifactorial structure. Component scales obtained from factor analysis generally conform to initial expectations: competence, positive affect, importance, and negative affect, although the first two are so highly related for individual sports competition that they form a single factor while for leadership they yield two distinct factors, and positive affect and importance items each load on the other factor.

Relationships between component scales of the MPAS scale confirm intuitive notions about sports competition and leadership. Given the traditionally masculine perception of these activities in Western culture, sports and leadership activity are perceived as more important by males than by females and arouse greater positive affect for males and greater negative affect for females. Given these are competitive rather than diagnostic activities, both men and women rate doing well as a more important goal than finding out about ability, and doing well in them is associated with greater affective arousal than is finding out about ability. Given the typical student is not oriented towards a professional career in sports, self-importance of leadership activity is higher than for individual sports competition for both men and women in this sample of college students.

Theoretically relevant relationships were also obtained. Eagerness to evaluate competence is positively associated with perceived competence and perceived importance, and perceived competence is positively related to self-importance, findings expected based on evolving theory concerning motivation and the self-system (Raynor & McFarlin, 1986), but inconsistent with Trope's (1986) views on motivation for self-assessment.

A general finding of the present research concerns the equivalent patterns of relationships obtained for variables assessed for individual sports competition and leadership activity. This was expected based on the preliminary research summarized earlier—relationships between theoretically-relevant variables were expected to be independent of the nature of the target activity. This replication is encouraging. The ultimate goal of this research is to validate empirically a way of looking at human motivation that leads to a general conceptual scheme, one that is applicable to any life activity. The next step in this research should be to administer to the same individuals several versions of the MPAS that are targeted to different kinds of activity to determine whether assessment across different domains yields a general index of motivation for a particular individual, or whether the rank-ordering of motivation for a particular set of individuals is specific to particular kinds of activity.

We now deal with results inconsistent with initial expectations. Items concerning doing well and finding out about ability did not load on distinct factors. Rather, within each factor, items concerning doing well and finding out are found with equal frequency. We will return to a more extended discussion of the distinction between doing well and finding out shortly. The most important violation of our initial expectations concerns the results of regression analysis which clearly showed that perceived competence rather than perceived importance accounts for a far greater proportion of variance in anticipated affective reactions. The data provide clear and convincing evidence, within the limits of correlational analysis of the efficacy of perceived competence as a variable involved in motivational arousal, a finding predicted by Nicholls (1984) conceptual analysis but not convincingly demonstrated, in our view, by the data marshalled thus far to support that position. Replication of the present results for a variety of different activities would be an important step toward placing perceived competence in the forefront of conceptually important variables in understanding the arousal of human motivation in life activity.

Doing Well vs. Finding Out as Goals of Achievement Activity

Explication of the primary goal of achievement-related striving has become a focus of controversy in research on achievement motivation. Both doing well in terms of meeting some criterion of success, and discovery or evaluation of (degree of possession of) abilities have been proposed as exclusive goals of achievement striving. Anticipated affective reactions to success and failure in striving to do well are considered the source of motivation in traditional theory of achievement motivation (Atkinson & Feather, 1966; Atkinson & Raynor, 1974) in competitive tasks where winning can be readily evaluated. This position suggests that the goal of doing well should be seen as most important and evoke greatest motivational arousal in competitive activity. However, Weiner's (1974) early attributional approach to achievement motivation suggested that information value is the primary source of motivation. The information-giving aspects of achievement activity determine motivation to undertake it. Feelings of "pride" and "shame" in success or failure are derived from the information gained from the task about level of ability. Affective value is secondary to information value as a goal or incentive for action. The testing of competence or the evaluation of skills is seen as the primary goal. This position suggests that finding out about ability should be seen as most important and evoke greatest motivational arousal in competitive activity.

Results using the MPAS clearly favor a position implying that doing well is more important and more motivationally arousing in individual sports competition and leadership activity than finding out about ability, for college men and women. However, we would not be surprised to find the reverse when the MPAS targets an activity that is commonly accepted as a diagnostic test of competence where feedback has no bearing on winning or losing per se. The data also imply that the goals of doing well and finding out are both meaningful for and relevant to understanding striving in these sports and leadership activities; the factor structure shows equal numbers of items loading on each of the empirically derived subscales of the MPAS.

Trope (1975; Trope & Brickman, 1975) suggests that diagnostic assessment is the goal of achievement activity. Maximizing information value by reducing uncertainty concerning one's own level of ability relative to others is the primary goal. This position is consistent with social comparison theory (Festinger, 1954).

Within this framework, all individuals are expected to show a desire to gain information concerning their own particular level of ability. Information value is predominant and affective value irrelevant, since individuals both high and low on a positive competence (ability) should be equally motivated to find out more about their particular level of possession of the attribute in question. This position implies that motivation to find out about level of possession is unrelated to degree of possession of that competence.

Nicholls (1984) recent conception utilizes both attribution and social comparison theory. Under ego-involved conditions, individuals are expected to be motivated to do as well as they can so as to demonstrate their competence, or to avoid demonstrating their incompetence. The primary goal of achievement activity is seen as demonstration of competence and avoidance of incompetence. The implication is that the higher the level of competence the greater the motivation to demonstrate that competence, and the higher the level of incompetence the greater the motivation to avoid demonstrating that incompetence.

Results using the MPAS clearly favor a position implying that the higher the level of possession of a positively valued competence the greater the importance of that competence to the individual and the greater the motivation to find out about degree of possession of that competence, a position advocated by Raynor and McFarlin (1986) in evolving theory concerning motivation and the self-system. The data reported here are consistent with the view that individuals are more motivated to demonstrate high rather than low sports and leadership competence because higher competence has greater positive affective value associated with it. They are also consistent with the view that perceived competence is the motivational variable which accounts for anticipated affective reactions in individual sports and leadership activity.

Recommendations Concerning the MPAS

Further use of the MPAS should, of course, be limited to research purposes; it is not a diagnostic tool. The total scale has acceptable psychometric properties but, to date, has limited conceptual validity. It is not meant as a substitute for the traditional n Achievement and Test Anxiety measures. Based on previous research on perceived competence and importance, we expect that the MPAS may relate to different motivational variables or show different relationships with previous behavioral measures. It would be inappropriate to pit traditional measures and the MPAS against each other in terms of construct validity within existing theory of achievement motivation. We make no claims for validity within existing theory developed using n Achievement and Test Anxiety.

The factor structure of the MPAS corresponds fairly closely to that intended, but not completely so. We have used conceptual scales rather than those derived from factor analysis to retain clarity in attempts to understand relationships between scales of the MPAS and with other variables. These conceptual scales have acceptable internal consistency. Time spent on exploring the relationships between the MPAS (and its components) and behavioral manifestations of motivation might be more fruitful than trying to obtain clean and simple factor structure, particularly since many of the items loading on different factors are substantially correlated. There is little doubt that items dealing with competence, importance, and positive affect refer to different conceptual variables. Their interrelationships seem more a matter of conceptual validity than lack of discriminant validity.

We recommend that research with the MPAS include both laboratory and field research. In principle, the scale can be targeted for different laboratory tasks in a way analogous to the way it can be targeted for different life activities. The most robust relationships obtained to date concern variables involved in career striving. Field research is clearly in order to expand the network of empirical relationships between the MPAS and other variables in this kind of life activity. Laboratory experimentation to deal with issues of determinants and processes should be guided by the results of assessments involved in career striving. Trivialization often occurs when a new measure is subjected either to a blind search for correlates or a search for causal linkages outside the context in which the measure was developed.

We are not sure that the distinction between traditional measures and the MPAS is that n Achievement and Test Anxiety assesses motives while the MPAS assesses values. At this point we would rather explore those empirical relationships that appear promising than to debate what the MPAS is measuring in terms of such distinctions. Theorizing will remain data-driven until a richer network of interrelationship has been established. Attempts to establish on cause-effect relationships and underlying mechanisms and processes should be tentative and speculative while the meaningfulness of scores on the MPAS become soundly grounded in robust and replicable findings. This strategy should prevent a premature return to theory-driven rather than data-driven research. It would insure that the discovery of empirical relationships is given its proper role in research on motivation in life activity.

The role of theory is to account for what is known in a coherent manner—as well as to provide a guide for future research. Science involves induction as well as deduction. When one or the other of these functions comes to dominate it is likely that a reaction sets in whose goal is to redress an imbalance between the two. Traditional research on achievement motivation has provided a solid base of empirical findings upon which has been built a substantive increase in understanding of human motivation. However, it is up to the next generation of researchers to insure that advances in empirical knowledge continue so that the study of motivation does not become an exclusive effort based on derivation from theory. Whether use of the MPAS will provide for such advance remains to be determined.

FOOTNOTES

[1]The authors wish to acknowledge the assistance of Lisa Wojcik in the planning of and data collection for these studies.

[2]Items 5, 6, 9, 12, 16, 18, 19, 20, 22, and 23 of the MPAS as numbered in Table 1 reflect incompetence or negative affect and, therefore, were reverse keyed to obtain the total MPAS score. Thus the higher the total score the greater the perceived competence, importance, and positive affect and the lower the perceived incompetence and negative affect.

REFERENCES

Alpert, R., & Haber, R. N. (1960). Anxiety in academic achievement situations. *Journal of Abnormal and Social Psychology, 61*, 207–215.

Atkinson, J. W. (1957). Motivational determinants of risk-taking behavior. *Psychological Review, 64*, 359–372.

Atkinson, J. W., & Birch, D. (1978). *Introduction to motivation* (2nd ed.). New York: Van Nostrand.

Atkinson, J. W., & Feather, N. T. (1966). *A theory of achievement motivation.* New York: Wiley.

Atkinson, J. W., & Raynor, J. O. (1974). (Eds.). *Motivation and achievement.* Washington, DC: Hemisphere.

Bandura, A. (1977). Self-efficacy: Toward a unifying theory of behavioral change. *Psychological Review, 84*, 191–215.

Brown, E. T. (1982). Parenting as a psychological career path for women. Unpublished doctoral dissertation, State University of New York at Buffalo.

Eccles, J., Adler, T., & Meece, J. L. (1984). Sex differences in achievement: A test of alternative theories. *Journal of Personality and Social Psychology, 46*, 26–43.

Festinger, L. (1954). A theory of social comparison. *Human Relations, 7*, 117–140.

Mandler, G., & Sarason, S. B. (1952). A study of anxiety and learning. *Journal of Abnormal and Social Psychology, 47*, 166–173.

Nicholls, J. G. (1984). Conceptions of ability and achievement motivation. In R. Ames & C. Ames (Eds.), *Research on motivation in education: Student motivation* (Vol. I) (pp. 39–73). Academic.

Nochajski, T. H. (1986). Effects of past orientation, future orientation, and resultant motive group on arousal and performance. Unpublished masters thesis, State University of New York at Buffalo.

Pearlson, H. B. (1982). Effects of temporal distance from a goal and number of tasks required for goal attainment on achievement-related behavior. In J. O. Raynor & E. E. Entin (Eds.), *Motivation, career striving, and aging* (pp. 131–150). Washington, DC: Hemisphere.

Raynor, J. O. (1969). Future orientation and motivation of immediate activity: An elaboration of the theory of achievement motivation. *Psychological*

Review, 76, 606–610.

Raynor, J. O. (1974). Future orientation in the study of achievement motivation. In J. W. Atkinson & J. O. Raynor (Eds.). *Motivation and achievement.* Washington, DC: Hemisphere.

Raynor, J. O. (1982a). A theory of personality functioning and change. In J. O. Raynor & E. E. Entin (Eds.), *Motivation, career striving, and aging* (pp. 249–302). Washington, DC: Hemisphere.

Raynor, J. O. (1982b). Self-possession of attributes, self-evaluation, and future orientation: A theory of adult competence motivation. In J. O. Raynor & E. E. Entin (Eds.), *Motivation, career striving, and aging* (pp. 207–226). Washington, DC: Hemisphere.

Raynor, J. O., & Brown, E. T. (1985). Motivation at different stages of striving in a psychological career. In D. A. Klieber (Eds.), *Advances in motivation and achievement* (Vol. 4): *Motivation and adulthood* (pp. 121–167). Greenwich, CT: JAI.

Raynor, J. O., & English, L. D. (1982). Relationships among self-importance, future importance, and self-possession. In J. O. Raynor & E. E. Entin (Eds.), *Motivation, career striving, and aging* (pp. 197–226). Washington, DC: Hemisphere.

Raynor, J. O., & Entin, E. E. (1982). *Motivation, career striving, and aging.* Washington, DC: Hemisphere.

Raynor, J. O., & Entin, E. E. (1983). The function of future orientation as a determinant of human behavior in step-path theory of action. *International Journal of Psychology, 18,* 25–49.

Raynor J. O., & McFarlin, D. B. (1986). Motivation and the self-system. In R. M. Sorrentino & E. T. Higgens (Eds.), *Handbook of motivation and cognition: Foundations of social behavior* (pp. 315–349). New York: Guilford.

Raynor, J. O., & Smith, C. P. (1965). Achievement-related motives and risk-taking in games of skill and chance. *Journal of Personality, 34* 176–198.

Raynor, J. O., Atkinson, J. W., & Brown, M. (1974). Subjective aspects of achievement motivation immediately before an examination. In J. W. Atkinson & J. O. Raynor (Eds.), *Motivation and achievement* (pp.155–171). Washington, DC: Hemisphere.

Spence, J. T., & Helmreich, R. L. (1983). Achievement-related motives and behavior. In J. T. Spence (Ed.), *Achievement and achievement motives: Psychological and sociological approaches* (pp. 34–72). San Francisco:

W. H. Freeman.

Trope, Y. (1975). Seeking information about one's ability as a determinant of choice among tasks. *Journal of Personality and Social Psychology, 32,* 1004–1013.

Trope, Y. (1986). Self-enhancement and self-assessment in achievement behavior. In R. M. Sorrentino & E. T. Higgens (Eds.), *Handbook of motivation and cognition: Foundations of social behavior* (pp. 350–378). New York: Guilford.

Trope, Y., & Brickman, P. (1975). Difficulty and diagnosticity as determinants of choice among tasks. *Journal of Personality and Social Psychology, 31,* 918–925.

Weiner, B. (1974). Achievement motivation and attribution theory. Morristown, NJ: General Learning.

Chapter Two

IN THE ATKINSON TRADITION: THE

MOTIVATIONAL FUNCTION OF EMOTION

Bernard Weiner

University of California at Los Angeles

One might anticipate that the study of motivation and emotion would be intimately linked. In support of this expectation, a psychological journal exists with the title *Motivation and Emotion*, and psychology courses at times carry this label. But theories of motivation and thoughts about emotion have not been united. Most motivational theories only incorporate the pleasure-pain principle, postulating that individuals strive to increase pleasure and to decrease pain. This is most clearly associated with the conceptions of Freud and Hull, but applies as well to the cognitive theorists such as Tolman and Rotter.

The crude delineation between just pleasure versus pain is inadequate to describe emotions, and is equally inadequate when attempting to construct a theory of motivation. For example, assume that one aggresses against another. If that other reacts with the negative affect of anger, the subsequent action might be quite different from the behavior generated by the equally negative affect of self-pity. In a similar manner, behaviors would be likely to be disparate if one reacted to aggression with distinctive positive affects. Joy when being hit is presumed to give rise to different actions than relief.

Implicit in the above examples is not only the fact that emotions must be distinguished from one another, but also that motivation is mediated by affective reactions. As indicated, I believe that aggression will give rise to different actions depending on whether it elicits anger, self-pity, joy, or relief. Emotion is therefore intimately involved in motivational processes.

My mentor, Jack Atkinson, was among the very few, if perhaps the only motivational theorist, to acknowledge emotions other than the all encompassing pleasure-pain principle. He stated that achievement strivings are guided by anticipations of pride and shame. Not only did he point out the relevance of two distinct emotions, but he also gave them a role in the motivational process. In Atkinson's theory, anticipated emotions guide or propel the organism toward or away from the goal.

In this chapter, I will give some other examples of motivational episodes that are guided by emotional reactions. To do this, I first have to examine very briefly some of the determinants of emotion. What gives rise to feelings such as pride and shame, or to anger, guilt, pity, gratitude, hope, and hopelessness? Inasmuch as I have discussed this in detail elsewhere (Weiner, 1982, 1985), here I only provide an overview of the determinants of some selected emotions. This also will give me more time to speculate about the linkages between emotions and action. All of these topics are examined from the perspective of an attribution theorist, that is, one who places strong emphasis on perceptions of causality for prior events. However, I believe that the general issue of what is the interface between motivation and emotion must be faced by all motivational theorists, regardless of their theoretical orientation. Hence, although attributions are my "main man," it was Atkinson who lead me down the "main street" of cognitions and emotions.

Attributions Related to Affects

In this section of the paper I will document the obvious: that how we feel depends to a large extent on what we think. I will restrict my attention to four affects: anger, pity, guilt, and shame. These four are selected because research has been conducted contrasting their motivational effects.

Anger

The attributional antecedent for anger is an ascription for a negative, self-related outcome or event to factors controllable by others (see Averill, 1983). In one illustrative study by Weiner, Graham, and Chandler (1982), subjects were asked to recount instances of their lives in which they experienced the emotion of anger. For this affect, 90% of the situations involved an external and controllable cause. For example, people are angry when others lie to them or cheat or when roommates fail to clean up the kitchen.

Pity

In contrast to the linkage between controllability and anger, among adults uncontrollable causes are associated with pity. In the retrospective recall research I conducted with my colleagues cited above (Weiner et al., 1982), it was found that typical instances eliciting pity are sights of the blind, crippled, aged, or others with uncontrollable shortcomings.

Guilt

A great number of philosophers and psychologists agree that guilt follows from acts that violate ethical norms and moral values. Guilt requires feelings of personal responsibility. Thus, one feels guilty for lying (but angry when being lied to). Within achievement-related contexts, lack of effort is the most controllable of the causes. Hence, ascription of failure to lack of effort should, and does, evoke guilt (Brown & Weiner, 1984; Jagacinski & Nicholls, 1984).

Shame

The attributional determinants of shame are equivocal in comparison to the definitive determinants of anger, pity, and guilt. I suggest that shame, and its corresponding affects of humiliation and embarrassment, are elicited when a cause of an outcome is internal but uncontrollable. Thus, failure because of low ability often elicits shame (Brown & Weiner, 1984; Jagacinski & Nicholls, 1984). Shame implies that a social comparison is being made and that one does not have what others do. Hence, experiences of being too (tall, short, uncoordinated, unattractive) will tend to elicit shame in the individual possessing these uncontrollable attributes (see Wicker, Payne, & Morgan, 1983).

Summary and Comparison

The attributional determinants of four affects: anger, pity, guilt, and shame, have been reviewed. These affects can be comprised within a two dimensional classification, including the direction of the affect and the controllability of the cause (see Table 1). Table 1 indicates that anger and pity are other directed, while guilt and shame are self-directed experiences. In addition, both anger and guilt are elicited by controllable causes, whereas pity and shame are evoked given uncontrollable causes. This has implications for the "fit" or association between emotional expressions of others and self-directed emotions (e.g., if the anger of others is accepted as justified, then one should feel guilty). But more about this later.

Table 1

Two Dimensional Classification for Affect

Causal Property	Affective Target	
	Self	Other
Controllable	Guilt	Anger
Uncontrollable	Shame	Pity

Feelings Related to Action

I will argue now that emotions are the synapses of motivational life, joining thinking with acting. The relations between thoughts about perceived control, emotional reactions, and actions are shown in Table 2. Table 2 reveals that anger tends to evoke retaliation or, in the words of Karen Horney, going against others; pity and guilt tend to elicit "retribution" and going toward others; and shame produces withdrawal and retreat or, using the Horney vocabulary, going away from others. I call these the 3 R's of motivation. Each affect, then, brings with it a general program for action; affects therefore summarize the past by providing an evaluation for what has occurred and suggest a prescription for the future, cueing what should be done.

Table 2

Relations Between Causal Thinking, Affect,

and Elicited Action

Causal Antecedent	Affect	Action Tendency
Personal failure controllable by others	Anger	Retaliation (going against)
Failure of another is uncontrollable	Pity	Restitution (going toward)
Failure of another is controllable by the self	Guilt	Restitution (going toward)
Failure of the self is uncontrollable	Shame	Retreat (going away from)

Now that I have made these rather bold statements, I imagine it is incumbent that some data are presented in their support. I will begin this task by examining the behavioral consequences of anger versus pity reactions in help-giving situations. Then I will return to my roots, the achievement domain, and bridge from anger and pity communications to inferred guilt and shame reactions.

Anger versus Pity

My colleagues and I (Betancourt, 1984; Meyer & Mulherin, 1980; Reisenzein, 1985; Weiner, 1980a, 1980b) have conducted a number of studies in the area of helping behavior that examine the general hypothesis that affects mediate between thought and action, as well as testing the more specific hypotheses that relate uncontrollability to pity and moving toward and controllability to anger and moving against. These studies typically (but not always) have made use of a role-playing methodology where subjects read particular vignettes and then are questioned about their affective reactions and what their behavior might have been in that situation. For example, in one series of investigations (Weiner, 1980b), the following scenario was given:

> At about 1:00 in the afternoon you are walking through campus and a student comes up to you. The student says that you do not know him, but that you are both enrolled in the same class. He asks

if you would lend him the class notes from the meeting last week, saying that notes are needed because he skipped class to go to the beach. (Alternate form: Notes are needed because of a severe eye problem). (Weiner, 1980b, p. 676)

Another scenario used (Weiner, 1980a) has been:

At about 1:00 in the afternoon you are riding a subway car. There are a number of other individuals in the car and one person is standing, holding on to the center pole. Suddenly, this person staggers forward and collapses. The person apparently is drunk. He is carrying a liquor bottle wrapped in a brown paper bag and smells of liquor. (Alternate form: The person is carrying a black cane and apparently is ill.) (p. 190)

In these investigations, perception of the controllability of the cause of the need (in these instances, "beach," "eye problem," "drunk," or "disabled,") ratings of pity and anger (which are known to be linked to perceived controllability), and the likelihood of helping were assessed.

The data revealed positive relations between perceived controllability, anger, and lack of help, as well as between perceived uncontrollability, pity, and help-giving. Thus, subjects tend to perceive the causes of the "eye problem" student and the disabled individual as uncontrollable, they report feeling pity, and indicate they would help. On the other hand, the causes of the "beach" student and the drunk are perceived as controllable, subjects report feeling anger, and indicate that they would not help.

These correlational data also provide evidence concerning the temporal organization of behavior, including the linkage between affect and action. The logic of the analysis is that if affect mediates the relation between thought and action, then partialling affect from the cause (controllability)–helping correlation will greatly modulate the magnitude of that correlation. On the other hand, partialling thoughts from the affect-helping relation should not influence the magnitude of that correlation. And that indeed has been the pattern of findings. The data from one pertinent study (Weiner, 1980b) are shown in Table 3. Table 3 reveals that helping relates negatively with perceived controllability ($r = -.37$), positively with feelings of pity ($r = .46$), and negatively with reports of anger ($r = -.71$). The relations between the two affects and helping are only slightly altered when perceptions of controllability are statistically taken from the relations, with the pity-helping correlation lowered more than that of anger-helping (see Row 2, Table 3). On the other hand, the relation between controllability and help-giving is reduced to near zero when the reactions of pity or anger are held statistically constant (see Column 1, Table 3). In sum, the data support the position that emotions, rather than causal perceptions, are the immediate motivators of behavior.

Betancourt (1983) and Reisenzein (1985) have more thoroughly supported

Table 3

Correlations of Variables with Judgments of Helping

with and without Variables Statistically Partialled

from the Analysis (Subway Scenarios, Weiner, 1980b, p. 192)

Partialled Variable	2	3	4
1. None	−.37*	.46**	−.71***
2. Controllability		.30	−.66***
3. Pity (sympathy)	−.02		
4. Anger (disgust)	.04		

this line of reasoning, making use of path analytic methodological techniques. The investigation by Reisenzein is particularly impressive in that he tested five alternative models. These five models are displayed in Table 4. Model 1 has been tested in most prior investigations; in Model 2, there is a direct as well as an indirect path between controllability and help—this model has received the best support in the prior research studies; Model 3 adds a path between anger and sympathy, for these affects may be mutually inhibitory or hedonically incompatible; in Model 4, the additional paths in both Models 2 and 3 are combined; and in Model 5 there is a direct path from the eliciting situation to the helping act. For example, it may be that falling in a subway elicits more help than a request for class notes because less "cost" is involved, it is more dramatic, physical needs are associated with stronger cultural norms to help, and so on.

Reisenzein (1985) tested these models with the class notes and subway scenarios already described. He reports that Model 1 significantly fit the data, and that it was not improved by the additional paths shown in Models 2–4. Model 5, however, which added a path from situation to helping, did slightly improve the fit of the model to the data. Thus, the "nonattributional" path reveals that, even in these selectively restricted situations, there are nonattributional determinants of helping. I suppose that should not surprise me, but in my lifespace attributions engulf the field.

From Anger and Pity to Inferred Guilt and Shame

The data regarding the relative influence of guilt versus shame on performance are sparse and are more tentative than the data pertaining to anger versus pity that were gathered in help-related domains. There are studies directly documenting that guilt does lead to retribution (e.g., Carlsmith and Gross, 1969), and investigations showing that guilt results in increments in achievement strivings,

Table 4

Various Models of Helping Behavior

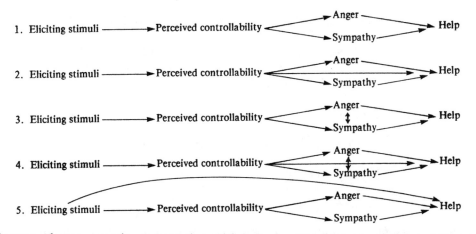

whereas shame reactions provoke withdrawal and decrements in achievement performance (Covington & Omelich, 1984). But in the present context I want to discuss some research by Graham (1984) documenting the disparate influence of anger versus pity communications on guilt and shame.

Graham (1984) had "teachers" communicate anger ("I'm really mad at you") or pity ("I feel sorry for you") toward children about 12 years old who had been induced to fail at an achievement-related task. This verbal feedback was accompanied by appropriate voice and postural cues. For example, anger was loudly expressed with hands extended, whereas the pity statement was said softly, with hands folded. The children subsequently were asked why the teacher thought they had failed, why they personally believed they had done poorly, and what they expected to do in the future. In addition, their persistence was assessed.

Now I want to backtrack somewhat and analyze the perceived process that Graham examined (see Table 5). Table 5 shows that an observer (e.g., a teacher) has a private evaluation of the target person, such as his or her ability or effort expenditure. Success and failure then give rise to an emotional experience and expression as a function of this belief system. Thus, for example, if a perceived smart person fails, the teacher might infer low effort, which would give rise to anger. Anger might be communicated in a number of ways. If the communication is received and correctly encoded, the actor (e.g., a student) will be able to infer the teacher's opinion of his ability and/or effort. This, in turn, has an impact on own self-attributions and affective reactions, expectations, and actions.

Now let me return to the investigation by Graham. Figure 1 shows the inferred experimenter ("teacher") attributions as a function of the affective feedback. It is evident from Figure 1 that when pity was expressed, low ability was the inferred cause of failure; lack of effort was linked with experimenter displays

Table 5

Communicated Affect-Self Attribution Process

Private evaluation of ⟶ Affective experience ⟶ Affective expression ⟶

    target person

Encoding of affect ⟶ Inferred opinion of others ⟶ Self-attribution ⟶

                              regarding self

Emotional reaction ⟶ Performance

Expectancy ⟶

FIGURE 1. Inferred experimenter attributions as a function of affect condition.

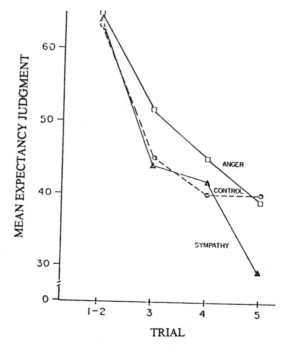

of anger; and there was no dominant causal inference when affective feedback was not delivered (the control condition). This documents that pity and anger expressions can be used to infer what others are thinking.

The next question Graham (1984) examined was whether this feedback also influences self-attributions for failure. It does, for self-ascriptions for failure to low ability were highest in the sympathy condition, while self-ascriptions to lack of effort were highest in the anger condition. According to the prior analysis, the participants should then be feeling ashamed in the ability condition and guilty in the effort condition, and this should respectively lead to low expectancy and task withdrawal, or to reasonably high future expectancies and increased vigor as a "retribution." Affective self-reports were not gathered in this study. But the expectancy data, shown in Figure 2, are as predicted. After five failure trials subjects in the anger feedback condition had higher expectancies of success than did subjects receiving pity feedback.

FIGURE 2. Expectancy judgments in the affect condition as a function of failure trials.

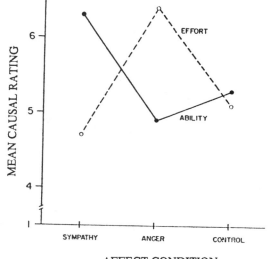

Unfortunately, the performance data were weak. In the right direction, I might add, but weak. Yet I must admit that we neither felt ashamed nor guilty about this. The conceptual analysis of this complex motivational episode, going from communicated emotions to self-ascriptions to inferences about self-generated emotions and then to expectancy and action was in large part supported. It is reassuring to know that we have things left to do.

Other Affect-Action Relations

The above analyses can be applied to any number of situations. For example, assume that one succeeds and that success is ascribed to volitional help from others. This is anticipated to give rise to gratitude. One might think that gratitude, in turn, promotes actions instrumental to the maintenance of the relationship, such as the purchase of a gift (the "retribution"). This sequence would be depicted as:

Outcome (success)————————> Attribution (help from others)

————————> Affect (gratitude)————————>

Action (gift purchase).

Or, consider a school setting in which a bright pupil fails because of a lack of effort. Inasmuch as this is a controllable cause, a teacher should experience some anger. Anger, in turn, is expected to give rise to some form of punishment. This sequence is depicted as:

Outcome (failure of a pupil)————————> Attribution (lack of effort)

————————> Affect (anger)————————> Action (punishment)

Many studies have confirmed that students failing because of a lack of effort indeed are more severely punished by teachers than those failing because of a lack of ability (see Weiner & Kukla, 1970, for one early investigation).

And let's consider still another example of an attribution-affect-behavior sequence. Imagine that an individual ascribes social rejection to some uncontrollable personal characteristic, such as physical unattractiveness. This should produce hurt feelings, shame, and humiliation. These affective experiences are likely to result in subsequent avoidance behavior in interpersonal contexts:

Outcome (social rejection)————————> Attribution (unattractiveness)

————————> Affect (shame and humiliation)————————> Action (withdrawal)

General Summary

It has been contended in this chapter that there is a temporal sequence to a motivational episode. The sequence is thinking to feeling to acting. Attributional analyses have pointed out how answers to why questions, or answers regarding the perceived cause of an event, are linked to quite specific affective reactions. These responses, in turn, provide a directional component to behavior.

I want to return now to my mentor and re-iterate his influence. Jack has always emphasized the conceptual analysis of behavior. His contributions in part lay in his very clear and systematic thinking about what motivation is. I have tried to follow in this lead, although I have to take responsibility for any failure. He also has stressed an active organism and focused on the direction of behavior as the key motivational issue. I share these beliefs. He also told me to theorize about a thinking-feeling organism. I have tried to do this. Finally, he conveyed that we should have a sense of history and try to build on our predecessors. I hope I have been able to do this. Thus, I can conclude by saying: "Ich bin auch ein Atkinsonian.

AUTHOR NOTE

This paper was written while the author was supported by Grant MH38014 from the Public Health Service, National Institute of Health. Reprint requests should be sent to Bernard Weiner, Department of Psychology, University of California, Los Angeles, CA 90024.

REFERENCES

Averill, J. R. (1983). Studies on anger and aggression. *American Psychologist, 38,* 1145–1160.

Betancourt, H. (1983). *Causal attributions, empathy, and emotions as determinants of helping behavior: An integrative approach.* Unpublished doctoral dissertation, University of California, Los Angeles.

Brown, J., & Weiner, B. (1984). Affective consequences of ability versus effort ascriptions: Controversies, resolutions, and quandaries. *Journal of Educational Psychology, 76,* 146–158.

Carlsmith, J. M., & Gross, A. E. (1969). Some effects of guilt on compliance. *Journal of Personality and Social Psychology, 11,* 232–239.

Covington, M. V., & Omelich, C. L. (1984). An empirical examination of Weiner's critique of attribution research. *Journal of Educational Psychology, 76,* 1214–1225.

Graham, S. (1984). Communicating sympathy and anger to black and white children: The cognitive (attributional) consequences of affective cues. *Journal of Personality and Social Psychology, 47,* 40–54.

Jagacinski, C., & Nicholls, J. G. (1984). Conceptions of ability and related affects in task involvement and ego involvement. *Journal of Educational Psychology, 76,* 909–919.

Meyer, J. P., & Mulherin, A. (1980). From attribution to helping: An analysis of the mediating effects of affect on expectancy. *Journal of Personality and Social Psychology, 39,* 201–210.

Reisenzein, R. (1985). A structural equation of Weiner's attribution-affect model of helping behavior. *Journal of Personality and Social Psychology.*

Weiner, B. (1980a). A cognitive (attribution)–emotion-action model of motivated behavior: An analysis of judgments of help-giving. *Journal of Personality and Social Psychology, 39,* 186–200.

Weiner, B. (1980b). May I borrow your class notes? An attributional analysis of judgments of help-giving in an achievement-related context. *Journal of Educational Psychology, 72,* 676–681.

Weiner, B. (1982). The emotional consequences of causal ascriptions. In M. S. Clark & S. T. Fiske (Eds.), *Affect and cognition: The 17th Annual Carnegie Symposium on Cognition* (pp. 185–209). Hillsdale, NJ: Erlbaum.

Weiner, B. (1985). An attributional theory of achievement motivation and emotion. *Psychological Review*.

Weiner, B., & Kukla, A. (1970). An attributional analysis of achievement motivation. *Journal of Personality and Social Psychology, 15*, 1–20.

Weiner, B., Graham, S., & Chandler, C. (1982). Causal antecedents of pity, anger, and guilt. *Personality and Social Psychology Bulletin, 8*, 226–232.

Wicker, F. W., Payne, G. C., & Morgan, R. D. (1983). Participant descriptions of guilt and shame. *Motivation and Emotion, 7*, 25–39.

Chapter Three

CONSCIOUS AND UNCONSCIOUS PROCESSES IN THE

PSYCHOLOGY OF MOTIVATION

Nathan Brody

Wesleyan University

In their book, *The Dynamics of Action*, Atkinson and Birch (1970) distinguish among three possible relations between phenomenal or conscious states and motivational states. They indicate that phenomenal states may stand in an epiphenomenal relation of parallelism to motivational states. In this view phenomenal states are outside the chain of causal influence. Alternatively, phenomenal states may exert a causal influence on motivational states. Finally, Atkinson and Birch propose a variant of their second position which asserts that all motivational states are influenced by phenomenal states. In this chapter I want to present arguments for a somewhat different way of construing the relations between phenomenal states and motivational states. I shall argue that phenomenal states do in point of fact exert an influence on motivational states. However, motivational states are only weakly related to their phenomenal manifestations. Thus, the phenomenal representation of the state is not to be construed as an exhaustive representation. In addition, I shall argue that in many if not all instances the influence of conscious motivational states or conscious components of motivational states is parallel to the influence of unconscious motivational states. Although I shall argue for the existence of unconscious motivational influences, I do not wish to argue that the influence of unconscious motivational states is in any fundamental sense different from the influence of conscious motivational states or conscious components of motivational states.

I realize that the topic I have chosen is a broad one. I obviously do not propose to treat it exhaustively (for a more extensive treatment see Brody, 1983). My chapter will have two parts. In the first part I will analyze the results of three experiments that provide data relevant to the influence of conscious and unconscious motivational states on behavior. In the second part of the chapter I will discuss recent research on the lateralization of affective perception, including some research that I have recently completed in collaboration with my students and colleagues at Wesleyan. I shall argue that these studies provide evidence in support of a structural spatial representation of independent processing of affect that helps us to understand the possibility of unconscious motivational influences.

The first study I shall discuss is a study reported by Zimbardo, Cohen, Weisenberg, Dworkin, and Firestone (1969). It is a study that figures prominently in Nisbett and Wilson's (1977) paper suggesting that verbal reports are rarely veridical and it is a study that is extensively discussed in a recently published critique of Nisbett and Wilson's paper (Quattrone, 1985). The Zimbardo et al. study is one of a series of studies that attempts to manipulate motivational states by dissonance instructions. In this study dealing with pain induced by electric shock, subjects are induced to endure an additional series of painful shocks after having been exposed to an initial series of painful shocks. Subjects in a high dissonance group are given few or inadequate reasons for continuing in the experiment. It is assumed that their knowledge that they have agreed to continue in the experiment is dissonant with their knowledge that they will have to endure painful shocks and they are not provided with a particularly compelling rationale for their additional exposure to the shocks. They are able to eliminate their state of dissonance if they ascertain that the shocks are not painful. Subjects in the low dissonance condition are given persuasive reasons for continuing as subjects in the experiment. Thus, their knowledge that they will have to endure painful shocks is not assumed to produce a state of high dissonance since they have a persuasive rationale for their actions. The subjects in the low dissonance condition are not assumed to be motivated to eliminate pain to the same degree as the subjects in the high state of dissonance. Zimbardo and his colleagues obtained both verbal and behavioral indices of the state of pain induced by the shocks. In agreement with their theoretical expectations Zimbardo et al. found on several of their indices that subjects assigned to their high dissonance condition appeared to have lower levels of pain than subjects assigned to their low dissonance condition.

In their analysis of this and related dissonance and attributional studies manipulating motivational states Nisbett and Wilson assert that the behavioral manifestations or indices of level of pain appear to exhibit larger or more complete reductions than the verbal reports about pain. In fact, they classify the Zimbardo et al. study as one in which there was a statistically significant reduction in various behavioral indices of pain combined with evidence of a non significant reduction in verbal reports indexing the level of pain experienced. Thus, Nisbett and Wilson argue that the behavioral indices provide a more sensitive and veridical indicator of the changes in the motivational state than the verbal reports. In his critique of the Nisbett and Wilson paper Quattrone argues that there is a large body of attributional and dissonance studies that rely on verbal report dependent variables. Thus, he asserts that it is not the case that dissonance and attributional induced changes in psychological states cannot be indexed by changes in verbal reports. Moreover, Quattrone takes issue with Nisbett and Wilson's interpretation of the Zimbardo et al. study and other related studies indicating that changes in the behavioral indices of psychological states occur in the absence of changes in verbal reports. He indicates that such results are either anomalous, attributable to inappropriate verbal indices, reflect effects of behavioral dependent variables on subsequent measures of verbal reports thus, in effect, contaminating the verbal reports, or are based on failure to examine thoroughly the details of the quantitative changes in both sets of measures. In this connection, Quattrone notes that in the Zimbardo study the subjects in the high dissonance condition do exhibit reductions in their verbal reports of pain relative to the subjects in the low dissonance condition. However, the changes are not quite statistically significant at the conventional .05 level. The fact that the changes in several behavioral indices are statistically significant does not establish that the difference between high and low dissonance groups between behavioral and verbal indices is statistically significant. The existence of a statistically significant difference and the absence of a statistically significant difference does not imply that the difference between the differences is statistically significant.

In order to understand the import of the Zimbardo et al. study for a resolution of the issues addressed by Quattrone and Nisbett and Wilson, it will be necessary to examine their data more carefully. Table 1 presents the actual verbal report data obtained in the Zimbardo et al. study. An examination of the data reported in Table 1 does indicate agreement with Quattrone that there is some evidence that subjects in the high dissonance group do exhibit larger decreases in their reported pain than subjects in the low dissonance group (−9 vs. −2). What is not discussed by Quattrone or Nisbett and Wilson is the difference in magnitude of reduction of verbal reports exhibited by subjects in the high dissonance group and subjects in the high moderate control group who are exposed to shocks of the same intensity during the pretest period and are then exposed to shocks of moderate intensity during the posttest period in the absence of an intervening choice to continue in the experiment. Not surprisingly, the control subjects respond to the reduction in the intensity of the shocks they experience by reporting that they have lower levels of pain. Also, the reduction in pain reported by subjects in the control group is clearly larger in magnitude than the reduction in pain reported by subjects in the high dissonance group (−26 vs. −9).

Table 1

Mean Perceived Pain and Physical Shock

Level of Sample Shocks

Group	N	Mean Shock (Volts)	Perceived Pain		Difference
			Precommitment	Postcommitment	
Control:					
High-Moderate	15	45–22	46	20	−26
High-High	15	44	50	47	−3
Dissonance:					
Low	20	38	49	47	−2
High	20	49	46	37	−9

Zimbardo, Cohen, Weisenberg, Dworkin & Firestone, 1969

Although the reduction in magnitude of reported pain is larger in the high moderate control group than in the high dissonance group, there is little or no difference between these groups in the several behavioral indices of pain. These two groups exhibit approximately equal magnitude of change in a learning task in which pain tends to increase the number of trials to criterion and in physiological indices of pain. These results indicate that subjects in the high dissonance condition exhibit changes in verbal reports that are clearly of smaller magnitude than do subjects in the control group who experienced shocks of lower intensity. However, the behavioral indices of pain support the inference that the magnitude of pain present is the same in subjects in the high dissonance condition and in the high moderate control group.

Quattrone has an additional criticism of the Nisbett and Wilson analysis of the Zimbardo et al. experiment. He claims that the analysis is logically untenable because of the ambiguity of the relationship between the experience of pain and the behavioral manifestations of pain. He argues as follows:

> when GSR data are used to infer an individual's experienced pain, it is not assumed that the experience of pain directly mediated or caused the GSR. . . . Because pain does not directly mediate the GSR, why should differences in inferred pain, produced by manipulations of choice and justification, be expected to lead to differences in the GSR? In other words, if one subscribed to the theory that dogs bark before an earthquake can a city be razed by exciting its kennels? . . . Yet a choice and justification manipulation designed to affect inferred pain (analogous to "exciting the kennels") was hypothesized and found to affect GSR (analogous to "razing a city"; Zimbardo, Cohen, Dworkin, & Firestone, 1969), and it is nothing more than pretense to claim to understand how the effect was obtained. (Quattrone, 1985, p. 20–21)

Quattrone's critique rests on the assumption that the psychological state that was manipulated in the Zimbardo et al. experiment must be a phenomenal state since the putative explanation of the change in the state of pain involves an appeal to processes of thought that could occur phenomenally. However, the Nisbett and Wilson analysis directly challenges the centrality of phenomenal states in the causal network surrounding this type of experiment. In effect, Quattrone's argument attacks a straw man. It is he who assumes that the state of pain that must be affected by dissonance manipulations is the experience of pain. A more plausible interpretation of the results of this experiment in line with Nisbett and Wilson's position is that the dissonance manipulation does not influence the experience of pain but rather a pain state whose meaning is not isomorphic with or exhausted by its phenomenal representations. Moreover, there is ample empirical justification, in part developed in the original Zimbardo et al. report of their experiment, for the particular behavioral manifestations of the state of pain used as dependent variables in their experiment. One can interpret the results of their experiment by arguing that the dissonance manipulations induced a pattern of reasoning in subjects of which they may not be aware. This, in turn, produced a change in the level of pain of which the subjects were also unaware, leading, in turn, to a series of diverse changes in the behavioral manifestations of the pain. Note that this argument does not imply that the influence of the, shall we say, partially unconscious state of pain was fundamentally different from the influence it would have if it were more completely phenomenally represented. The claim here is only that the influence of the state of pain does not require its complete phenomenal representation. It can be argued on additional grounds that the behavioral effects of the pain state are not in point of fact mediated by the phenomenal representation of the state of pain since, as noted by Nisbett and Wilson, the correlation between the magnitude of changes in the verbal reports about pain and the behavioral changes was close to zero.

The second experiment that I would like to discuss is one of a series of studies initiated by Lloyd Silverman and his colleagues designed to test empirically hypotheses derived from psychoanalytic theory. In the study reported by Silverman and Spiro (1968), schizophrenic subjects were presented with a subliminal or supraliminal picture designed to intensify unconscious conflicts. The picture presented was that of a charging lion with bared teeth. The subliminal status of the stimulus was ascertained by the subject's inability to discriminate between different stimuli with better than chance accuracy under the viewing conditions used in the experiment. An additional stimulus condition was used in the experiment—the presentation of the stimulus supraliminally with the additional requirement that subjects verbally describe the stimulus. Following exposure to the stimuli, the experimenters obtained a number of measures of the psychopathological state of their subjects. Among the indices of psychopathological state that they observed were word associate behavior, pathological overt behaviors, reports of pathological body experiences and accuracy of story recall. The subjects exposed to the subliminal stimulus tended to exhibit increases in psychopathology relative to the subjects exposed to the supraliminal stimulus on several indices of psychopathology. However, subjects who were exposed to the supraliminal stimulus with the requirement that they verbally describe the stimulus exhibited the same magnitude of increase in psychopathology as they did under conditions in which they were exposed to the stimuli subliminally.

The Silverman and Spiro study was designed to demonstrate the importance of unconscious conflicts on behavior. Paradoxically, it demonstrates that the influence of unconscious states is parallel to the influence of conscious states if the conscious states are made salient. Evidently, under conditions of supraliminal stimulus presentation without instructions to vocalize, the schizophrenic subjects simply ignore or do not attend to the stimulus.

The last experiment I will discuss in this series is designed to demonstrate the importance of phenomenal states. It is an experiment dealing with the familiar overjustification effect pioneered by Deci (1975). In this paradigm subjects are given an extrinsic reward for performing a task and are then given an opportunity to engage spontaneously in the rewarded activity. It is usually found that subjects who are presented with the reward are less likely to engage spontaneously in the activity that has been extrinsically rewarded. Subjects are assumed to reason that they have engaged in the activity for the reward and that the activity is of little extrinsic interest to them. Pittman, Cooper and Smith (1977) attempted to manipulate the cognitions that were assumed to be involved in the overjustification phenomenon. Their subjects were assigned to groups that received rewards combined with false physiological feedback. These subjects were informed that their pattern of physiological response was indicative either of an intrinsic or an extrinsic interest in a game. In addition, subjects were assigned to two additional groups that either received an extrinsic reward or did not receive a reward. The false physiological feedback did influence the verbal reports of the subjects about their extrinsic or intrinsic interest in the game, as is indicated by the data in Table 2. It is clear that the subjects assigned to the group receiving false physiological feedback indicative of an intrinsic interest in the game express the highest level of intrinsic interest. Pittman, Smith, and Cooper also obtained behavioral data—the number of trials on which their subjects spontaneously chose to play the game during a free choice period. An examination of these data, presented in Table 2, indicates that subjects assigned to the false physiological feedback group receiving an intrinsic cue exhibited greater interest in the task than subjects in the false physiological feedback group receiving an extrinsic cue, thus supporting the hypothesis of the study. However, there is an additional finding present in these data that is not discussed by Pittman and his associates. Note that subjects who did not receive a reward exhibited the highest level of interest in the task during the free choice period, as indexed by their behavior of choosing spontaneously to play the game. The number of trials they played the game was significantly higher than the number of trials the subjects who received a reward combined with an intrinsic cue played the game. However, subjects who did not receive a reward expressed lower, although not significantly lower, intrinsic interest in the game than subjects who received a reward combined with an intrinsic interest cue. Therefore, the behavioral differences between these groups cannot be attributed to differences in their cognitions as indexed by their verbal reports. It appears that the presentation of an extrinsic reward decreases intrinsic interest independent of subject's beliefs as expressed verbally about their intrinsic interest. There are any of a number of ad hoc subsidiary hypotheses that might be invoked to explain these results. Perhaps cognitions about intrinsic interest do not mediate the behavioral effects of reward. This hypothesis appears to be partially incorrect since manipulations of these cognitions did in point of fact change behavior. Alternatively, the behavioral effects might be mediated by other cognitions that were not assessed in this study. The explanation I would favor is as follows: Changes in cognition do influence behavior. The motivational state induced by the presentation of a reward is only imperfectly indexed by cognitions about the state that are phenomenally represented. Hence, the total motivational influence of the state contains unconscious components.

Let me suggest several conclusions based on this brief review of three experiments. Motivational states have unconscious components and hence may be incompletely indexed by verbal reports about the state. Unconscious influences on behavior may exist for several different processes. Individuals may not be aware of the stimuli that influence them. The effects of subliminal stimuli in the Silverman and Spiro study would appear to support that conclusion. Of course, the conclusion is supported by an abundant literature not discussed here. The processes of reasoning that may be initiated by a stimulus or an experimental manipulation may occur without phenomenal representation. This conclusion is suggested if not

Table 2

Verbal Reports and Behaviors Following

Manipulation of Intrinsic and Extrinsic Cues

Groups:	No Reward No Cue	Reward No Cue	Reward Extrinsic Cue	Reward Intrinsic Cue
Verbal				
Mean arousal attributed to intrinsic interest	47.3	40.2	36.0	55.3
Behavioral				
Mean number of trials	18.2	4.2	2.4	10.5

Pittman, Cooper & Smith, 1977

strongly supported by Nisbett and Wilson's review of literature indicating that subjects do not spontaneously report the processes of reasoning that they are alleged to engage in whose hypothetical occurrence is presumed to constitute the putative explanation of their behavior. Thus, subjects in the Zimbardo et al. study do not, when questioned, reproduce a dissonance explanation of their behavior and, indeed, are found to deny such an explanation when it is presented to them. The psychological processes that are initiated as a result of manipulations of psychological states that lead to behavioral changes occur outside of awareness. That is, subjects are not aware of the connection between changes in their state of pain and in their basal skin conductance levels. Schizophrenics may not be aware of the processes relating arousal of psychological conflicts to changes in the various behavioral indices of psychological disturbance they exhibit.

Although I have interpreted these experiments as providing evidence for the existence of unconscious motivational influences, no claim is made that unconscious influences are fundamentally different from the influences of conscious motivational states. Indeed, each of the experiments discussed provides evidence for the presence of parallel motivational influences of phenomenal states. Quattrone has noted that there is large body of research demonstrating dissonance and attributional manipulations in which the dependent variable is a verbal report. So too, in the Zimbardo et al. experiment dissonance manipulations did appear to at least weakly influence verbal reports about pain. In the Silverman and Spiro study the effects of supraliminal stimuli accompanied by vocalization were parallel to the effects of subliminal stimuli. In the Pittman, Cooper and Smith study the effects of manipulations in cognitions about intrinsic interest led to changes in behavior that counteracted the effects of extrinsic rewards. Note that these experiments do not support an epiphenomenal position that assumes that phenomenal states are without behavioral consequences. Rather they support the view that phenomenal states have behavioral consequences that are often parallel to the effects of unconscious states.

In the second part of this chapter I want to describe three experiments dealing with the lateralization of the perception of affect. The discussion of lateralization effects in the context of a discussion of conscious and unconscious motivational influences is justified, in part, because such studies provide a structural model or metaphor for the independent registration of information in different parts of the brain and thus provide one way of understanding unconscious influences.

The first study I would like to discuss was performed by Dawson and Schell (1982). It was based on phenomena first reported by Corteen and Wood (1972). In their study Corteen and Wood associated words with electrical shock. After the initial conditioning phase of their study Ss were presented with a shadowing task in which the previously shocked words along with control words were presented to one ear while Ss were instructed to shadow words presented to the other ear in a dichotic listening task. They found that the previously shocked words presented to the unattended ear that subjects claimed they were not aware of produced electrodermal responses indicative of an emotional response to the stimuli.

The Corteen and Wood study may be interpreted as providing evidence of unconscious influences on behavior. However, the study has generated controversy. There is a reported failure to replicate the study (see Wardlaw & Kroll, 1976) and there are suggestions in the literature that the phenomena they reported may be attributable to momentary lapses of attention. In their study, Dawson and Schell attempted to institute a number of controls for the possibility of attentional lapses. In addition, they varied the ear to which the emotional stimuli were presented. They found that evidence of electrodermal responses indicative of an emotional response to the stimuli in the absence of any apparent attention to, or state of awareness of, the stimulus that was presented could be obtained if the emotional stimuli were presented to the left ear. If the emotional stimuli were presented to the right ear, the effect did not appear. Dawson and Schell note that the left hemisphere is involved in the control of speech. Hence the shadowing task must engage the left hemisphere. When the stimuli to be shadowed are presented to the right ear, the left hemisphere receives the words to be shadowed directly on the assumption that the predominant transmission pathways to the hemispheres are contralateral for auditory stimuli. The right hemisphere is then assumed to be free to mediate the emotional response to the stimuli. It should also be noted that there is evidence that the right hemisphere is specialized for the processing of affective stimuli (Bryden & Ley, 1985). If the right ear receives the emotional stimuli, they are then sent directly to the left hemisphere. The words to be shadowed in this case would be sent initially to the right hemisphere and then must be subject to interhemispheric transfer to the left hemisphere for the control of the verbal shadowing responses. The apparent involvement of the left hemisphere in shadowing words does not leave that hemisphere free to mediate the emotional response to the stimulus.

Dawson and Schell's study appears to suggest that individuals can have an emotional response to a stimulus that they are not aware of. In addition the lack of awareness may be understood in terms of a spatial structural model that represents the emotional stimulus as literally having a particular location that under certain circumstances renders it immune from a verbal representation.

The second study I shall discuss is one of a series of studies performed by Davidson and his colleagues dealing with the lateralization of affective states. Davidson, Perl, and Saron (1983) tested a hypothesis relating individual differences in tendencies to be repressive to hemispheric assymetries. They assumed that individuals classified as repressors might have less functional cooperation between the hemispheres. In particular, they assumed that such individuals would be less likely to transfer affective information from the right hemisphere to the left hemisphere than individuals who were classified as nonrepressors. The tendency to hold affective information in the right hemisphere would create a functional independence between an affective experience and the ability to describe that experience verbally. Such a dissociation between affect and verbal report would appear to be centrally related to repression. In order to test this hypothesis, Davidson, Perl and Saron tachistoscopically presented their subjects with faces depicting various emotional expressions. Their subjects were required to identify the emotional expression of each face. The stimuli were lateralized and were presented to either the right or left visual field. They assumed that stimuli presented to the left visual field would require an interhemispheric transfer of information from the right to the left hemisphere. Such stimuli are initially transmitted to the right hemisphere since the contralateral pathways are dominant. The information would have to be transferred to the left hemisphere for the verbal report. If repressors have difficulty transferring affective information from the right to the left hemisphere, they should perform poorly relative to non-repressors when the faces were presented to the left visual field. They should not, however, have deficits for stimuli presented to the right visual field since no interhemispheric transfer of information is required in this instance. Davidson, Perl, and Saron obtained results that supported their hypothesis. There were no differences between individuals classified as repressors on the basis of performance on a paper and pencil test and individuals classified as non-repressors in judging stimuli presented to the right visual field. However, individuals classified as repressors had less accurate identification of the emotional expression of faces than individuals classified as non-repressors when the faces were presented in the left visual field. Although these results support the hypothesis, they are subject to a different interpretation. It may be the case that repressors are less accurate in the perception of affect than non-repressors when the affective stimuli are presented to the right hemisphere. That is, Davidson, Perl, and Saron assume that both groups of subjects perceive affect equally well when affective stimuli are presented to the right hemisphere. They differ on the ability to transfer affective information to the left hemisphere. In any case, this study demonstrates a possible relationship between a personality dimension assumed to be related to response to unconscious emotional states and a structural model of interhemispheric transfer of information.

The last study that I would like to discuss is one of a series of studies on lateralized priming that I have performed in collaboration with my colleagues and students at Wesleyan (Brody, Goodman, Halm & Sebrechts, 1985). In these studies subjects are required to judge whether a word is either positive or negative in affective meaning. The stimulus words are presented tachistoscopically to the right or left visual field. The words are preceded by prime stimuli that are also lateralized. In the data I shall present, the prime stimuli were, in one experiment, happy, sad, or neutral schematic faces and in another experiment, positive, negative or neutral words. In the experiment in which words were used as prime stimuli, the duration of the prime stimuli was varied. The prime stimuli were presented at 10, 30, or 60 milliseconds. At 10 milliseconds the stimuli were subliminal. That is, our subjects were not able to discriminate with above chance accuracy whether the prime stimulus that preceded the target stimulus was positive or negative. At 60 milliseconds the prime stimuli were supraliminal and our subjects were aware of the stimuli and were instructed to ignore them and to judge the target stimuli. We found that the effects of the prime stimuli were comparable across variations of duration and variations in whether the prime stimulus was either a face or a word.

FIGURE 1. *Semantic prime scores for lateralized prime and target stimuli.*

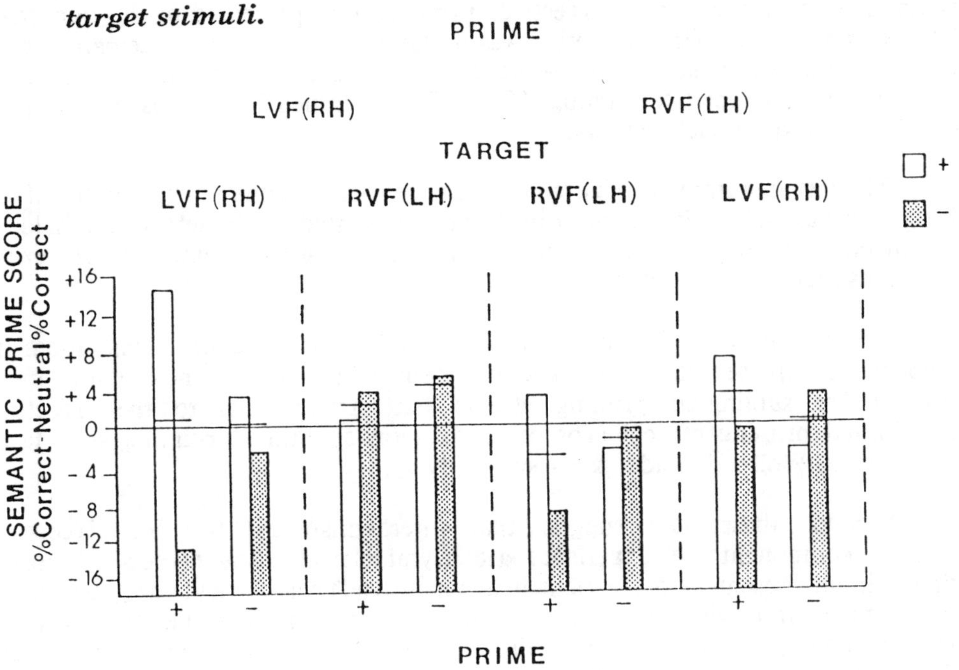

Figure 1 presents the principle results of these experiments. The data presented in Figure 1 are semantic prime scores indicating the extent to which a particular affective prime stimulus (either a positive or negative face or word) has led to changes in the accuracy of judgment of the target words relative to the effects of a neutral prime stimulus presented to the same visual field for the same targets. Examine the data presented in the first quadrant of Figure 1. Semantic prime scores are presented for left visual field primes of left visual field targets. There is a strong semantic prime effect for positive prime stimuli in this case. Note that positive prime stimuli presented to the left visual field increase the accuracy of judgment of positive targets delivered to the left visual field and decrease the accuracy of judgment of left visual field negative targets. Since 50% accuracy would constitute chance judgments and 100% accuracy would be perfect judgment, the magnitude of this semantic priming effect is quite large relative to the scale of possible effects. It should be noted that under most conditions the accuracy of judgment in these tasks is approximately 75%.

Examine the second quadrant in Figure 1. This quadrant presents data for the effect of left visual field prime stimuli on targets presented to the right visual field and thus deals with interhemispheric transfer effects. Note that the strong positive semantic priming effect does not exhibit interhemispheric transfer. Positive primes presented to the left visual field do not increase the accuracy of judgment of positive targets and decrease the accuracy of judgment of negative targets presented to the right visual field.

Examine the data in the third quadrant of Figure 1. This quadrant presents semantic prime scores for the effects of prime stimuli presented to the right visual field on right visual field targets. Again there is evidence of a semantic prime effect for positive prime stimuli—although in this case the semantic priming effect is weaker than the positive priming effect that is obtained for left visual field prime stimuli of left visual field targets.

The last quadrant of Figure 1 presents semantic prime scores for the effects of right visual field prime stimuli on targets presented to the left visual field. In this instance there is some evidence that the positive prime stimuli exhibit interhemispheric transfer effects.

These data may be interpreted to imply several conclusions about the independent representation of affective knowledge. First, these data present evidence for subliminal priming effects that are parallel to the effects of supraliminal priming effects (for other data on subliminal priming see Marcel, 1983; Fowler, Wolford, Slade, & Tassinary, 1981).

Second, these data suggest that interhemispheric transfer effects for affective components of experience are asymmetrical. The effects of positive prime stimuli presented to the right hemisphere (left visual field) are restricted to right hemisphere targets and do not transfer to left hemisphere targets. However, left hemisphere positive prime stimuli do appear to influence, albeit weakly, both left and right hemisphere targets.

Although right hemisphere prime stimuli do not have a semantic prime influence on left hemisphere targets, they do appear to exert a generalized influence on right hemisphere targets. Examine the second quadrant of Figure 1 again. Note that each of the semantic prime scores is positive, indicating that affective primes, whether they are positive or negative, lead to greater accuracy of judgment than neutral prime stimuli. There is in point of fact a statistically significant difference ($p < .01$) between the accuracy of judgment of targets presented to the right visual field preceded by affective primes presented to the left visual field, as opposed to the accuracy of judgment of these targets when preceded by neutral primes delivered to the left visual field.

The asymmetric interhemispheric transfer effects obtained in these studies may be interpreted by reference to the effects of studies of brain damaged subjects. Damage to the left hemisphere is associated with states of depression. One might assume that the left hemisphere is specialized for signaling positive affect. Damage to the right hemisphere is associated with an indifference reaction and an inability to experience any affective state. It may be assumed that the right hemisphere is specialized for signaling the presence of emotional states (Heilman, Bowers, & Valenstein, 1985). The results in this experiment are congruent with these clinical findings. That is, the left hemisphere was found to transfer the effect of positive primes to left hemisphere targets. The right hemisphere did not transfer specific information about an affective stimulus to the left hemisphere but it did appear to prepare the left hemisphere to process affective stimuli and thus did appear to signal the presence of an emotional stimulus.

The studies presented in the second part of this chapter provide evidence for the independent representation of affective experience and verbal reports about these experiences. They suggest that, at least under certain limited and specialized laboratory conditions, affective experiences may not be subject to complete interhemispheric transfers. The functional significance of this independence in ordinary experience when no special attempts are taken to create disassociations remains to be determined. It does appear to me, however, that the laterality studies I have reviewed do help us to understand the influence of unconscious motivational states that were outlined in the first part of this chapter.

52

REFERENCES

Atkinson, J. W., & Birch, D. (1970). *The dynamics of action*. New York: Wiley.

Brody, N. (1983). *Human motivation: Commentary on goal-directed action*. New York: Academic Press.

Brody, N., Goodman, S. E., Halm, E., Krinzman, S., & Sebrechts, M. (1985). Lateralized affective priming of lateralized affectively valued target words. Submitted for publication.

Bryden, M. P., & Ley, R. G. (1983). Right-hemispheric involvement in the perception and expression emotion in normal humans. In K. M. Heilman & P. Satz (Eds.), *Neuropsychology of human emotion*. New York: Guilford.

Corteen, R. J., & Wood, B. (1972). Autonomic responses to shock-associated words in an unattended channel. *Journal of Experimental Psychology, 94,* 308–313.

Dawson, M. E., & Schell, A. M. (1982). Electrodermal responses to attended and nonattended significant stimuli during dichotic listening. *Journal of Experimental Psychology: Human Perception and Performance, 8,* 315–324.

Fowler, C. A., Wolford, A., Slade, R., & Tassinary, L. (1981). Lexical access with and without awareness. *Journal of Experimental Psychology: General, 110,* 341-362.

Heilman, K. E., Bowers, D., & Valenstein, E. (1985). Emotional disorders associated with neurological diseases. In K. M. Heilman & E. Valenstein (Eds.) *Clinical neuropsychology*. New York: Oxford.

Marcel, A. J. (1983). Conscious and unconscious perception: Experiments in visual masking and recognition. *Cognitive Psychology, 15,* 197–237.

Nisbett, R. E., & Wilson, T. D. (1977). Telling more than we can know: Verbal reports on mental processes. *Psychological Review, 84,* 231-259.

Pittman, T. S., Cooper, E. E., & Smith, T. W. (1977). Attribution of causality and the overjustification effect. *Personality and Social Psychology Bulletin, 3,* 280–283.

Quattrone, G. E. (1985). On the congruity between internal states and action. *Psychological Bulletin, 98,* 3–40.

Silverman, L. H., & Spiro, R. H. (1968). The effects of subliminal, supraliminal and vocalized aggression on the ego functioning of schizophrenics. *Journal of Nervous and Mental Disease, 146,* 50–61.

Wardlaw, K. A., & Kroll, N. E. A. (1976). Autonomic responses to shock-associated words in a nonattended message: A failure to replicate. *Journal of Experimental Psychology: Human Perception and Performance, 2,* 357–360.

Zimbardo, P. G., Cohen, A., Weisenberg, M., Dworkin, L., & Firestone (1969). The control of experimental pain. In P. G. Zimbardo, *The cognitive control of motivation.* Glenville, IL: Scott, Foresman and Co.

Chapter Four

MOTIVATIONAL CHAOS: A SIMPLE MODEL

Julius Kuhl

University of Osnabrück

In psychology, the use of formal models is controversial. Some psychologists believe that the premature construction of formal models blinds us to the complexities of the phenomena to be explained, while others maintain that only formal models can achieve what science is all about: Replace our everyday intuitions about the world by precise formal statements whose implications can be tested empirically. Although descriptive methods are more adequate for capturing the complexities of behavior in natural settings than formal models, the former provide little explanatory value. However, descriptive and formal approaches are complementary rather than contradictory. Ideally there should be an optimal balance between documentation of behavioral phenomena and development of formal models explaining those observations. In most areas of social psychology this balance has not yet been achieved. Documentation of phenomena fills far more journal space than formal modelling. In the area of social motivation the development of formal models is more advanced than in most other areas due to the work of Atkinson and his associates (1957; 1958; 1981; Atkinson & Feather, 1966; Atkinson & Birch, 1970; 1978).

This work contains many examples for one of the most intriguing facets of formal modelling: Numerous testable hypotheses were derived that had never been tested before because they run counter to most investigators' intuitions. For example, highly achievement-oriented subjects do not aspire toward very difficult tasks, as might be expected on intuitive grounds, but toward intermediately difficult tasks as derived from Atkinson's (1957) risk-taking model. People do not maximize time spent in activities they prefer, disregarding non-preferred activities, but they allocate some proportion of time to *all* action alternatives perceived according to a "matching principle" derived from the *Dynamics of Action* (Atkinson & Birch, 1978). Subjects do not stick with their most preferred behavior (e.g., preferred difficulty level at an achievement task) even if the expectancies and incentives affecting their decisions do not change (Kuhl & Blankenship, 1979a, b). On the basis of Atkinson and Birch's theory, variable behavior is expected even when the personal and situational determinants remain constant.

Many psychologists fail to recognize the heuristic power of formal modelling, its function to make us aware of counter-intuitive implications of intuitively compelling assumptions. In this chapter, I would like to discuss the implications of one assumption that is also contained the the *Dynamics of Action* (Atkinson & Birch, 1970), namely the assumption regarding the "recursiveness" reflexivity of psychological processes. In Atkinson and Birch's theory, the strength of a motivational tendency at a given point in time affects one of its determinants (i.e., consummatory force) at a subsequent point in time. The stronger an organism is motivated to perform an activity, the faster will its motivation be reduced once the activity is enacted. The hungrier I am, the faster I will reduce my hunger when eating (e.g., by taking bigger bites than in a less hungry state). It is worthwhile to focus on the assumption of reflexivity because some of its more general implications disprove an argument advanced by scholars who are reluctant to accept formal modelling.

Doesn't the explanation of complex real-life phenomena require models that would be too complex to handle even by the most advanced mathematical techniques? Physicists, who were among the first to take advantage of new insight regarding the mathematical implications of reflexive or "recursive" models, discovered that they could account for very complex phenomena (e.g., "chaotic" turbulences) on the basis of very simple models once they added the property of recursiveness to these models. Could it be that some of the simple models psychologists have been elaborating for many years—often up to the point that the model had to be discarded because of its complexity—could account for complex phenomena without adding more and more parameters simply by making them reflexive? To deal with this question we need to discuss the concepts of reflexivity and interdependence in psychological models in some detail.

The Concepts of Reflexivity and Interdependence

Interdependence and reflexivity are two difficult characteristics of psychological processes. How can we ever predict the outcomes of a complex system presumably comprising a multitude of processes if we assume that all processes are *interdependent*, that is the outcome of one subsystem affects other subsystems, and *reflexive*, that is the outcome of each subsystem affects the future state of the same subsystem? It is only natural that many psychologists have found it useful to focus on one subsystem (e.g., memory) and disregard others (e.g., emotion). In this chapter, I would like to explore some of the effects of a simple way to incorporate the features of interdependence and reflexivity in our models. As it turns out, adding these features to some of the most frequently used (non-monotonic) models may have dramatic effects. The elaborated model explains the transition from stable and consistent behavior to virtually chaotic behavior as a function of a slight variation of one parameter beyond a critical point. As this parameter may be interpreted as being a function of a trait-like dispositional factor in some of the models, we will see how consistent as well as inconsistent behavior may be attributable to the same stable dispositional factor only by incorporating the assumptions regarding the reflexivity and interdependence of psychological processes in our models.

Let us take the cognition-emotion relationship as an example. If not our models, then our intuitions tell us that emotions affect cognitions and vice versa. The more emotional and motivated I feel about reaching some goal, the more confident I become that I will be able to reach it. Conversely, the greater my expectation to accomplish a desired goal state, the more motivated I feel to strive for it. These two intuitions from everyday experience are corroborated by numerous experimental results, for instance in achievement motivation research (Atkinson, 1957; Heckhausen, 1967; Heckhausen, Schmalt & Schneider, in press; Weiner, 1980). However, in many areas of psychological research the prevailing models do not take account of the dynamic features of cognition-emotion *interdependence*. Most psychological theories focus on one "subsystem," and neglect the other(s), for example, the focus is either on cognitive processes (Anderson & Bower, 1973; Anderson, 1983; Atkinson & Shiffrin, 1968; Craik & Lockhart, 1972; Kintsch, 1974; Norman & Rumelhart, 1975; Reitman, 1973) or on emotional and/or motivational processes (Atkinson & Birch, 1970; Izard, 1977; Plutchik, 1980). Even models that do describe interactions between two sets of parameters which might be interpreted as more cognitive (e.g., expectation of control) or more emotional, (e.g., incentive or value of expected consequences) treat those parameters as isolated components of a "static" (e.g., multiplicative) interaction rather than as truly interdependent constituents of a dynamic process (e.g., Ajzen & Fishbein, 1973; Atkinson, 1957; Heckhausen, 1977; Vroom, 1964).

While one might consider the existing interactive models as first, though insufficient, approximations to a description of interdependent processes, a consideration of *reflexive* relationships is lacking completely in our formal models. Yet the idea regarding the reflexive nature of cognitions and emotions is intuitively very compelling. I become angry at somebody insulting me and it seems as if the fact that I notice that I am angry makes me feel more and more angry. I am moderately confident that I will be able to solve a new problem, and it seems as if the mere perception of my positive expectations is (positively) fed back into my expectancy judgments building up an increasing sense of confidence.

A common concern is that a formal model would become too complex if it were to include interdependent and reflexive processes. Indeed, even mathematical experts who have only recently started to investigate the formal characteristics of interdependent and reflexive (recursive) functions in a systematic way, do not seem to be able to describe these characteristics in terms of general equations permitting the derivation of all the implications by hand. Instead, they have to settle with computer simulation "experiments" to discover more and more unforeseen characteristics of those functions (May, 1976).

In current research, even the most elaborated (non-reflexive) models seem to be unable to account for some of the inconsistencies observed, for instance in subjects having high anxiety or depression scores. Anxious subjects often show abrupt and virtually unpredictable changes in their behavior. Their risk-taking, their expectancy of control estimates as well as their performance scores are frequently so inconsistent that their behavior cannot be accommodated even though the models are more and more elaborated in an attempt to explain the inconsistencies (Heckhausen, 1977; Heckhausen, Schmalt & Schneider, 1985). In fact, some investigators seem to be so much dissatisfied with the increasing complexity in psychological models that they start from scratch reintroducing some of the old simple concepts under new labels only to find out after some research that simple models do have to be elaborated in an effort to understand some of the puzzling inconsistencies in behavioral data (e.g., Abramson, Seligman & Teasdale, 1978; Seligman, 1975).

As I pointed out earlier, I will examine a strategy here which differs in some respects from the elaboration strategy. Could it be that the simple models we start with contain some deficiencies which cannot be remedied by adding more and more parameters? Is there any model that would account for inconsistent behavior without falling back on short-circuited explanations such as attributing behavioral inconsistency to inconsistencies in the latent determinants (cf. Mischel, 1968)? The hypothesis which I would like to elaborate here is that the neglect of the interdependence and reflexivity of mental processes in our models has been a major reason for the problems mentioned earlier (e.g., failure to account for cross-situational variability in behavior).

A Recursive Model of Achievement Motivation

As I plan to spell out some of the implications of the concepts of interdependence and reflexivity as specifically as possible, I will present a brief introduction to one specific area of research in which those concepts may be applied before discussing the formal characteristics of a simple recursive model.

Atkinson's Model of Achievement Motivation

Models of social motivation in general attempt to describe the relationship between the strength of a motivational tendency to engage in a specified action and several cognitive variables. Most current models assume a one-way relationship, i.e., cognitive factors affecting strength of motivation but not vice versa. In the field of achievement motivation research, the most successful model has been the one proposed by Atkinson (1957). This model describes strength of motivation to strive for success on a given task (T_r) in terms of a parabolic (inverted-U shaped) function of its central cognitive parameter, i.e., the subjective probability of success (P_s):

$$T_r = (M_S - M_F) \times P_s \times (1 - P_s), \qquad (1)$$

where P_s ranges between 0 and 1 and ($M_S - M_F$) designates the difference between the strength of the motives to achieve success (M_S) and to avoid failure (M_F).

The parabolic feature of this model derives from the assumptions that (a) strength of motivation is a function of the algebraic product of expectancy and value ("incentive") parameters and (b) incentive of success (I_s) may be described as an inverse linear function of the subjective probability of success, that is $I_s = (1 - P_s)$. Experimental data support some of the model's implications, e.g., that *success-oriented* subjects (for whom $M_S > M_F$) (a) prefer intermediate risks, i.e., where $P_s \approx .5$ (Atkinson & Feather, 1966; Atkinson, 1974; Heckhausen, 1977; Heckhausen, Schmalt & Schneider, 1985; Kuhl, 1982); (b) persist longer than failure-oriented subjects (for whom $M_F > M_S$) when confronted with repeated failure on allegedly easy tasks (Feather, 1961; 1962; Nygard, 1977); and (c) perform better than failure-oriented subjects on intermediately difficult tasks (Karabenick & Youssef, 1968).

Although these implications of the model are roughly corroborated by aggregate data, the model did rather poorly when applied to individual data (Kuhl, 1977; 1982; Schneider, 1973; 1978). To account for some of the variance still unexplained, several elaborations have been proposed to incorporate into the model such factors as perceived responsibility for outcomes (Feather, 1967), instrumentality of immediate outcomes for the attainment of future goals (Raynor, 1969), perceived goal distance (Gjesme, 1981), and personal standards for self-evaluation (Kuhl, 1978). Although these elaborations account for a greater proportion of variance than the original one, risk-taking data still show many unexplained inconsistencies (Heckhausen, 1977).

Applying the Concept of Reflexivity

We are now prepared to examine to what extent some of these inconsistencies may be explained by adding a reflexive feature to the model. This is done very easily by assuming a one-dimensional recurrence relation, the general structure of which is:

$$X_{n+1} = f(x_n). \qquad (2)$$

Applying this equation to the original model of achievement motivation (Equation 1) results in a sequence of iterative applications of Equation 1. In each of these iterations the new ordinate value (i.e., Y_{n+1}) is computed by inserting the previously obtained ordinate value (i.e., Y_n) as the new argument (i.e., X_{n+1}) of the equation. That is, the outcome of the model (Y_n) is fed back into the model by using it as a new abscissa value (X_{n+1}).

What happens when we add this assumption of recursiveness to the model? Let us discuss some of the general implications before applying Equation 2 to the theory of achievement motivation. Since the implications of the recursive model cannot be derived by hand, mathematicians exploring the properties of these models use computer-simulation techniques. However, there is a simple graphic method of visualizing the implications of this recursive model (cf. Hofstadter, 1981). This method is illustrated in Figure 1. We start with the value $x_1 = 0$. Applying the function $f(x) = x(1-x)$ we find the value for $f(x_1)$ at the intersection of the vertical line starting at x_1 with the inverted U-shaped curve. We find the next abscissa value x_2 by drawing a horizontal line from that intersection to the diagonal which depicts the recursive relationship expressed in Equation 2. The abscissa value corresponding to this intersection point is x_2. The value of $f(x_2)$ can be found on the curve again and a horizontal line drawn from that point to the diagonal yields x_3. Applying these steps repeatedly results in a series of x-values approaching an asymptote. The important counterintuitive property of the recursive model is depicted in Figure 2.

FIGURE 1

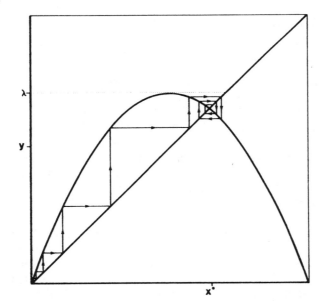

In this figure, the peak of the U-shaped curve is slightly higher than in Figure 1. Applying the same procedure to find successive values of x_1, x_2 . . . , results in a totally different sequence of values. Rather than approaching one asymptote, the x-values alternatively approach two asymptotes. Further slight increases of the peak of this function yields cases with x-values alternating between 4, 8, 16, 32, . . . asymptotes. In sum, slight increases of the maximum of the curvilinear function produce an increasing number of asymptotes which successive x-values are approaching in a fixed order. This sequence of x-(or $f[x]$) values may appear "chaotic" to a naive observer who is not aware of the deterministic (and totally predictable) nature of the underlying process. This brief description of one of the most simple "chaos-models" (cf. May, 1976) illustrates the heuristic

FIGURE 2

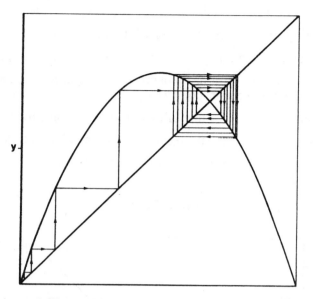

value of formal modelling which is especially useful in making us aware of counter-intuitive implications of our assumptions. Capitalizing on this advantage of formal modelling, Atkinson (1957) introduced the well-known model of achievement motivation, at a time when most research in this area was based on ad-hoc intuitions. Feather's (1962; 1963) work on persistence is one of the finest examples of the huge number of research findings that were made possible by the application of Atkinson's model of achievement motivation. Let us explore some implications of Atkinson's original model when it is extended by the recursive relationship defined in Equation 2.

Applications to Atkinson's Theory of Achievement Motivation

Theoretically, applying Equation 2 to Equation 1 represents one of the simplest ways of accounting for cognition-motivation interdependence. It should be noted that the use of the terms *interdependence* and *reflexivity* depends to a certain degree on a general assumption about the human mind. Whether Equation 2 is considered to describe reflexivity or interdependence depends on the conceptual nature of the processes it refers to. For example, if both P_s and T are conceived of as aspects of the same mental subsystem, for instance, in terms of motivationally relevant cognitions, (i.e., expectancy and intention), Equation 2 describes a "reflexive" aspect of that subsystem. If P_s and T are considered to describe aspects of separate subsystems (e.g., expectancy describing a cognitive state and motivational tendency describing a separate state), Equation 2 describes the assumed nature of the interdependence between those two subsystems. In general, if one tends to emphasize the *modularity* of mental processes (Fodor, 1983), one would talk about the *interdependence* between various subsystems, whereas a more holistic approach suggests a *reflexivity* interpretation of Equation 2 (e.g., Anderson, 1983; Kuhl, 1983b; Leventhal, 1980). Equation 2 can be applied to the theory of achievement motivation if we confine ourselves to tasks that maximize the causal relevance of effort, that is where performance is mainly affected by motivation. Figure 3 illustrate this case.

When an individual is confronted with a task, the starting value for the probability of success (P_s) may result from the individual's "first guess" based on previous experiences with this task or similar tasks. Let us say the task appears rather easy to the subject (cf. the dashed line in Figure 3 starting at $P_s = 0.8$). This starting value results in an initial strength of the motivational tendency to approach that task (T_1) which causes a proportionate increase in P_s. When applying Equation 2 to describe this process, we start with the simplifying assumption that any increase in P_s equals the previous increase in T before considering less restrictive cases. This assumption is plausible for effort-dependent tasks only, that is when performance is a direct function of strength of motivation (T) for the task. To the extent that the subject is aware of the effects of variations in effort on task performance, these effects should be reflected in appropriate changes of their success expectations (P_s). Let us first focus on the middle (dashed) curve in Figure 3 (i.e., points B_1 to B_4).

FIGURE 3

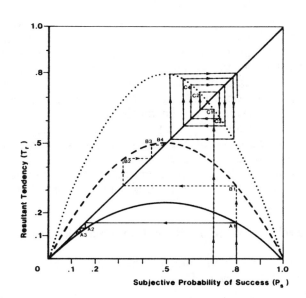

According to the original theory of achievement motivation, a P_s-value of 0.8 results in less than maximum motivation (T_1). If performance primarily depends on the amount of effort invested, performance will be rather low. As a result, the individual will revise her/his current success expectation accordingly ($P_{s_2} \approx 0.2$). For subsequent trials, the model predicts a gradual increase of motivation/ performance and, as a result, an increase of success expectancy. Motivation and performance scores, as well as subjective probability of success, are expected to stabilize at a value around 0.5. Interestingly, this point of stable motivation and success expectancy is invariant to the starting value of P_s. Irrespective of the individual's first guess of success probability, her/his motivation and success expectancy will eventually stabilize at the same level.

Now consider the lowest curve in Figure 3 which describes an individual having a rather low motive to achieve success (cf. Equation 1). The model predicts a gradual decrease of motivation and success expectancy. This is quite plausible for an effort-centered task: If subjects invest less and less effort, their performance will decrease and success expectancy will drop accordingly. Note that we are talking about a type of subjective probability that is conditional on intended or invested effort. (This conditional probability may or may not co-exist with a rather high, ability-centered probability of success based on the (imaginary) case of maximum effort investment).

The counterintuitive thing happens when the success motive exceeds a critical value, as illustrated by the dotted curve in Figure 3. In this case, the values of T and P_s—after first showing a gradual increase similar to the middle curve— suddenly start alternating and approaching two asymptotes. It can be shown that further increases in motive strength produce 4, 8, 16, 32 . . . asymptotes: Indices of task motivation, performance, level of aspiration, and success expectation would appear totally inconsistent whenever the peak of the motivation curve exceeds a critical level. This is the case of "motivational chaos" produced by a simple deterministic model. The occurrence of this phenomenon depends on the relationship between the maximum of the motivation curve and the slope of the recursiveness function (cf. Equation 2) rather than on the peak of the motivation function *per se*. When the slope of the line of the recursiveness is less than 1, motivational instability would occur even for the middle curve in Figure 3. In general, whenever the line of recursivity intersects with the motivation curve at a point beyond (i.e., to the right of) the peak of the latter, motivational instability ensues.

Level of Aspiration: Some Preliminary Results

There is an interesting application of the recursive model to the level-of-aspiration paradigm. In a level-of-aspiration experiment, subjects state the performance level aspired prior to each trial. It is usually assumed and found that the performance level achieved at a given trial strongly influences the level of aspiration set for the subsequent trial. Although this is a clear case of a recursive process, the models used to analyze level-of-aspiration data never took the recursiveness aspect into account. Applying a recursive model opens some interesting new perspectives on this old experimental paradigm which has been almost totally abandoned in motivation research. To keep things simple, let us focus on the case in which the same inverted-U-shaped function describes the relationship between strength of motivation and performance (cf. Atkinson, 1974). Let us further assume that strength of motivation (i.e., amount of effort invested) is a direct function of level of aspiration: The higher a subject's level of aspiration, the more effort she or he exerts in achieving it. On the basis of these assumptions, we can apply the model depicted in Figure 3 with level of aspiration as the new abscissa and level of performance as the new ordinate. The peak of the curve now describes the degree to which performance is a function of level of aspiration. The dotted line in Figure 3 describes a task at which effort has (or is believed to have) a very strong effect on performance. In this case highly "inconsistent" standard-setting is expected. The lower graph in Figure 4 illustrates the sequence of levels of aspiration corresponding to the dotted curve in Figure 3. With a moderate effect of effort on performance, standard-setting should gradually approach a stable level (cf. Figure 1 or dashed line in Figure 3). The sequence of levels of aspiration expected in this case is illustrated in the upper graph of Figure 4. Testing the recursive model requires an experimental situation which satisfies the assumptions of recursiveness (i.e., performance affecting subsequent level of aspiration) and curvilinearity (i.e., performance as an invested-U-shaped function of motivation). A computer task was developed that was to approximate these two conditions as closely as possible. This task requires subjects to push a button whenever a certain letter (e.g., an X) appears on the screen of a microcomputer. Subjects can choose the speed at which a random series of single letters is shown on the screen. Performance scores are computed on the basis of number of critical letters identified per time unit. Obviously, maximum performance can be attained at a moderate speed only because, at low speeds, not many critical letters are displayed within a given time period and, at high speeds, not many critical letters can be identified. At each trial a random series of letters is displayed in the center of the screen (i.e., one at a time) at the speed selected by the subject. Subsequently, the subject's "performance score" is displayed on the screen. This can be either based on the actual number of critical letters identified per time unit or it can be a fictitious feedback derived from the ideal curve (cf. Figure 1). The model can be tested by manipulating and/or assessing the peak of the performance curve or the slope of the line of recursiveness. The model predicts a continuous oscillation of level of aspiration between two or more asymptotes if the peak of the curve is very high and/or the slope of the line of recursiveness is rather flat. We are currently developing methods for manipulating and assessing the critical parameters of the model. Even before these methodological problems are solved, the recursive model raises some interesting questions that can be studied in a rather straightforward manner. One question is: Are the two different temporal patterns of standard-setting (cf. Figure 4) identifiable in level-of-aspiration data? Until now, analysis of such data has been confined to rather simple measures such as mean goal discrepancy (i.e., level of aspiration minus performance obtained), number of typical shifts (i.e., increase of level of aspiration after success and decrease after failure), and number of atypical shifts. The recursive model makes us focus on the general characteristics of the time course of standard-setting.

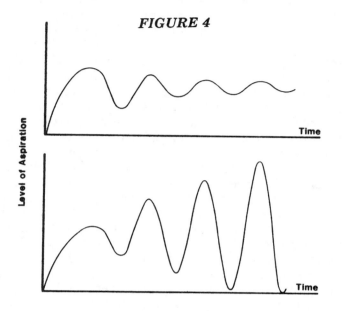

FIGURE 4

In our first study we investigated this question. In addition, we were interested in finding out whether two personality scales (described later) differentiate between the two cases mentioned above. Thirty-three subjects performed the letter-identification task described above. For each trial the computer recorded performance scores displayed on the screen and the subjects' level of aspiration for the subsequent trial.

An inspection of the time course of level-of-aspiration data yielded a surprisingly easy classification of subjects into one of the two categories predicted by the recursive model. The first category (cf. upper part of Fig. 4) refers to the case that standard-setting eventually approaches one stable level. Recall that this case is expected when the line of recursiveness intersects with the performance curve left of (or at) the latter's maximum. This first category could be subdivided into cases with and cases without the initial phase of oscillation. The two upper graphs in Figure 5 illustrate these two cases. The lowest graph in Figure 5 shows the data from a subject having an increasing rather than a decreasing amplitude of oscillations. Categorizations were obtained from several raters. Interrater agreement varied between 82% and 95%. We had administered the Achievement Motive Scale (Gjesme & Nygard, 1970), which yields separate measures of the motive to achieve success and the motive to avoid failure, and the Action-Control-Scale (Kuhl, 1985), which assesses three aspects of "action vs. state orientation." These two scales were included in the study because we suspected that they might discriminate between the different cases of the recursive model. We know from many studies, that subjects having a low resultant motive to approach success show high goal discrepancies; that is, their level of aspiration is markedly higher or lower than the performance level actually achieved. In contrast, success-oriented subjects tend to have realistic aspirations (Atkinson, 1958; Heckhausen, 1977). Since an unrealistic level of aspiration affects the slope of the line of recursiveness (cf. Figure 3), it should affect the probability of "chaotic behavior."

The Action Control Scale was included because it was suspected that "action vs. state orientation" may be related to the degree of recursiveness. State orientation is defined as a tendency to focus on current, past, or future states rather than on action plans (Kuhl, 1983; 1984; 1985). State-oriented individuals often engage in recursive thinking leading to "cognitive loops" which render the enactment of intentions very difficult. If state-oriented subjects are more likely to focus on their current performance, their standard-setting should be more affected by their current performance level and, as a result, they should be more likely to display oscillating standard-setting (cf. lower part of Figure 4) than action-oriented subjects.

The results are in line with these assumptions. A discriminant analysis yielded a perfect discrimination between the three cases mentioned earlier (cf. Figure 5) on the basis of the five scores provided by the two scales. As can be seen from Table 1, this discrimination was mainly attributable to the fact that subjects showing increasing oscillations (cf. Case 3 [= subject No. 8] in Figure 5) had lower action-orientation scores (i.e., were more state-oriented), lower scores of "hope for success," and higher scores for fear of failure than subjects belonging to the remaining Groups 1 and 2. Orthogonal contrasts between pairs of groups showed that, for an overall score of action orientation (summing across the three subscales), the difference between Group 1 (stable level of aspiration without initial oscillation) and Group 3 (increasing oscillation of level of aspiration) approached significance, t (19) = 2.0, p .06. With regard to the Achievement Motive Scale, only the measure of "hope for success" yielded a significant difference, namely between Group 3 and the pooled remaining two groups (p .05). A final decision as to whether or not these results are really attributable to the processes postulated by the recursive model cannot be made on the basis of the present data alone. Further experimentation is needed to examine the constraints of the validity of the recursive model. Nonetheless, the current data illustrate the heuristic utility of the recursive model. Whereas traditional level-of-aspiration research has focused on rather narrow indices (e.g., mean goal discrepancy), the recursive model has interesting implications for the broader aspects of the temporal changes in level of aspiration that have been ignored in previous research. The transition from a stable to a very variable time course of standard-setting seems to be—at least in part—attributable to personality factors. This finding supports Atkinson's (1981) claim that perfectly stable personality traits can produce extremely variable behavior even when situational variables are held constant. This claim was derived from *Dynamics of Action* (Atkinson & Birch, 1970), a theory which is much more comprehensive than the recursive model discussed here. The analysis has shown that the property of recursiveness, which is only one of several "dynamic" features in Atkinson and Birch's theory, is already sufficient to support Atkinson's claim.

FIGURE 5

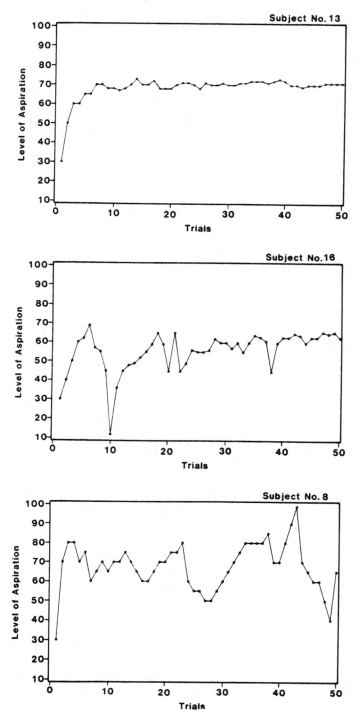

Table 1

Mean Scores on Five Personality Scales

for Three Groups of Subjects

Group	1	2	3
	Stable Level of Aspiration (LA) (without initial oscillation)	Stable LA (after initial oscillation)	Unstable LA (increasing oscillation)
Scale			
Hope for success	50.0	46.3	43.9
Fear of failure	28.5	31.9	32.2
Action Orientation (performance-related)	11.4	10.3	8.1
Action Orientation (following failure)	11.5	9.7	7.3
Action Orientation (decision-related)	10.7	10.7	9.4

REFERENCES

Abramson, L. Y., Seligman, M. E. P., & Teasdale, J. D. (1978). Learned helplessness in humans: Critique and reformulation. *Journal of Abnormal Psychology, 87*, 49–74.

Ajzen, I., & Fishbein, M. (1973). Attitudinal and normative variables as predictors of specific behaviors. *Journal of Personality and Social Psychology, 27*, 41–57.

Anderson, J. R. (1983). *The architecture of cognition.* Cambridge, MA: Harvard University Press.

Anderson, J. R., & Bower, G. H. (1973). *Human associative memory.* Washington: Hemisphere.

Atkinson, J. W. (1957). Motivational determinants of risktaking behavior. *Psychological Review, 64*, 359–372.

Atkinson, J. W. (1958). *Motives in fantasy, action, and society.* Princeton, NJ: Van Nostrand.

Atkinson, J. W. (1974). Strength of motivation and efficiency of performance. In J. W. Atkinson & J. O. Raynor (Eds.), *Motivation and achievement.* (pp. 193–218). Washington, DC: Winston.

Atkinson, J. W. (1981). Studying personality in the context of an advanced motivational psychology. *American Psychologist, 36*, 117–128.

Atkinson, J. W., & Birch, D. (1970). *The dynamics of action.* New York: Wiley.

Atkinson, J. W., & Birch, D. (1978). *Introduction to motivation.* New York: Van Nostrand.

Atkinson, J. W., & Feather, N. T. (1966). *A theory of achievement motivation.* New York: Wiley.

Atkinson, R. C., & Shiffrin, R. M. (1968). Human memory: A proposed system and its control processes. In K. W. Spence & J. T. Spence (Eds.), *The psychology of learning and motivation* (Vol. 2). New York: Academic Press.

Craik, F. J. M., & Lockhart, R. S. (1972). Levels of processing: A framework for memory research. *Journal of Verbal Learning and Verbal Behavior, 11*, 671–684.

Feather, N. T. (1961). The relationship of persistence at a task to expectation of success and achievement-related motives. *Journal of Abnormal and Social Psychology, 63*, 552–561.

Feather, N. T. (1962). The study of persistence. *Psychological Bulletin, 59*, 94–115.

Feather, N. T. (1963). Persistence at a difficult task with alternative task of intermediate difficulty. *Journal of Abnormal and Social Psychology, 66*, 604–609.

Feather, N. T. (1967). Valence of outcome and expectation of success in relation to task difficulty and perceived locus of control. *Journal of Personality and Social Psychology, 7*, 372–386.

Fodor, J. A. (1983). *The modularity of mind*. Cambridge: MIT Press.

Gjesme, T. (1981). Is there any future in achievement motivation? *Motivation and emotion, 5*, 115–138.

Gjesme, T., & Nyga, R., (1970). *Achievement-related motives: Theoretical considerations and construction of a measuring instrument*. Unpublished manuscript. University of Oslo.

Heckhausen, H. (1967). *The anatomy of achievement motivation*. New York: Academic Press.

Heckhausen, H. (1977). Achievement motivation and its constructs: A cognitive model. *Motivation and Emotion, 1*, 283–329.

Heckhausen, H., Schmalt, H. D., & Schneider, K. (1985). *Achievement motivation in perspective*. New York: Academic Press.

Hofstadter, D. R. (1985). Strange attractors: Mathematical patterns delicately poised between order and chaos. *Scientific American, 5*, 22–43.

Izard, C. E. (1977). *Human emotions*. New York: Plenum.

Karabenick, S. A., & Youssef, Z. I. (1968). Performance as a function of achievement levels and perceived difficulty. *Journal of Personality and Social Psychology, 10*, 414–419.

Kintsch, W. (1974). *The representation of meaning in memory*. Hillsdale, NJ: Erlbaum.

Kuhl, J. (1977). Meß-und prozeßtheoretische analysen einiger person- und situationsparameter der leistungmotivation). Bonn: Bouvier.

Kuhl, J. (1978). Standard setting and risk preference: An elaboration of the theory of achievement motivation and an empirical test. *Psychological Review, 85*, 239–248.

Kuhl, J. (1982). The expectancy-value approach in the theory of social motivation: Elaborations, extensions, critique. In N. T. Feather (Ed.), *Expectations and actions: Expectancy-value models in psychology* (pp. 125–160). Hillsdale, NJ: Erlbaum.

Kuhl, J. (1983). *Motivation, konflikt und handlungskontrolle* (Motivation, conflict, and action control). Heidelberg: Springer.

Kuhl, J. (1984). Volitional aspects of achievement motivation and learned helplessness: Toward a comprehensive theory of action control. In B. A. Maher (Ed.), *Progress in experimental personality research* (Vol. 12), (pp. 99–170). New York: Academic Press.

Kuhl, J. (1985). Volitional mediators of cognition-behavior consistency: Self-regulatory processes and action versus state orientation. In J. Kuhl & J. Beckmann (Eds.), *Action control: From cognition to behavior.* Heidelberg, New York: Springer-Verlag.

Kuhl, J., & Blankenship, V. (1979a). Behavioral change in a constant environment: Moving to more difficult tasks in spite of constant expectations of success. *Journal of Personality and Social Psychology, 37*, 551–563.

Kuhl, J., & Blankenship, V. (1979b). The dynamic theory of achievement motivation: From episodic to dynamic thinking. *Psychological Review, 86*, 141–151.

Leventhal, H. (1980). Toward a comprehensive theory of emotions. In L. Berkowitz (Ed.), *Advances in Experimental Social Psychology, 13*, 139–207.

May, R. M. (1976). Simple mathematical models with very complicated dynamics. *Nature, 10*, 459–467.

Mischel, W. (1968). *Personality and assessment.* New York: Wiley.

Norman, D., & Rumelhart, D. (1975). *Explorations in cognition.* San Francisco: Freeman.

Nygard, R. (1977). *Personality, situation, and persistence.* Oslo: Universitetsforlaget.

Plutchik, R. (1980). *Emotion: A psychoevolutionary synthesis.* New York: Harper & Row.

Raynor, J. O. (1969). Future orientation and motivation of immediate activity:

An elaboration of the theory of achievement motivation. *Psychological Review*, *76*, 606–610.

Reitman, W. (1973). Problem solving, comprehension, and memory. In G. J. Dalenoort (Ed.), *Process models for psychology*. Rotterdam: University Press.

Schneider, K. (1973). *Motivation unter Erfolgsrisiko*. Göttingen: Hogrefe.

Schneider, K. (1978). Atkinson's "risk preference" model: Should it be revised? *Motivation and Emotion*, *2*, 333–344.

Seligman, M. E. P. (1975). *Helplessness: On depression, development, and death*. San Francisco: Freeman.

Weiner, B. (1980). *Human motivation*. New York: Holt, Rinehart and Winston.

Vroom, V. H. (1964). *Work and motivation*. New York: Wiley.

Chapter Five

MATHEMATICAL MODEL OF THE

BEHAVIORAL STREAM MEASUREMENT

David Birch

University of Illinois

Motivation theory is coming of age and it carries the unmistakable stamp of Jack Atkinson. In this chapter I intend both to help the rest of you to document Atkinson's influence on the psychology of motivation and to argue that motivation theory is coming of age.

The primary difficulty those of us who study motivation have had in coming together on a single theory of motivation is that what we need, quite properly and of necessity and are only now getting, is a theory that will embrace many theories. The many theories I speak of do not necessarily compete for the same domain, though this will happen at times; rather they are theories about different aspects of the psychology of motivation. What I have in mind is captured by these three, double-barrelled questions:

1. What are the phenotypic behavioral units of analysis appropriate to the study of motivation and how do we know when we have hold of one?

2. How do we represent phenotypic motivational units at the genotypic level and what can we say about their origins?

3. What rules do we propose for the transformation from the potential for action found in the genotype to the behavior we observe and what do these rules lead us to look for in our data?

I believe these questions can be tied together by a single concept, one that permits us to speak in terms of a unifying theory of motivation. The concept is that of *elaborated tendency* and I first learned about it from Jack. I can even remember, roughly, where and when.

Long, long ago Jack and I spent several noon hours each week for many years talking about motivation. Our talks began in Haven Hall (so you have an idea just how long ago it was) and continued throughout our subsequent moves to

Mason Hall and the Perry Building. (We also talked about motivation while we looked for lost golf balls, but I can't say this led to much despite the sizeable amount of time we spent at it.) On nice days during the summer we would go out to the Huron Valley Swim Club to take a swim before eating a sandwich and talking about motivation. We did this fairly often and, I must say, in all my experience the water there was always cold enough to cool beer and never warm enough for swimming. At any rate, one day (and I can even picture the picnic table) Jack said with just about as much context as I have given you now, "Maybe the rat begins eating in the start box."

It turns out that what he meant was that perhaps we should not think of a goal-oriented activity as an instrumental response learned and maintained by the receipt of a goal object or even as a Tolmanian Means-Ends-Readiness, which did indeed leave the rat lost in thought at the choice point as Guthrie pointed out, but rather that our concept of a motivational unit should be one that included both instrumental and goal behaviors in nondecomposable form. Maybe what we see in the goal-directed activity of a rat in the maze is the expression of an elaborated tendency to eat. A hungry rat never before in the maze has a tendency to eat aroused by deprivation. Then, as a consequence of repeated experience in the maze, the tendency to eat changes in character; it becomes the tendency to run and eat, or even, if you set it up that way, to run, turn left, turn right, press a lever and eat. If you asked what, from the perspective of motivation, is the rat doing from entrance into the start box to exit from the goal box, the answer would be "expressing an elaborated tendency to eat." What we see looks different at different points in the maze, but motivationally the rat is doing just one thing.

Notice that as we apply this idea more generally, it means we should distinguish motivationally between "riding the bus to work" and "riding the bus to the movie" even though these look very much alike, and between "riding the bus to work" and "walking to work"—which are different elaborations of the same original tendency. In each case we are dealing with distinct elaborated tendencies. At the same time, however, we can aspire to determine empirically the families that elaborated tendencies fall into. Jack and I proposed that relations of substitution and displacement might be a useful direction to take here.

Thus, my argument is that the fruitful behavioral units of study in motivation are to be found in the expression of elaborated tendencies for action. These are the phenotypic behavioral units asked about in the first part of Question 1. We will return to the second part of Question 1 after we develop some other ideas.

Question 2 has been addressed recently most comprehensively by Nuttin in his book *Motivation, Planning, and Action* (1984) and by Heckhausen and Kuhl (in press) in their paper "From wishes to action: The dead ends and short cuts on the long ways to action." But many others have developed theoretically one or another aspect of the genotypic nature of an elaborated tendency. This is most certainly an important thing to do; we need to learn as much as possible about the elaboration of tendencies and about the processes which result in different elaborations for different tendencies. Today's theories about the origin of elaborated tendencies tend to be cognitive and this makes good sense. Back in 1968, however, I proposed how an elaborated tendency might be conceptualized from the standpoint of S-R theory; the resulting unit resembled Hebb's cell assembly but was based on classical Hullian theory (Birch, 1968). We should, of course, continue to formulate all types of theories of elaborated tendencies and do our best to preserve the better ones.

What I want to stress most at this point is that when we inquire about an individual motivational tendency, we are asking about its elaboration and about the activity that we would observe if that tendency were being expressed. Let me illustrate a part of what I am talking about with some data I am currently working with in collaboration with Grayson Cuqlock. I shall leave out procedural details unless someone asks and talk only about the elaboration of a motivational tendency and its manifestation in ongoing activity. The experimental context comes out of the dual task paradigm in pursuit tracking.

This paradigm requires a subject to perform a tracking task as well as possible under single task conditions where tracking is all the subject is to do and under dual task conditions where an additional task must be undertaken concurrently with tracking and performed at an experimenter determined criterion level. I am interested in comparing single and dual task tracking performance but not with respect to tracking effectiveness, as is usually asked about in these experiments. Instead, I want to consider the nature of the tracking activity, and by implication the nature of its elaborated tendency. Specifically, my aim is to determine whether single and dual task tracking should be viewed, motivationally, as one activity occurring under two sets of conditions or as two distinct activities. Is *what* the subject is doing the same under the different conditions even though *how* the subject is going about doing it may be quite different?

To try to get an answer we will turn back the clock even farther than I have so far, this time to Spearman (1927) and the tetrad difference, which in the days before multiple factor analysis was used to look for patterns in a 4 x 4 correlation matrix. Very briefly, if the tetrad difference = $t_{1234} = (r_{12})(r_{34}) - (r_{13})(r_{24})$ = 0, the four scores involved in the correlations can be written in terms of a single common factor plus specific factors. (In Spearman's context the single common factor was g, the general factor of intelligence.) What is important for us is that if the tetrad difference equals zero there is no evidence of a special clustering of 1 with 2 and 3 with 4. This is better understood with the aid of Table 1.

I have let 1, 2, 3 and 4 be OE-S, SUM-S, OE-D and SUM-D, respectively, in Table 1 where S and D refer to single and dual task tracking and OE and SUM to two different additional tasks that were used to set up two different dual conditions. Notice first the high correlations in the top matrix of Table 1 and the near zero tetrad differences that are present for AIE (average integrated error) which is just the average distance between the target and the cursor calculated over the tracking interval. It is apparent that there is no reason to entertain other than a

Table 1

Correlation Matrices and Tetrad Differences for Average Integrated Error (AIE) and

Three Measures (Period, Amplitude and Coherence) Resulting from the Spectral

Analysis of Tracking

	1 OE-S	2 SUM-S	3 OE-D	4 SUM-D	
AIE					
1 OE-S	—	.96	.96	.84	$t_{1234} = (.96)(.87)-(.96)(.80)$ $= .0635$
2 SUM-S		—	.91	.80	$t_{1243} = (.96)(.87)-(.84)(.91)$ $= .077$
3 OE-D			—	.87	$t_{1342} = (.96)(.80)-(.84)(.91)$ $= .0135$
4 SUM-D				—	
PERIOD					
OE-S	—	.84	−.16	.07	$t_{1234} = (.84)(.61)-(-.16)(-.14)$ $= .4887$
SUM-S		—	−.24	−.14	$t_{1243} = (.84)(.61)-(.07)(-.24)$ $= .5277$
OE-D			—	.61	$t_{1342} = (-.16)(-.14)-(.07)(-.24)$ $= .0389$
SUM-D				—	
AMPLITUDE					
OE-S	—	.79	.39	.44	$t_{1234} = (.79)(.78)-(.39)(.68)$ $= .3489$
SUM-S		—	.65	.68	$t_{1243} = (.79)(.78)-(.44)(.65)$ $= .3312$
OE-D			—	.78	$t_{1342} = (.39)(.68)-(.44)(.65)$ $= -.0177$
SUM-D				—	

Table 1 (continued)

	1	2	3	4
	OE-S	SUM-S	OE-D	SUM-D

COHERENCE

OE-S	—	.65	−.62	−.04	$t_{1234} = (.65)(.52)-(-.62)(-.22)$
					$= .2008$
SUM-S		—	−.30	−.22	$t_{1243} = (.65)(.52)-(-.04(-.30)$
					$= .3253$
OE-D			—	.52	$t_{1342} = (-.62)(-.22)-(-.04)(-.30)$
					$= .1245$
SUM-D				—	

single common factor for all four conditions. Moreover, the high correlations suggest that most of the variability in the AIE scores is due to individual differences related to the common factor with only a small amount of variability left over for factors specific to the four conditions. I should point out, also, that there are sizeable and statistically significant differences in the mean AIE scores for the single and dual task conditions reflecting the overall effectiveness of the experimental manipulations.

These data lead me to suggest that, motivationally, there is one elaborated tendency operating across the conditions rather than different tendencies for single and dual task tracking. This makes sense when we go back to the instructions (the source of the elaborated tendency) which state that, if they are to succeed, subjects should do the best they can whenever they are tracking. Our instructions are quite explicit about this and we can expect that the quality of each subject's tracking performance, whether in the single or dual task condition, is some combination of the strength of the elaborated tendency to track and succeed that we aroused and the subject's tracking skill. Both of these apparently are quite stable across the conditions.

Our instructions were not explicit about *how* the subjects should carry out the tracking. *What* they were to do was explicit, but the manner or style with which it was to be done was not. Thus, we might expect less uniformity from subject to subject and condition to condition in the how of the tracking than in the what. We made a spectral analysis of the tracking performance to check on this. In effect, what the spectral analysis does is to take the traces of the target and the cursor across time and by Fourier analysis determine the differences between those traces in terms of period, amplitude and coherence (the squared correlation between the two traces). The tetrad differences for each of these measures separately are also contained in Table 1.

I see evidence for different styles in single and dual task tracking in these data. For all three measures the tetrad differences are quite different from zero when the two single and the two dual task scores are paired in the tetrad and near zero when they are not paired. Thus, a single common factor does not account well for the correlations based on any of the three spectral measures, but separate factors for single and dual task tracking in each case will do so. The difference between *the one elaborated tendency* to track well so as to succeed that is common to both the single and dual task conditions when the AIE measure is used, and the *unlike styles of tracking* in the two conditions seen with the spectral measures, is the difference between identifying the elaborated motivational tendency for tracking and describing in detail the structure of the movements that constitute tracking as it is going on.

This discussion is designed to lead to another distinction, one I refer to as the difference between considering the characteristics of an activity as it is ongoing and attempting to understand the fabric of the stream of activities across time. The motivational characteristics of ongoing activities are to be found in elaborated tendencies; the fabric of the stream of activities is to be found in the rules governing the interaction of elaborated tendencies as asked about in Question 3. The fabric of the stream of activities is what Jack and I addressed in the dynamics of action.

As we shift the discussion from the description of a single activity to the fabric of the stream of activities, we need to switch consideration from watching an ongoing activity to attending to that juncture between successive activities that Jack and I called a change of activity in the dynamics of action. Once we have both descriptions of ongoing activities, including their origins, and understanding of changes of activity, we have most of what we want in a comprehensive theory of motivation.

One of the most important things the dynamics of action does is to give an unambiguous statement of the linkage between what we observe in behavior and the central concept of the theory, tendency—something never intended to be observed directly. It was Jack, early on, who proposed in one of our sessions that the observation that Activity A is ongoing should mean theoretically that the tendency to engage in Activity A is strongest out of the set of tendencies for all the activities that could be ongoing. If we accept that, it follows that if, as we watch, Activity B replaces Activity A, it must mean that the tendency to engage in Activity B has become stronger than the tendency to engage in Activity A and is now the strongest in the set. It was from this that we developed the theory of the dynamics of action to give an account of what might be happening to strengths of tendencies over time to produce isolated changes of activity. It was then a natural step to go on to inquire about the whole succession of changes of activity that constitutes the stream of behavior.

The identification of the ongoing activity with the dominant tendency is not the only identification that might be made between observable behavior and unobservable theory, but *some explicit* identification must be made if we are to avoid confusion. When Toates (1980), for example, is led to say that a dominant activity can allow non-dominant activities to occur by certain processes of control, he is making a kind of statement not allowed by the dynamics of action. In the dynamics of action it is *not possible* for a non-dominant activity (i.e., an activity with a non-dominant tendency) to be ongoing; it is not possible by definition. What is not only possible but to be expected is that very often the ongoing activity is complex, reflecting the complexity of the elaboration of the underlying tendency. Thus, it may take most of the day to express the very elaborated tendency to go to the football game. This single activity may include dressing appropriately, going to brunch, driving to the stadium, etc., but we need to think of the elaborated tendency, however complex it may appear to the eye, as the motivational unit which is participating in the stream of behavior. Identifying the motivational units that are present in the stream of behavior is what I want to get to next.

The theoretical development follows these steps. We begin by extending the analysis of a single change of activity to encompass the stream of activities using the dynamics of action. This gives the kind of computer printout you have seen in the past and will, very shortly, see more of. Nice as these graphics are, they do not make easy or critical contact with the quantitative data we can obtain on the stream of behavior, data that are rich in relationships based on time and frequency.

The next step I have taken is to use the dynamics of action as the psychological foundation for a model of the stream of behavior I have called a model of fixed activation time scheduling (Birch, 1984; in press). The tie between the dynamics of action and the model is through a parameter called activation time. Each activity being coded in the stream has an activation time (the only parameters in the model) which is the time it takes the tendency for that activity to become dominant again following upon its having become non-dominant. You can see this as the off-time in Figure 1.

As an idealization the off-time, which is not quite a constant throughout the duration of the stream in the dynamics of action even for constant conditions, is treated as a constant activation time, perhaps best thought of as a kind of average value. The model proposes that the stream is generated by activities counting down their activation times and bumping out the ongoing activity.

For the version of the model I want to use, the exact and the approximate equations for the total duration $T(A_i)$ and the frequency $N(A_i)$ for each activity in a stream of three activities are these:[1]

Total Duration

$$T(A_1) = a_2 a_3 \left(1 + \frac{1}{a_1 + a_2} + \frac{1}{a_1 + a_3}\right) \approx a_2 a_3$$

$$T(A_2) = a_1a_3(1 + \frac{1}{a_1 + a_2} + \frac{1}{a_2 + a_3}) \approx a_1a_3$$

$$T(A_3) = a_1a_2(1 + \frac{1}{a_1 + a_3} + \frac{1}{a_2 + a_3}) \approx a_1a_2$$

Frequency

$$N(A_1) = (a_2 + a_3 - 1)(1 + \frac{1}{a_1 + a_2} + \frac{1}{a_1 + a_3}) \approx a_2 + a_3$$

$$N(A_2) = (a_1 + a_3 - 1)(1 + \frac{1}{a_1 + a_2} + \frac{1}{a_2 + a_3}) \approx a_1 + a_3$$

$$N(A_3) = (a_1 + a_2 - 1)(1 + \frac{1}{a_1 + a_3} + \frac{1}{a_2 + a_3}) \approx a_1 + a_2$$

It is easy to derive from the approximations, which should be quite good if the activation times are not too small, that the relative rates for any two activities, evaluated in terms of their respective off-times, should be the same as their relative durations. That is, we find

$$\frac{T(A_1)}{T(A_2)} = \frac{\dfrac{N(A_1)}{T - T(A_1)}}{\dfrac{N(A_2)}{T - T(A_2)}} \quad \text{and} \quad \frac{T(A_1)}{T(A_3)} = \frac{\dfrac{N(A_1)}{T - T(A_1)}}{\dfrac{N(A_3)}{T - T(A_3)}}, \text{ where } T = T(A_1) + T(A_2) +$$

$T(A_3)$. It is not so easy to see but can be proved that, if the exact equations are used, it is expected that for $a_1 < a_2 < a_3$ these inequalities will hold:

$$1 < \frac{T(A_1)}{T(A_2)} < \frac{\dfrac{N(A_1)}{T-T(A_1)}}{\dfrac{N(A_2)}{T-T(A_2)}} \quad \text{and} \quad 1 < \frac{T(A_1)}{T(A_3)} < \frac{\dfrac{N(A_1)}{T-T(A_1)}}{\dfrac{N(A_3)}{T-T(A_3)}}$$

These are demanding requirements made on the frequency and duration data by the model since there is no a priori reason that the frequency and duration of activities should be other than independent. That is, it is possible, in principle, for an activity to occur frequently with either a short or a long duration each time or infrequently with either a short or a long duration each time. Thus, a plot of relative duration against relative rate can be diagnostic of the fit of the model to the data.

Bill Timberlake some fifteen years ago (Timberlake, 1969) collected extensive stream of behavior data on rats. He coded the rat's free behavior into mutually exclusive and exhaustive categories of exploration, grooming and pausing and I have taken these data and plotted the Relative Rate-Relative Duration values in natural log units for all three pairs of activities. The next three figures show the result.

Each plot contains approximately 320 points obtained from 8 animals over 40 days with a day's session ten minutes long. The research design included a

FIGURE 1. Hypothetical stream of seven activities as generated by the interactions among the tendencies for the activities (from Birch, in press).

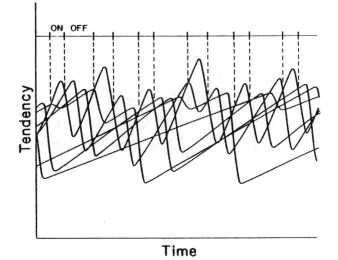

FIGURE 2. Relative rate versus relative duration in natural log units for exploration and grooming (from Timberlake, 1969).

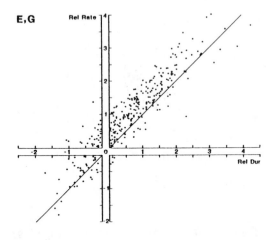

FIGURE 3. Relative rate versus relative duration in natural log units for exploration and pausing (from Timberlake, 1969).

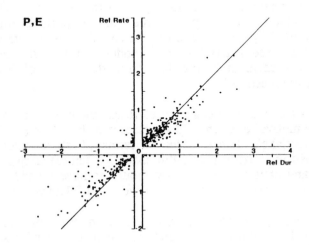

FIGURE 4. Relative rate versus relative duration in natural log units for grooming and pausing (from Timberlake, 1969).

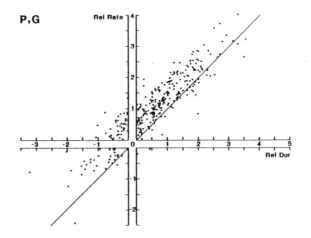

standard condition on Days 1–20 and 31–40 and a changed set of conditions on Days 21–30. The changed conditions had an effect on the stream of behavior but none that I can discern on the fit of the model to the data.

All three plots (Figure 2 for exploration and grooming, Figure 3 for exploration and pausing, and Figure 4 for grooming and pausing) show basically the same things: (a) A 45° line represents the data quite well as a first approximation, (b) the bulk of the deviations from the 45° line are above the line as expected from the exact equations, and (c) relatively few points fall in the second and fourth quadrants where ideally from the perspective of the model there should be no points. It seems to me that important duration-frequency relationships required by the model are to be found in these data and that I should take seriously the fixed activation time model and its rules as the conceptual framework to be used in analyzing data from the stream of behavior. Here we have my answer to Question 3.

Given this confidence, I can proceed to use the model as a tool in attempting to decide on the motivational units in the stream of behavior (back to Question 1). I reported Timberlake's data to you in terms of three categories, exploring, grooming and pausing but, in truth, Bill coded for ten categories, five exploratory, four grooming and pausing. How many should he have coded? How many are in the motivation of the rat and how many in the eyes of Timberlake?

I'm not going to answer that last question now because I haven't made the analyses yet, but I will illustrate the method I plan to use with some hypothetical data set out in Figure 5.

FIGURE 5. Summary values for duration and frequency and accompanying relative rate-relative duration plots for two hypothetical streams of four activities and for a selected example in which Activities 3 and 4 are combined.

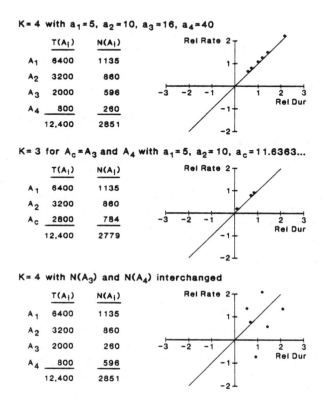

K= 4 with a_1=5, a_2=10, a_3=16, a_4=40

	T(A_i)	N(A_i)
A_1	6400	1135
A_2	3200	860
A_3	2000	596
A_4	800	260
	12,400	2851

K= 3 for A_c=A_3 and A_4 with a_1=5, a_2=10, a_c=11.6363...

	T(A_i)	N(A_i)
A_1	6400	1135
A_2	3200	860
A_c	2800	784
	12,400	2779

K= 4 with N(A_3) and N(A_4) interchanged

	T(A_i)	N(A_i)
A_1	6400	1135
A_2	3200	860
A_3	2000	260
A_4	800	596
	12,400	2851

At the top of Figure 5 a stream of four mutually exclusive and exhaustive activities (K = 4) with activation times of 5, 10, 16, and 40 is summarized. The model specifies the time and frequency values given in the table. One can, by using the equations in reverse, so to speak, recover the activation times from the time and frequency values. This is the sort of thing we would want to do with real data. To the side is the Relative Rate-Relative Duration plot for the hypothetical data showing the good fit we expect.

The values in the table are perfectly fit by the model as they should be. Now let us proceed to combine A_3 and A_4 into a single activity A_c as shown in the middle table. We see that $T(A_c) = T(A_3) + T(A_4)$ but that $N(A_c) = N(A_3) + N(A_4) - N(A_3A_4) - N(A_4A_3)$ since we are no longer distinguishing A_3 and A_4.

$N(A_3A_4)$ and $N(A_4A_3)$ are the frequencies of the A_3 to A_4 and A_4 to A_3 transitions, respectively, given by the model. The fit is once again perfect and, in fact, it is possible to discover that $\frac{1}{a_c} = \frac{1}{a_3} + \frac{1}{a_4} - (\frac{1}{a_3})(\frac{1}{a_4})$. The Relative Rate-Relative Duration plot is again located adjacent to the table and shows the expected fit once again.

So far, we have an example where the model fits the data for $K = 4$ and continues to fit for $K = 3$ where A_c equals A_3 and A_4 combined. It will always be the case that, within the limits of what we are asking of the model with these tests, the combined classes data will be fit if the original data are fit.

Now let's continue with $K = 4$ but interchange $N(A_3)$ and $N(A_4)$ as if these were the data we were facing. This is shown in the bottom table. The model no longer fits, as can be seen in the accompanying Relative Rate-Relative Duration plot. However, if we form, as before, A_c by combining A_3 and A_4 into a single class we will end up with the $K = 3$ table we have already seen where the fit is perfect. In this example we would be led to the conclusion that, from the standpoint of the motivational units functioning in the stream of behavior as defined by the fixed activation time model, we should not distinguish A_3 and A_4 but code only their composite A_c.

We are now in a position to generalize this method and ask, for example, with respect to the Timberlake data, how many motivationally meaningful units of exploring and grooming behavior should Timberlake have been coding according to the model? The method will work whether we apply it blindly or guided by particular hypotheses. Once we have the units, we most certainly want to know the nature and origin of the elaborated tendencies responsible for the behaviors we are observing. This, of course, calls upon theories concerned with the elaboration of tendencies for activities, as I have already stressed, not upon a theory directed to understanding the fabric of the stream of activities.

Perhaps you have a better idea now than when I began of why I think motivation theory is coming of age, why I think we can have a comprehensive motivational theory. Jack Atkinson has given us the concept of elaborated tendency and the meaning, theoretically, of an ongoing activity, the two basic ingredients of a comprehensive theory of motivation. With these in hand all the rest can follow.

FOOTNOTE

Parts of this research were supported by Contract DAAG29–83-K0138 with the U.S. Army Research Office.

[1]These equations come from a special case of the general model of fixed activation time scheduling (Birch, 1984). The particular assumption that leads to the equations is that each conflict in the stream is immediately converted into a mini-stream, composed of the activities involved in the conflict, for the duration of the conflict in the higher order stream. For example, a conflict between Activity 1 and Activity 2, which arises because these two activities have completed their activation times together, is converted into a mini-stream in which the two activities alternate until Activity 3 completes its activation time and becomes dominant again in the overall stream. The derivations of the equations for duration and frequency that follow from this particular assumption about the resolution of conflicts in the stream of behavior are not given here. The unpublished notes containing the derivations are available from the author upon request.

REFERENCES

Birch, D. (1968). Shift in activity and the concept of persisting tendency. In K. W. Spence & J. T. Spence (Eds.), *The psychology of learning and motivation: Advances in research and theory (Vol. II)*. New York: Academic Press.

Birch, D. (1984). A model of fixed activation time scheduling. *Journal of Mathematical Psychology, 28,* 121–159.

Birch, D. (in press). From the dynamics of action to measuring the stream of behavior. In J. Kuhl and J. W. Atkinson (Eds.), *Motivation, thought, and action*.

Heckhausen, H., & Kuhl J. (in press). From wishes to action: The dead ends and short cuts on the long way to action. In M. Frese & J. Sabini (Eds.), *Goal-directed behavior: Psychological theory and research on action*. Hillsdale, NJ.

Nuttin, J. (1984). *Motivation, planning, and action*. Leuven/Louvain: Leuven University Press.

Spearman, C. (1927). *The abilities of man*. New York: The MacMillan Co.

Timberlake, W. (1969). Continuous coding of general activity in the rat during exposure to a constant environment and to stimulus change. Unpublished doctoral dissertation, University of Michigan.

Toates, F. M. (1980). *Animal behavior – A systems approach*. New York: Wiley.

Chapter Six

USES OF THE COMPUTER IN MOTIVATIONAL PSYCHOLOGY

Virginia Blankenship

Oakland University

In this chapter I will illustrate three uses of the computer in motivational research: (a) simulation for hypothesis generation; (b) presentation of stimuli for empirical testing of those hypotheses; and (c) modelling of empirical results for parameter estimation. My research program combines the Atkinson and Birch (1970) dynamics of action model and classical achievement motivation theory (Atkinson, 1957; Atkinson & Feather, 1966) and Lewinian level of aspiration theory (Lewin, Dembo, Festinger, & Sears, 1944).

Simulation-Generated Research Hypotheses

In order to generate research hypotheses using the dynamics of action model, coordinating definitions must be established within a particular substantive domain. Atkinson and Birch (1974, 1978) have provided those coordinating definitions within the achievement motivation domain. By defining the instigating force in terms of the motive to succeed (M_S) and the subjective probability of success (P_S): $F_S = M_S \times P_S \times (1 - P_S)$, and inhibitory force in terms of the motive to avoid failure (M_F) and the P_S: $I_F = M_F \times P_S \times (1 - P_S)$, the way is set for generating research hypotheses representing individual differences in the motive to succeed and the motive to avoid failure. Revelle and Michaels (1976) refined the coordinating definition of the consummatory value of achieving by proposing that the consummatory value of success is greater than the consummatory value of failure: $c_S > c_F$.

To demonstrate the procedure for generating testable hypotheses, I will outline my empirical research investigating the consummatory value of success at easy and difficult tasks (Blankenship, 1982). As in any experiment, the research hypothesis must be stated and the experiment designed so that the results are interpretable. This means that two or more causal factors must not be confounded. Within the dynamics of action simulation, some of the parameters of the model must be held constant, some must be ignored, and only one parameter can be systematically varied.

Table 1 illustrates the decision process involved in setting parameter values for this experiment, where the null hypothesis was that no difference exists between the consummatory value of success at an easy task and the consummatory value of success at a difficult task. Classic achievement motivation theory allows the choice of two levels of difficulty, an easy task with P_S equal to .7 and a difficult task with P_S equal to .3, for which the instigating forces to engage in those tasks are equal. By selecting subjects with high achievement motivation (as indicated by the Thematic Apperception Test, TAT, Atkinson, 1958), and low test anxiety (as measured by the Test Anxiety Questionnaire, TAQ, Mandler & Sarason, 1952), inhibitory force and force of resistance can be ignored.

Table 1

Outline of Decision Process for Setting

Simulation Parameter

Dynamics of Action

Parameter:	Decisions:	Rationale:
Initial Tendency Level	Ongoing = F/c Alternate- =0	Comparison of Stabilized to Instigated Activities
Instigating Force	Hold Constant	$F_{S(E)} = F_{S(D)}$
		$P_{S(E)} = .7$
		$P_{S(D)} = .3$
Inhibitory Force and Force of Resistance	Ignore	Choose Ss with Hi M_S and Lo M_F
Consummatory Value	Systematically Vary	Focus of Experiment
Substitution and Displacement	Ignore	Activities are Unrelated
Selective Attention and Consummatory Lags	Hold Constant (Choose Standard Values)	Not Varied in Experimental Design

In order to justify the decisions to ignore substitution and displacement parameters, I will have to jump ahead a bit and describe to you the experimental situation. Sixty-one male subjects who scored high on the measure of motive to achieve success and low on the measure of fear of failure were tested individually on the computer as they divided their time between two activities; rating jokes as to their funniness, an opinion task with no success/failure outcomes, and playing a target-shooting game with success or failure feedback. Both activities were presented on a computer monitor. For the target-shooting game, subjects were given a target a certain number of yards away and required to enter an angle between 1 and 45 degrees, the angle between the barrel of a cannon and level ground. Based on a trajectory equation, the shot was determined to hit the target or to be a number of yards short of or beyond target. In this experiment subjects were allowed a second shot if they missed with the first shot. If the second shot was still outside the allowed error limit, the trial was declared a failure and the subject was told by the computer that "The target escaped." Twenty-nine of the subjects were randomly assigned to the Easy Condition and were allowed to divide their time among joke-rating and the easy level of the target-shooting game, and 32 subjects were randomly assigned to the Difficult Condition, constrained to joke-rating and the difficult level of the game. All of the subjects received successes on approximately 5/10 trials because the game was designed to decrease the target size if the success rate rose above 5/10 and to increase the target size if the success rate fell below 5/10. The subject was unable to infer the target size or to determine that the target size was fluctuating. On each trial, success/failure feedback was strictly honest.

The joke-rating activity involved reading a one-line joke and rating it on a scale from 1 to 9, where 1 indicated "not funny at all" and 9 indicated "hilariously funny." Subjects were encouraged to use the full range of the scale, and they were reminded that the joke ratings were strictly their own opinions. Subjects were asked to start rating jokes and were told that they could switch to the easy task (if they had been randomly assigned the easy condition) or to the difficult task (if they had been assigned the difficult condition) whenever they wished, and that they could switch back and forth between the two activities as often as they wished. The dependent measures were latency to the achievement task, and duration of time spent at the achievement task the first time it was chosen.

It is clear now that the two tasks, joke-rating and target-shooting, were unrelated, the first being an opinion task and the second an achievement task. This allows us to ignore the substitution and displacement parameters which apply only between members of families of related activities. Finally, we held constant the selective attention and consummatory lag parameters since their systematic variation was not included in the experimental design. They were set to standard values, since simulations cannot be run without values for these parameters.

Figure 1 contains two simulations based on the dynamics of action (Bongort, 1975; Seltzer, 1973; Seltzer & Sawusch, 1974). In the upper simulation, consummatory value is set to .03 and in the bottom simulation, consummatory value is set to .07. All other parameters are equal between the two simulations.

The initial tendency level for the non-achievement (joke-rating) activity, the instigating force for rating jokes, the initial tendency level for the achievement (target-shooting) activity, and the instigating force for target-shooting are equal in the two simulations. These simulations represent the situation where a subject begins rating jokes and can switch to the achievement task whenever he wishes. The simulations indicate that, because the instigating force for an easy task of P_S = .7 is equal to the instigating force for a difficult task of P_S = .3, the time to the achievement task (latency) should be the same for subjects in the Easy Condition and subjects in the Difficult Condition. However, at the point where the achievement activity is initiated, the difference in consummatory value leads to the prediction that the group given the achievement task (Easy or Difficult) with the higher consummatory value will stay at the achievement task a shorter amount of time (bottom simulation) than the group given the achievement task with the lower consummatory value.

FIGURE 1. Simulations of easy or difficult achievement task (F = 21) with c = .03 (top) and c = .07 (bottom).

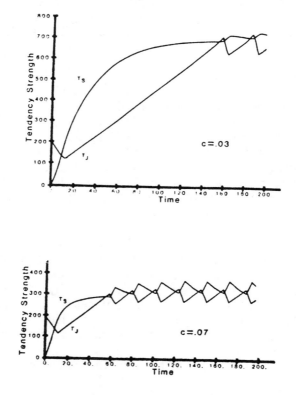

Computer Presentation of Stimuli

I have already described the situation where the subject is asked to begin rating jokes on the computer and is told that he can switch to the easy or difficult task (depending upon which condition he had been randomly assigned to) whenever he wishes. Inside the computer is a real-time clock which can be addressed when activity changes are made. As the subject plays the game, the computer is keeping track of how much time is spent on each activity, time measures which can be used to calculate latency to the achievement task, duration of the first achievement activity, and frequency of the achievement and nonachievement activities. When the 15-minute testing period is complete, these time measures are stored on a computer disk for subsequent coding.

Table 2 lists the empirical results, median latency to the achievement task for the Easy and Difficult Conditions, median duration of the first achievement activity, and mean prediction of number of successes expected given ten more trials at the assigned difficulty level. Seventy-seven subjects (including 16 subjects who received success feedback at a rate of 7/10 or 3/10) provide data for the latency measures. From the simulations (Figure 1) it was predicted that no difference would exist between the Easy and Difficult Conditions on latency to the achievement task. The results support this prediction. On the other hand, the predicted difference in first duration is highly significant with the subjects in the Easy Condition spending just 6.75 minutes at the achievement task and the subjects in the Difficult Condition spending 9.38 minutes at the achievement task (Mann-Whitney $U = 258$, $p < .005$). The difference between mean predicted number of successes given ten more trials for the two groups is also highly significant, $t(59) = 5.96$, $p < .0001$, indicating that although both groups received 5/10 successes they perceived the tasks differently. This difference in perception is supported by differing attributions (Weiner et al., 1971) with the Easy Group attributing success to task ease to a greater degree than the Difficult Group and the Difficult Group attributing failure to task difficulty as opposed to bad luck to a greater degree than the Easy Group (Blankenship, 1982, p. 911).

Modelling Empirical Results

The third step in simulation research is to model empirical results. Figure 2 contains two simulations showing the preferred activities of the Easy and Difficult Conditions. In modelling results, the same considerations are made as in simulating for hypothesis generation except that more constraints are put on the choice of parameter values. In modelling the results of the experiment designed to investigate the consummatory value of success at easy and difficult tasks, 150 time units were chosen to represent the 15-minute time period of the experiment. Parameter values had to be chosen which would allow for a latency of approximately 29 time units and first durations of 67.5 and 93.8 time units for the easy and difficult tasks, respectively. The initial tendency values and instigating forces can be approached mathematically using the time-spent formula (Atkinson & Birch, 1974, p. 327) and the formula for time to activity change (Atkinson & Birch, 1970, p. 21). Since selective attention was not varied in the experiment, a standard value of .8 was

Table 2

Time to Initiate Achievement Task (Latency), First Duration of Achievement Task, and Number of Successes Predicted Given 10 More Trials at Easy and Difficult Tasks

Condition	Mean Latency	Median First Duration	Mean Predictions
Easy Task	2.97	6.75	6.52
	(37)	(29)	(29)
Difficult	2.78	9.38	4.44
Task	(40)	(32)	(32)
	$t(75) = .40$	Mann Whitney	$t(59) = 5.9$
	$p = .69$	$U = 258$	$p < .0001$
		$p < .005$	

used; and minimal values were chosen for the initiation and cessation consummatory lags. In order to model the first durations of 67.5 and 93.8 time units, consummatory values of .036 (for the Easy Condition) and .030 (for the Difficult Condition) were necessary. The simulations also indicate that the subjects assigned the easy task would be expected to change activities more often in the 15-minute testing period than subjects assigned the difficult task. This was found to be the case. Subjects in the Easy Condition changed activities an average of 2.90 times, while subjects in the Difficult Condition changed activities an average of only 2.06 times, $t(59) = 2.49$, $p < .05$.

The purpose of modelling for parameter estimation is to provide a basis for further simulation and hypothesis generation. As just noted, the modelling of differential durations for Easy and Difficult tasks led to the further hypothesis that subjects in the Easy Condition would make more activity changes than subjects in the Difficult Condition. The estimation of consummatory values of success for easy and difficult tasks also allowed for simulations of substitution and displacement relationships between an intermediate achievement task and the easy or difficult task (Blankenship, 1968a).

FIGURE 2. Simulations modelling results for subjects in the easy condition (top simulation, F = .7, c = .036) and subjects in the difficult condition (bottom simulation, F = .7, c = .030).

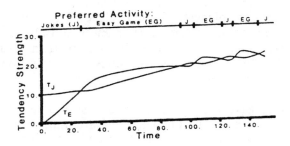

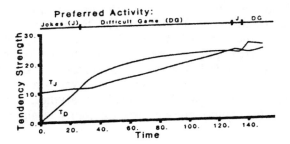

Computer Measure of Resultant Achievement Motivation

My more recent research was designed to develop a computer-based measure of resultant achievement motivation based on the number of atypical shifts a subject makes in a sequence of achievement choices. The investigation of individual differences has always been a major focus of achievement motivation research. While thematic coding of fantasy stories has been shown to be a valid measure of the achievement motive even though it lacks high internal consistency as measured by classic indicators (Atkinson, Bongort, & Price, 1977), method variance between fantasy story writing and playing games on computers has been a source of frustration in my pursuit of investigating the dynamics of achievement activities. In order to reduce that frustration, I have developed a computer-based measure of resultant achievement motivation which has a respectable level of reliability and validity.

Lewin and his colleagues, Dembo, Festinger, and Sears (1944), were the source of inspiration for this research. Level of aspiration was presented as a choice situation determined by valences of success and failure and the probability of future success. The level of aspiration for a new task was assumed to be set at that objective which had the highest weighted valence, based on the combination of positive valences of succeeding and negative valences of failure. An atypical shift could result from higher negative valences for failure than positive valences for success (i.e., fear of failure), which raised the level of aspiration to an unrealistic level (Levin et al., 1944, p. 365).

Festinger (1942) gave subjects a synonym test and an information test and recorded their levels of aspiration following goal attainment and non-attainment. His subjects made atypical shifts 8% of the time following goal attainment and 7% of the time following non-attainment. Moulton (1965) combined level of aspiration and achievement motivation theory by demonstrating that fewer subjects classified as high in resultant achievement motivation (RAM) (based on TAT – TAQ measures) made atypical shifts than subjects classified as low RAM. His subjects worked on an anagram task of intermediate difficulty and were given success or failure feedback. When subjects were subsequently allowed a free choice between easy and difficult tasks, 36% of the low RAM subjects made an atypical shift while only 3% of the high RAM subjects made an atypical shift. Moulton's subjects made just one free choice. The power of the atypical shift distinction to classify subjects as high or low RAM would be increased as the number of choices increased (cf. Nunnally, 1978). I set about to develop a measure of resultant achievement motivation based on the number of atypical shifts made when a subject is allowed 21 free choices among three difficulty levels of a target-shooting game on a computer.

Littig (1963) discovered that high RAM males were less responsive to point incentives in skill games than low RAM subjects. This led me to include in the free choice situation point incentives on half the trials and no points on the other half. A chi-square statistics could then be calculated indicating the extent to which a subject responded differentially to point and no-point trials, with a low chi-square indicating low responsiveness and, therefore, high RAM, and a high chi-square indicating high responsiveness and low RAM.

The first experiment in this series investigated validity of the atypical-shift and differential-responsiveness-to-incentive measures of RAM. In Session One 62 subjects (31 males and 31 females) made 21 choices among three difficulty levels (P_S = .7, .5, and .3) of a target-shooting game on the computer. The target-shooting game was the same as described previously. On half the trials (the first trial and subsequent odd-numbered trials) points were offered. On the other half of the trials no points were offered (Blankenship, 1986b, in revision). Points were awarded for the easy, intermediate, and difficult levels (P_S = .7, .5, and .3) so that the P_S x I_S values were equal (points = 15,21, and 35, respectively). The computer kept track of the choices made, the success/failure outcomes, whether points were offered or not, and the amount of time spent at each of the difficulty levels. After the subject had left the laboratory, the research assistant printed summary data of the session, including the number of atypical shifts made, the chi-square indicator of differential incentive responsiveness, and the percentage of time spent at each of the three difficulty levels of the game.

One week later the subject returned and was allowed to divide his/her time among the three difficulty levels of the target-shooting game and watching a color design develop on the computer monitor. Following a short practice period, subjects were asked to start watching the color design. Whenever they wished, they could switch to any of the three levels of the target-shooting game, and could switch back and forth among the color design and three difficulty levels as often as they wished for a 15-minute testing period. The computer summarized percentage of time spent at the four activities, latency to the target-shooting game, and the difficulty level of the first achievement task choice.

The null hypothesis for this experiment is that subjects classified as high RAM and subjects classified as low RAM on the basis of the atypical shift and responsiveness to incentive measures will not differ in the latency to the achievement task and in the amount of time they spend at the non-achievement (color design) activity. Since high RAM and low RAM subjects differ both on the amount of instigating force to achieve and the amount of inhibitory force, the high RAM subjects would be expected to spend less time at the non-achievement task than the low RAM subjects. Figure 3 contains four panels which represent the activity choices among one non-achievement task and the easy, intermediate, and difficult levels of an achievement task for four hypothetical individuals with high F_S and low I_F (Panel 1), high F_S and high I_S (Panel 2), low F_S and low I_S (Panel 3), and low F_S and high I_F (Panel 4). In all combinations, high F_S and I_F values are three times the magnitude of low F_S and I_F values. The forces to achieve at easy, intermediate, and difficult tasks were assigned values of 10.5, 12.5, and 10.5, respectively, for high values and 3.5, 4.17, and 3.5, for low values, values which are proportional to P_S x $(1-P_S)$. The point at which one of the positively sloped lines crosses the flat line represents the choice of one of the three achievement tasks. As Table 3 indicates, this change to the achievement task occurs after 33.2 time units in the first panel, after 52.8 time units in the second panel, after 110.5 time units in the third panel, and after 184.4 time units in the fourth panel. Panels 1 and 4, representing high RAM and low RAM, contain the most striking differences in latency to the achievement task and in percentage of time spent at the non-achievement task, and are the basis for the two hypotheses, that high RAM subjects will go to the achievement task after a shorter time period and that they will spend less time at the non-achievement task.

Subjects were split at the median on number of atypical shifts and at the

FIGURE 3. Simulations of activity choices among one non-achievement task (represented by flat line with initial tendency strength of 200) and three levels (easy, intermediate, and difficult) of the achievement task for individuals with $M_S > M_F$ (Panel 1), $M_S = M_F$, both high (Panel 2), $M_S = M_F$, both low (Panel 3) and $M_S < M_F$ (Panel 4). In each panel the first positively sloped line to cross the flat line represents the intermediate level of the achievement task.

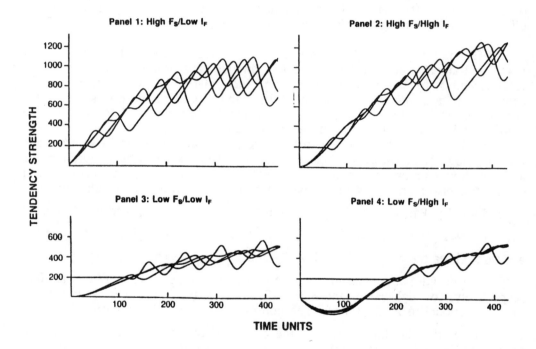

median on chi-square values computed on a contingency table of frequencies of choices among the three difficulty levels on point versus no-point trials. A three-way factorial analysis of variance was performed (atypical shift by incentive by gender) with percentage of time spent at the color design (non-achievement) task as the dependent variable. The main effect for atypical shift and the main effort for gender were not significant. The main effect for incentive was significant, with subjects who were responsive to incentives spending a greater percentage of their time at the non-achievement task a week later than subjects who were unresponsive, a finding consistent with the predictions. A three-way analysis of variance using latency to the achievement task as the dependent variable resulted in no significant main effects or interactions.

Table 3

Predictions Based on Dynamics of Action Simulations

of 500 Time Units

		Latency to Ach. Task (time units)	Percentage of Time Spent (after achievement task initiated)			
F_S	I_F		Color	Easy	Int.	Diff.
1. Hi	Lo	33.2	22.7	19.8	31.7	25.8
2. Hi	Hi	52.8	17.8	25.9	29.6	26.8
3. Lo	Lo	110.5	35.8	16.7	23.8	23.8
4. Lo	Hi	184.4	32.6	19.6	27.1	20.7

Results which are given in Table 4 are based on high RAM categories and low RAM categories constructed so that subjects so categorized were consistently categorized by the two measures, number of atypical shifts and responsiveness to incentive. The Mixed Group was categorized as high RAM on one measure and low RAM on the other. There was considerable convergence of the two measures ($r = .34$, $n = 62$, $p < .005$). As one can see, there was no significant difference in latency, but there was a significant difference in time spent at the non-achievement task, with the high RAM subjects spending less time at the non-achievement task (watching a color design) than low RAM subjects.

While the choices offered in the two sessions were different, it is possible to calculate stability of the criterion measures, percentage of time spent at the three levels of the achievement task. Percentage of time spent in the easy task in session one correlated $r = .44$, $p < .001$, with percentage of time spent in the easy task in session two one week later. Stability for the intermediate task was much lower, $r = .18$, $p = .08$, and somewhat lower for the difficult task, $r = .31$, $p < .01$. A very interesting gender difference appeared in the stability coefficients. For males test-retest reliability for the easy task was $r = .63$ ($n = 31$, $p < .001$); for females

Table 4

Observed Behaviors, Experiment I

	Latency (in seconds)	Percentage of Time Spent			
		Color	Easy	Int.	Diff.
SESSION 2					
High Ram (n=23)	63.4	10.6	8.7	40.2	40.5
Mixed (n=16)	65.5	16.3	16.0	39.1	28.2
Low Ram (n=23)	73.9	19.0	17.7	27.8	35.5
		$p=.05$			
Males (n=31)	67.6	16.7	12.8	32.8	37.7
Females (n=31)	68.0	13.7	15.0	37.8	33.5
SESSION 1					
Males (n=31)	—	—	18.6	30.1	51.3
Females (n=31)	—	—	27.6	44.5	27.8
				$p<.05$	$p<.005$

$r = .31$ (n $= 31$, $p < .05$). For the difficult task higher stability was evident for females, $r = .52$, $p = .001$, than males, $r = .07$, $p = .35$. While no gender differences appeared in session two on percentage of time spent in the achievement tasks, gender differences were found in session one with females spending slightly more time at the easy task than males, significantly more time at the intermediate task, and significantly less time at the difficult task. This pattern of results suggests a very interesting phenomenon; that subjects are more consistent (males at the easy task, females at the difficult task) in the activities they tend to avoid.

Test-Retest Reliability

Interviews with subjects in Experiment 1 indicated that the high correlation between the atypical shift measure and the responsiveness to incentive measure could have arisen from the fact that the points and no-points were offered on alternating trials. Some subjects indicated that they chose the easy level on no-point trials so they could get back quickly to the point trials on which they were more likely to pick the difficult level with a higher number of points offered. This strategy could maximize the chi-square difference between choices on the point and no-point trials while at the same time leading to increased atypical shifts because of the choice of the easy task even when the subject had succeeded on the previous difficult (and point-offered) trail, resulting in a high correlation between the two measures. In the subsequent test-retest reliability experiment, point and no-point trials were offered in blocks. Sixty-seven subjects (52 females and 15 males) served as subjects in the second experiment. Thirty-four subjects were randomly assigned to the points-first condition, and 33 subjects were assigned to the points-last condition.

The game was also changed in two other significant ways. The decision was made to limit the subject to one shot so that the amount of time spent at success and failure trials could be made more equal. With two shots possible, if the subject succeeded on the first shot, the amount of time spent at success-outcome trials would be shorter on the average than time spent at failure-outcome trials where two shots were always necessary. In this research I was interested in investigating differences in decision times following success and failure and in game times following success and failure between subjects with high RAM and low RAM. To make these measures meaningful, base-line times for the success and failure trials had to be equalized, so the target-shooting game was changed to allow for just one shot.

The other way the game was changed was that five, rather than three, levels of the target-shooting game were offered: very easy, P_S = .9; moderately easy, P_S = .7; intermediate, P_S = .5; moderately difficult, P_S = .3; and most difficult, P_S = .1. Further, the training session for the target-shooting game was computerized, so that following a brief introduction to make sure the subject knew how to use the computer, the research assistant could leave the room and allow the subject to learn the game alone.

Subjects were tested individually at two sessions a week apart. At each session they made 21 choices among five difficulty levels of the target-shooting game. Decision times and games times were recorded, along with the choices, success/failure outcomes, and point/no-point conditions on the 21 trials. Null hypotheses were that there would be no significant correlations between number of atypical shifts a week apart and incentive-responsiveness measure of RAM at sessions a week apart.

Table 5 lists the test-retest reliability correlations between number of atypical shifts at Time 1 and Time 2. For the entire sample the correlation was r = .46 (n = 67, $p < .001$). For points-first condition the correlation was r = .53 (n = 34, $p < .001$), and for the points-last condition the correlation was r = .39 (n = 33, $p < .02$). The correlations for chi-square measure of incentive responsiveness were lower; for the entire sample the correlation was r = .23, (n = 67, $p < .05$); for the points-first condition r = .33 (n = 34, $p < .03$); and for the points-last condition r = .04 (n = 33, $p = .41$). With both indicators the points-first condition resulted in a more reliable measure.

It was at this point that I began to suspect that my focus should change from

Table 5

Test-Retest Reliability of RAM Measures

(One Week Apart)

(n = 67)

	Pearson Correlation	Percent Consistently Classified High and Low
Atypical Shift	.46	57%
Typical Shift	.65	82%
Atypical minus Typical Shift	.41	64%

number of atypical shifts to number of typical shifts. In my research design subjects were allowed not to shift. This was not allowed in the Festinger (1942) and Moulton (1965) studies. The non-shifters were categorized as high RAM when number of atypical shifts was used, but were categorized as low RAM when the number of typical shifts was used. Once focus has shifted from atypical shifts to typical shifts, it becomes clear that the nature of sequential choices made by a person with high resultant achievement motivation involves the processing of success/failure outcomes and the subsequent choices of a difficulty level based on past outcome and realistic future challenge. The non-shifter is perseverating in the face of differential outcomes; that is, the non-shifter is either ignoring outcomes or processing outcomes but not responding to them. This strategy (or lack of strategy) would be more indicative of low RAM.

When points and no-points were offered in blocks instead of on alternating trials, convergent validity of the atypical shift measure and the incentive responsiveness measure fell to $r = -.08$ (n = 67, $p = 26$) for Time 1 and $r = -.03$ (n = 67, $p = .41$) for Time 2.

Experimentally-Created Computer Anxiety

The most recent experiment in this program involved the experimental manipulation of computer anxiety through the simulation of a computer breakdown. As the dynamics of action simulations summarized in Table 3 indicate, subjects with high RAM are expected to have a shorter latency to an achievement task than subjects with low RAM (line 1 versus line 4). The dual effect of higher instigating force to achieve and lower inhibitory force to avoid failure work to increase the latency for low RAM subjects. Further, low RAM subjects are expected to be more easily aroused to failure threatening stimuli, such as the breakdown of a computer. Therefore, if an experimental group experiences a computer breakdown in the midst of an experiment, the low RAM subjects in that condition would be expected to take longer to go to an achievement task in a free choice situation following the restart of the computer.

Fifty-nine subjects (46 females and 13 males) were determined to be high RAM and low RAM on the basis of the number of typical shifts they made on 21 choices among five difficulty levels of the target-shooting game, with point trials offered first and no-point trials offered last. When they were returned to the laboratory a week later, they were offered three activities, watching a color design, rating jokes as to their funniness, and playing the intermediate level of the target-shooting game. The null hypothesis was that there would be no difference between the high RAM and low RAM subjects in the computer breakdown condition and two control conditions.

Two control conditions were necessary to make the results of this experiment interpretable. One control group would experience an interruption at the same time in the experimental procedure that the breakdown was experienced by the experimental group. Following a training period and just before the testing period, the computer would print "And now for the important part." In the breakdown condition the computer screen would go blank and no key input would cause it to restart. The subject would be forced to get the research assistant who was seated outside the experimental room and have the computer restarted. In the interruption condition, the computer instructed the subject to "Please get the research assistant to input a secret code." For these two groups, the procedure was exactly the same. The research assistant entered the room, pressed the return key twice, moved to the other side of the computer, and entered a Control-A, which immediately restarted the computer. The research assistant then said, "It's all right now. I'll be outside if you need me," and walked out. If the subject persisted in asking questions, the experimenter said (quite truthfully), "I don't know what happened." The third condition, a second control condition, proceeded immediately to the 15-minute free choice testing period without any interruption or breakdown. The last digit of the milisecond timer was used to randomly assign subjects to one of the three conditions.

In the free choice testing period, subjects were asked to start watching the color design. When they wished to change activities, they could choose the joke-rating activity or the intermediate level of the target-shooting game. They were free to switch back and forth among these three activities as often as they wished. The computer kept track of the amount of time spent at each of the activities, the decision times, the success/failure outcomes of the target-shooting games, and the joke-ratings (from 1 to 9). No points were offered in the target-shooting game.

The results of a two-way analysis of variance (condition by Hi-Low RAM) are presented in Table 6. When subjects are divided on the basis of the number of typical shifts they made (as opposed to the number of atypical shifts), subjects classified as high RAM went to the achievement task sooner than subjects classified as low RAM. These differences are consistent across all conditions and are particularly strong in the computer breakdown condition.

Table 6

Latency to the Achievement Task Hi RAM vs. Lo RAM

Based on Number of Typical Shifts

(Time in Seconds)

	Experimental Condition		
	Control (No Interrupt)	Control (Interrupt)	Breakdown
Hi RAM	109.64	174.16	187.64
	(11)	(11)	(8)
Lo RAM	309.05	406.11	617.39
	(13)	(7)	(8)

For condition: $F(2,53) = 2.05$, $p = .14$

For Individual Differences: $F(1,53) - 11.25$, $p = .001$

Structural Differences Among the Experimental Situations

At this point it is instructive to characterize the various experimental conditions and to point out how minor differences in activities offered lead to more or less successful demonstrations of the dynamics of achievement behavior. The success of the last experiment is due in large part to the increased power and sensitivity of the design which allowed subjects to avoid the achievement task while still responding to the demand characteristics of the experiment to remain active throughout the testing session. Specifically, in the first experiment of this series subjects in the free choice situation (second session) could choose only between the color design activity and three levels of the achievement activity. Latency measures were constrained because when subjects tired of watching the simple color design, they had no choice but to play the target-shooting game. In Experiment 3 they could avoid the achievement task and still remain active by rating jokes. The importance of avoidance behavior had been suggested in Experiment 1 with the higher reliability of avoided activities for males and females. Experiment 1 with just one non-achievement activity and three levels of the achievement activity is the perfect design if the dependent variable of interest is risk preference. It is not adequate to test hypotheses relating to latency to the achievement task and percentage of time spent at non-achievement and achievement task.

Advantages and Disadvantages of Computer Use

As the last experiment illustrates, sometimes a research hypothesis is not exactly on target. When data have been collected by the computer and saved on disk, it is possible to re-analyze the data and extract information that was not originally anticipated. An example of this advantage is the suggestion I received that the dynamic involved in the last experiment was not avoidance of the achievement task per se, but rather the reluctance of the subject in the breakdown condition to touch the computer at all. This explanation of the results had not occurred to me, but once the suggestion was made it was possible for me to go back to the data and perform a two-way analysis of variance on time to touch the machine using condition and high-low RAM as the factors. As Table 7 indicates, it was not reluctance to touch the computer that explained the differential latency to the achievement task. As predicted, the inhibitory effect was specific to the achievement task and not generalized to touching the computer.

Table 7

Time to Touch the Machine Hi RAM vs. Lo RAM

Based on Number of Typical Shifts

(Time in Seconds)

Experimental Condition

	Control (No Interrupt)	Control (Interrupt)	Breakdown
Hi RAM	44.03	34.89	65.79
	(11)	(11)	(8)
Lo RAM	39.22	28.89	41.16
	(13)	(7)	(8)

For condition: $F(2,53) = 1.157$, $p = .32$

For Individual Differences: $F(1,53) = .99$, $p = .33$

We have long known that affiliation motivation can combine with achievement motivation and result in performance decrements due to over-motivation (cf. Horner, 1968). With the computer the subjects can be left to work alone in a room without the need for an experimenter with a stop watch to be present who might arouse affiliation and/or approval motives. Further reaction times and decision times are much more precisely measured with the computer. Presentation of stimuli can be made contingent on response, an advantage that will allow us to probe reasons subjects have for making particular choices at particular times. Following a failure outcome, for example, a subject can be asked to attribute the cause to lack of effort or bad luck. This will make the combination of cognitive and dynamic aspects of achievement motivation more accessible to research.

There are also some pitfalls that await the person who uses the computer without sufficient background. The most important danger is that an artifact will be introduced into the experiment based on some programming decision. For example, if the computer program consistently takes a longer branch requiring more computing time for one condition of the experiment, a consistent difference will appear in the data which will favor a shorter time for the other condition. The consistency of the computer, one of its greatest advantages, becomes a disadvantage if it consistently adds a constant to one time measure. The only way to guard against such an artifact is to run each program with instantaneous responding built in so that consistent differences can be discovered and controlled for. For example, in the RAM testing experiment, I collected decision time and game time data based on pre-programmed responses made by the computer and added timing loops to equalize the baseline game times for success and failure trials. Because the failure trial required that the program calculate the amount by which the target was missed, the failure trials took longer than the success trials. This was equalized by adding a delaying loop in the feedback loop on the success trails.

Random numbers are tricky in computers as well. Most microcomputers have a random number function, but unless a random seed can be produced, the same random numbers in the same sequence will be provided each time. This is comparable to starting at the same spot in a random number table each time. The time clock provided a solution for assigning subjects randomly to the conditions of Experiment 3. The digit of the millisecond counter of the Mountain Apple Clock was the basis for assigning subjects. Computer clocks vary; some do not provide easy access to millisecond output.

In summary, it pays to know your computer and to know enough about programming to tell if your program is indeed doing what you want it to do. Computer simulation and modelling and computer presentation of stimuli demand that you be very specific about your assumptions and that your coordinating definitions be soundly based in a substantive domain. With proper caution, the computer will be an exacting tool to further motivational research.

REFERENCES

Atkinson, J. W. (1957). Motivational determinants of risk-taking behavior. *Psychological Review, 64*, 359–372.

Atkinson, J. W. (Ed.) (1958). *Motives in fantasy, action, and society*, Princeton, NJ: Van Nostrand.

Atkinson, J. W., & Birch, D. (Eds.) (1970). *The dynamics of action*. New York: Wiley.

Atkinson, J. W., & Birch, D. (1974). The dynamics of achievement-oriented activity. In J. W. Atkinson & J. O. Raynor (Eds.), *Motivation and achievement*. Washington, DC: V. H. Winston.

Atkinson, J. W., & Birch, D. (1978). *An introduction to motivation* (2nd ed.). New York: Van Nostrand.

Atkinson, J. W., & Feather, N. T. (1966). *A theory of achievement motivation*. New York: John Wiley & Sons.

Atkinson, J. W., Bongort, K., & Price, L. H. (1977). Explorations using computer simulation to comprehend TAT measurement of motivation. *Motivation & Emotion, 1*, 1–27.

Blankenship, V. (1982). The relationship between consummatory value of success and achievement task difficulty. *Journal of Personality and Social Psychology, 42*, 911–924.

Blankenship, V. (1986a). Substitution in achievement behavior. In J. Kuhl and J. W. Atkinson (Eds.), *Motivation, thought, and action*, in press.

Blankenship, V. (1986b). *A computer-based measure of resultant achievement motivation*, in revision.

Bongort, K. (1975). *Most recent revision of computer program for dynamics of action*. Unpublished computer program, University of Michigan.

Festinger, L. (1942). Wish, expectation, and group standards as factors influencing level of aspiration. *Journal of Abnormal and Social Psychology, 37*, 184–200.

Horner, M. (1968). *Sex differences in achievement motivation and performance in competitive and noncompetitive situations*. Unpublished doctoral dissertation, University of Michigan.

Lewin, K., Dembo, T., Festinger, L., & Sears, P. S. (1944). Level of aspiration. In J. McV. Hunt (Ed.), *Personality and the behavior of disorders*. New

York: Ronald.

Littig, L. W. (1963). Effects of motivation on probability preferences. *Journal of Personality, 31*, 417–427.

Mandler, G., & Sarason, S. B. (1952). A study of anxiety and learning. *Journal of Abnormal and Social Psychology, 47*, 166–173.

Moulton, R. W. (1965). Effects of success and failure on level of aspiration as related to achievement motives. *Journal of Personality and Social Psychology, 1*, 399–406.

Nunnally, J. C. (1978). *Psychometric theory* (2nd ed.). New York: McGraw-Hill.

Revelle, W., & Michaels, E. J. (1976). The theory of achievement motivation revisited: The implications of inertial tendencies. *Psychological Review, 83*, 394–404.

Selzer, R. A. (1973). Simulation of the dynamics of action. *Psychological Reports, 32*, 859–872.

Selzer, R. A., & Sawusch, J. R. (1974). Computer program written to simulate the dynamics of action. In J. W. Atkinson & J. O. Raynor (Eds.), *Motivation and achievement*. Washington, DC: V. H. Winson.

Weiner, B., Frieze, I., Kukla, A., Reed, L., Rest, S., & Rosenbaum, M. (1971). *Perceiving the causes of success and failure*. New York: General Learning Press.

Chapter Seven

MOTIVATION AND EFFICIENCY OF COGNITIVE PERFORMANCE

William Revelle

Northwestern University

It is fitting in a book written in honor of Jack Atkinson's lifelong contribution to the study of personality and human motivation to consider the motivational determinants of cumulative achievement. In this chapter I will show how parts of the theoretical framework outlined by Atkinson can be filled in to answer the question of what determines cumulative achievement. Figure 1 (adapted from Atkinson and Birch, 1978) gives an overview of the richness of Atkinson's theory, and will serve as an outline of this chapter.

Achievement over a lifespan is logically the cumulation of many separate accomplishments. High achievement is a function of the number of accomplishments and the quality of the average accomplishment. Each of these single acts may differ in absolute quality; frequency and number of outstanding achievements will also differ between people. Evariste Galois and Albert Einstein are known for a few profound insights; Thomas Edison and George Carver are remembered for a lifetime of high productivity. Hank Aaron and Walter Payton have set records in professional sports based partly upon high average levels of performance, but based also upon long and productive careers.

The level of performance on a single task is a function of ability and the efficiency with which the task is performed. Efficiency, in turn, depends upon the nature of the task, and the strength of motivation to engage in that task. Tasks can differ in their difficulty, their importance, and their intrinsic interest. In addition, tasks can differ in the type of cognitive resources they require. Recent work in cognitive psychology allows us to analyze tasks in terms of various components of information processing, and to consider how motivation can effect efficiency in a number of different ways. Efficiency can be analyzed in terms of the tradeoff between spending time doing one class of tasks (e.g., achievement) versus another class (e.g., affiliation), in terms of task choice (whether to do the experimenter defined task or to do the subject defined task), in terms of strategic tradeoffs between working rapidly and working accurately, and in terms of tradeoffs between cognitive resources (e.g., those required for short term memory versus sustained information transfer).

Time spent on a task is a function of the strength of motivation to engage in

FIGURE 1. The multiple determinants of cumulative achievement. (Adapted from Atkinson and Birch, 1978).

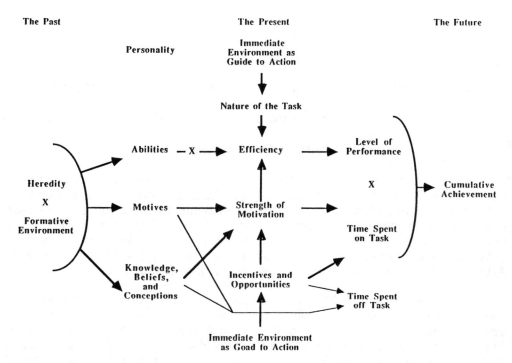

that task, as well as the incentives and opportunities to do the task or to do something else. Alternative measures of motivation include choice, latency, persistence, frequency, and total time spent, and can be seen as different levels of measurement of the same underlying construct.

All of these analyses depend upon decomposing the strength of motivation into two components: direction and intensity. Some motivational effects are best explained by their directional characteristics, others (particularly the effect of motivation upon components of information processing) are best understood in terms of their intensity. Central to this decomposition is Atkinson and Birch's (1970) analysis of the dynamics of motivation as a function of time.

Strength of Motivation: The Implications of the Dynamics of Action

Perhaps Atkinson's major contribution to the study of cumulative performance was his work with David Birch which introduced the dimension of time to the analysis of motivational strength and direction. This work was an outgrowth of earlier work by Lewin and other Gestalt psychologists (e.g., Zeigarnik, 1927/1938), Feather (1961), as well as a paper with Cartwright (Atkinson and Cartwright, 1964). The fundamental idea was the recognition that the initiation of an activity should be analyzed in the same manner as the persistence of an activity: the latency of onset of an activity is equivalent to the persistence of not doing that activity.

Although a seemingly simple point, this realization provides a common language for the analysis of choice, persistence, latency, frequency, and time spent. That is, the simple act of choosing to initiate B rather than C after doing A can be analyzed in terms of the choice (B or C), the persistence of A, and the latency of B. If choices are allowed in an unconstrained manner, it is possible to find the frequency of choosing B over C, as well as the total time spent in activities A, B, or C.

In addition, by changing from a static to a dynamic perspective, the issue of what behavior was occurring before the current one becomes of vital importance. That subjects recall more unfinished tasks than finished tasks (Zeigarnik, 1927/1938), or that non-anxious subjects perform better following failure than following success (Weiner & Schneider, 1971) is understandable within a dynamic framework, but hard to understand within a static perspective.

The Dynamics of Action (DOA)

An early formulation of this dynamic model (Atkinson, 1964) considered that the strength of tendency to do r in order to achieve the goal g, $(T_{r,g})$ was greater if there were some unsatisfied "inertial" tendency to achieve success. The inertial tendency was associated with Lewin's need or intention which was thought to persist until satisfied.

Formal specification of this model was provided by Atkinson and Birch (1970) who realized that the combination of inertial tendencies and changes over time could be expressed by differential equations. This meant that the analysis should change from specifying motivational tendency to specifying rates of change in tendency. An advantage of the dynamic model was that it forced investigators to investigate the time course of the behavioral stream. No longer was it possible to assume trial to trial or task to task independence, but rather it was necessary to be explicit in how to treat the different amounts of satisfaction one obtained by succeeding versus failing on a task in order to understand performance on the subsequent trial.

A simple application of the inertial tendency assumption was the demonstration by Revelle and Michaels (1976) that some data which seemed to contradict the conventional theory of achievement motivation (Atkinson, 1957) could be well fit with the addition of inertial tendencies. As Heckhausen (1967) and Hamilton (1974) had shown, persons with a high need for achievement tend to prefer tasks with a probability of success somewhere between .3 and .4 rather than the .5 predicted by Atkinson (1957). Further problematic data had been reported by Locke (1968) who had shown that subjects try harder the harder the goal that they set. When the assumption of inertial tendencies ($T_{sk} = T_{s1} + c_f T_{sk-1}$ following failure but $T_{sk} = T_{s1}$ following success) was added to the traditional (Atkinson, 1957) theory [$T_{s1} = M_s P_s (1-P_s)$], Revelle and Michaels (1976) showed that Hamilton's data and Locke's data could be fit quite well.

A more elegant extension of this point was made by Kuhl and Blankenship (1979 a,b) who completely integrated the Atkinson (1957), Atkinson and Birch (1970), and Revelle and Michaels (1976) perspectives. Kuhl and Blankenship (1979a) provide an excellent theoretical treatment of the relationship between the traditional theory of achievement motivation (Atkinson, 1957) and the dynamics of action (DOA, Atkinson & Birch, 1970). Kuhl and Blankenship (1979b) provide empirical support for the prediction that risk preferences should shift over time from an initial preference for intermediate difficulty to a later preference for more difficult tasks. (See also Schneider and Posse's (1982) suggestion that such shifts can be understood in terms of a win-shift, lose-stay strategy.)

Although analytical solutions to the DOA model could only be estimated asymptotically, by approximating the model in terms of a set of difference equations, it was possible to develop computer simulations of the model. Many of us can remember the excitement of testing alternative theoretical assumptions by comparing how the "spaghetti" behaved as assumptions were varied. These simulations showed both the strengths and the weaknesses of the model. It was clear from the simulations that several parameters of the model (the instigating and consummatory lags) which are necessary to make it work have rather fuzzy coordinating definitions in the theory. Yet another difficulty in the DOA is that although the decision rule of what leads to a change in behavior is well specified, it is less clear how the decision is made.

Stimulus-Need-Response Model 1

An alternative model to the DOA, which maintains many of the same assumptions but is mathematically simpler, can be derived from concepts developed by British "control theorists" of animal behavior (e.g., McFarland, 1974, Toates & Halliday, 1980). This model has one exogeneous independent variable (the input stimulus), an intervening variable (a need or covert response), and one observable output variable (the overt response). The basic assumption in this model is that a stimulus excites a need, a need excites a response, and a response reduces the need. This may be shown figurally as a box or flow diagram (Figure 2).

This path model may be formalized in terms of the following two differential equations relating stimulation (S), need (N), and response (R) with the constraint that $R \geq 0$:

$$dN = mS - cR \tag{1}$$

$$dR = eN - iR \qquad (2)$$

FIGURE 2. A control system model of the interrelationships of stimulus, needs, and responses. Stimulus and response are observable variables, need is an unobserved latent variable.

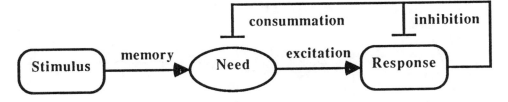

The coefficients are: m, the strength of the memory associating the stimulus to the need; c, the amount of the consummatory effect of the response on the need; e, the strength of the excitation that a need induces in a response; i, the inhibition or fatigue that making a response has upon that response. The constraint $R \geq 0$ is imposed by assigning all negative values of R to 0. When equations (1 and 2) are simulated and need and response are plotted against time, need and response will achieve stable values (Figure 3).

As should be obvious from the equations, with constant stimulus S, need will achieve an asymptotic level: $N = iR/e$. At this level, response strength will have value $R = mS/c$, and thus, by substitution, need will have the value of $N = imS/ec$. This system is equivalent to several of the systems discussed by Bolles (1980) who showed how a system can achieve an equilibrium without necessarily having a homeostatic set point.

Generalized Stimulus-Need-Response Model (SNR)

Such a system becomes more complicated (and more interesting) if we consider S, N, and R to be vectors of stimuli, needs, and responses, and introduce the concept of response incompatibility. If doing A is incompatible with doing B (an interesting example of such incompatibility is found in the newt which breaths at the surface of ponds, but copulates under water, Halliday, 1980), then responses can be said to inhibit each other and we have a system which may be seen graphically (Figure 4) or may be expressed by the differential equations:

$$dN = mS - cR \qquad (3)$$

$$dR = eN - iR. \qquad (4)$$

The coefficients are matrices, the elements of which are: m, the strength of the memory associating a stimulus to a need; c, the amount of a consummatory effect of a response on a need; e, the strength of the excitation that a need induces

FIGURE 3. Need and response intensity as a function of time. The stimulus (S) has an initial value of 8, and is then changed to 2 and finally to 6. Both need and response intensity achieve new equilibrium values after the change in stimulus intensity.

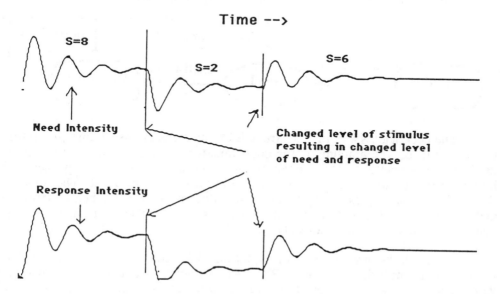

in a response; *i*, the inhibition or fatigue that making a response has upon that and other responses. The constraint $R \geq 0$ is imposed by assigning all negative values of R to 0.

If the inhibition matrix is diagonal, then responses are mutually compatible and all responses can occur at the same time. Thus, each need may achieve a steady state. However, if the responses are incompatible, then only one response occurs at a time and the needs do not achieve a steady state. Instead, needs grow and decline over time as first one and then another response is expressed (Figure 5).

The benefits of the matrix representation is that it recognizes that a stimulus actually can be formed as a complex pattern of stimuli, and similarly, that a single response may be formed from a pattern of simpler acts. In addition, the matrix representation introduces the concept of a state space, in which it is possible to consider how behavior changes an individual's location in a multidimensional space, the dimensions of which are the separate needs. If responses are mutually incompatible (mutually inhibitory), producing a response which reduces one need will simultaneously lead to a move away from homeostatic balance along the other need dimensions.

FIGURE 4. A generalized control system model of stimuli, needs, and responses. Mutual inhibition between responses is shown. The generalized effect of stimuli on multiple needs, the excitatory effect of needs on multiple responses, and the consummatory effect of responses on multiple needs are not shown.

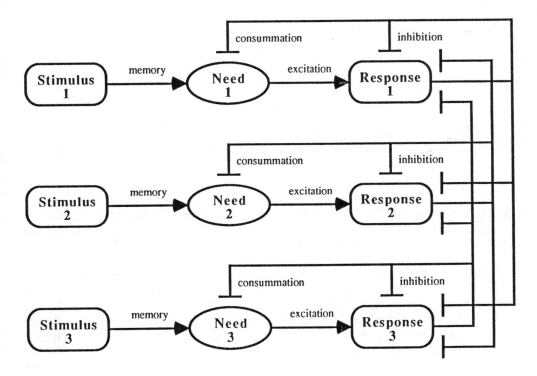

A further benefit of the matrix representation is simplicity. For instance, all relationships between stimuli and needs are summarized in the m (memory) matrix. The diagonal elements correspond to the direct effect a stimulus has upon a need; the off-diagonal elements correspond to generalization effects. That is, to the extent that two stimuli are similar, they should have similar effects upon a need. Similarly, the diagonal elements of the c (consummation) matrix reflect the degree to which doing an activity reduces the need to do that activity; the off diagonal elements may be thought of as representing substitutions: the extent to which doing an act reduces other needs. The diagonal elements of the e (excitation) matrix represent direct excitatory effects of needs upon responses; the off diagonal

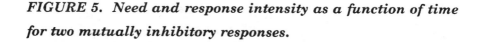

FIGURE 5. Need and response intensity as a function of time for two mutually inhibitory responses.

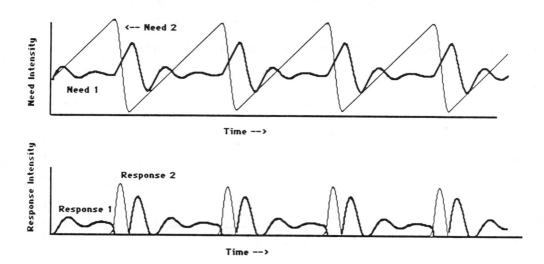

elements represent possible displacement effects. Finally, the diagonal elements of the *i* (inhibition) matrix represent fatigue effects; the off diagonals represent the degree to which two responses are incompatible.

It is important to note that these matrices need not be symmetric. Thus, an anxious response might inhibit working on an exam, but working on the exam does not necessarily inhibit one's anxiety. This suggests that formulations such as Gray's (1982) Behavioral Activation System/Behavioral Inhibition System (BAS/BIS) can be captured within the structure of the excitation and inhibition matrices. Furthermore, the matrices need not be square nor of the same rank. That is, a vector of ten stimuli might only excite three or four needs, which in turn elicit only one of two responses.

As a final note, by representing the SNR model as two matrix difference equations, it is easy to simulate the model on even the simplest micro-computer. The basic model requires slightly more than 100 lines of Pascal and executes on an Apple II computer. The graphics for this chapter used a more convenient (and somewhat longer) version of the model, running on a Macintosh and originally written in MacPascal.

Stimulus-Need-Response as a Distributed Motivation Model

Recent work in cognitive science has suggested that it is appropriate to think of human information processing as a massively parallel operation in which memory is distributed across millions of nodes or connections. The SNR model is in some sense an analog of such a memory model in that different needs grow and decay in simultaneous response to many different stimuli. Although responses tend to be in sequential order, there is parallel processing of stimuli. The mechanism behind the shift from parallel processing of stimuli and needs to sequential output of responses is in the "winner take all" effect of mutual inhibition. If two responses are mutually incompatible (mutually inhibit each other), the response with the slightly greater initial strength will dominate and suppress the other. It is only when the need to do the suppressed response grows strong enough that the suppressed response will become active and suppress, in turn, the previously dominant response.

Stimulus-Need-Response vs. Dynamics of Action

The SNR model can be viewed as a reparameterization of the DOA. The instigating forces of DOA are equivalent to stimuli in SNR. Action tendencies of DOA are equivalent to the needs of SNR. In DOA, the dominant action tendency is expressed in behavior which in turn reduces the action tendency; in SNR needs excite responses which in turn reduce needs. What then is the difference? DOA needs to introduce lags (both instigating and consummatory) for the time from when an action tendency becomes dominant to when doing the action will have a consummatory effect and reduce the action tendency, and for the time from stopping an activity to the time that consummation is stopped. Functionally, these lags are equivalent to the distinction between needs and responses. Response strength lags behind need strength, and changes in need do not occur until after responses are produced.

Another difference between the two models is in the treatment of *negaction*. There are two types of stimuli in DOA, instigating forces and inhibitory forces. Instigating forces lead to action, inhibitory forces lead to negaction, which is then subtracted from action to produce resultant tendency strength. Although there is no formal equivalent to negaction in SNR, it is easy to create responses which behave like negaction. For example, a test could lead to two different needs, achievement and anxiety, which in turn could excite two different responses, approach and avoidance. If the avoidance response inhibited the approach response, but was not in turn inhibited by the approach response, the delay in initiation of the achievement-approach response would mimic the effects of negaction in DOA. (See also Gray, 1982 for a discussion of how anxiety affects the behavioral inhibition system).

Perhaps the greatest difference between the two models is in the decision rule of which response to make. In DOA the stronger resultant tendency is always expressed in action. That is, if A is chosen over B, then $T_a > T_b$. In SNR, on the other hand, the strongest response is always expressed in action, but the strongest need is not necessarily expressed. If A is chosen over B, this means that the inhibitory effect of doing A is greater than the excitatory effect of the need to do B

($iR_a > eN_b$). This implies that increasing the response strength of an activity without changing need strength will increase its persistence.

There are logically two different choice situations: Doing A and then choosing to change behavior to initiate B, or doing some ongoing activity O, and then choosing to initiate B rather than A. In general, DOA assumes local independence (the choice between A and B should be independent of the other alternatives) and treats both of these situations the same. In DOA, changing from A to B implies that Ta < Tb, just as does choosing to stop continuing to do O and to initiate B rather than A. SNR, on the other hand, does not assume local independence, but notes that the ongoing activity affects choice. That is, changing from A to B implies that the need to do B is greater than the inhibitory effect on B of doing A. Changing from O to initiate B rather than A implies that the need to do B is greater than the inhibitory effect of doing O on B, and that the need to do A is less than the inhibitory effect of doing O on A. It does not imply that the need to do B is greater than the need to do A. One can have very strong needs to initiate an activity A, but if doing that activity is incompatible with (inhibited by) the current activity, not initiate A, but rather initiate a less desired but more compatible (less inhibited) activity B. Although it is possible in DOA to consider compatibilities between action tendencies, doing so breaks down the direct correspondence between choice and tendency.

(Consider the situation of someone discussing a complex idea with some colleagues while sitting in a bar drinking beer. After several beers one can very much want to go to the rest room but, because leaving the table is incompatible with continuing the discussion, defer going and instead have another beer. In DOA, we need to say that the tendency to drink the beer is stronger than the tendency to go to the rest room. In SNR, by emphasizing the inhibitory effects of the ongoing activity, we only can conclude that having another beer is less inhibited by the conversation than is going to the rest room. We are unable to say that the need to drink beer is greater than the need to go to the rest room. An interesting prediction that follows from SNR is that if the conversation becomes less interesting, the likelihood of going to the rest room will increase.)

A second characteristic of the SNR decision rule is that it is a natural consequence of the mathematics. The effect of mutual inhibition is to lead to a winner take all decision rule which does not need a separate comparator examining the strengths of all competing action tendencies. Mutual inhibition is, of course, a standard characteristic of the brain physiology and is a natural way to implement a decision maker (McDougall, 1903, Ludlow, 1980).

An important characteristic of both the DOA and SNR models of motivation and choice is that they imply that stable personality characteristics (traits) affect the rate of change of behavior rather than behavior per se. If individual differences in achievement motivation, anxiety, impulsivity, or sociability are associated with the coefficients in equations 3 and 4, then these stable dimensions of individual differences produce differences in the rates at which behavior changes rather than the behavior itself. But, by affecting rates of change, they will also affect choice, latency, persistence, frequency, intensity, and the total time spent in an activity.

Two Components of Motivation

An important characteristic of both dynamic models (DOA and SNR) is that they lead us to separate motivational strength into two components: direction and intensity. Direction can be associated with choice or preference, intensity perhaps can be associated with physiological arousal. What is interesting about both components is that different ways of indexing motivation will lead to different conclusions about motivational strength. Because most of the theorizing of Atkinson and his associates has centered around the directional component of motivation, it is fruitful to spend some time considering alternative measures of direction.

Direction. The most obvious measure of direction is choice. A consequence of both of these dynamic models is that the longer one has been doing an activity A, the more likely one is to switch to another activity. Ongoing activities will tend towards stable response and need strengths (see Figure 5), while needs for other actions will grow until they are strong enough to be initiated. The likelihood of continuing in the next time unit as will be a negatively decreasing function of time. This differs from a simple stochastic process, in which the likelihood function should be flat. This implies that choice is not independent of the situation, but rather depends upon how long one has been doing an activity.

Two measures of motivational strength other than choice are latency and persistence. Latency may be measured by how long it takes to initiate A and is equivalent to the off-time of A. Persistence may be defined as how long A is on once it is initiated, and is equivalent to the latency of not A. In a situation with only two possible acts, of course, persistence of A is equivalent to the latency of B.

Choice, latency, and persistence are measures taken at one change in behavior. Two other measures of direction, requiring averaging across many changes of behavior, are frequency and time spent. Frequency is merely how many times an act was initiated or chosen. Time spent is the sum of the persistences. These two measures are not interchangeable nor even necessarily correlated. An individual can do something frequently, but not spend very much total time doing it. For example, I sleep 8 hours or one third of a day, but I only go to sleep once a day. During a day I might talk to 20 different people, but only spend 1 hour talking to people. (See Figure 5 for an example of a 2 choice situation in which both activities occur equally often but one takes up 80–90 % of the time.)

Intensity. The second motivational component is intensity. Unfortunately, while direction is easily indexed (although not consistently) by choice and persistence, there is no easy index of intensity. Furthermore, our intuitive definitions are not very helpful, for by saying that someone is trying hard, do we mean that he or she is spending a great deal of time, or exerting a great deal of energy? It is tempting to equate physiological arousal with intensity, but given the complexities of the concept of arousal, one is loath to make hard and fast definitions. It is possible to show that manipulations thought to affect physiological arousal such as stimulant drugs, the time of day, or sleep deprivation affect tasks differently from manipulations that seem to affect task choice or persistence such as incentives, success or failure feedback, or ego threat (Humphreys & Revelle, 1984).

Task Variables Affecting Efficient Performance

In addition to the strength of motivation, another important determinant of efficient task performance is the nature of the task to be performed. Unfortunately, much of the research concerned with motivational effects upon performance has either used an overly simplistic analysis of task variables, or has used none at all. Tasks tend to be chosen because they have been used before or for convenience but not for any important theoretical reason. In addition, very little contact has been made with relevant theories of cognitive psychology or of information processing.

Rather than accuse others of careless disregard for task parameters, it is appropriate to cite some of my own research for examples of such naive practices. In a study of how introversion-extraversion and arousal affected performance, Revelle (1973) chose tasks because they had been used before in studies of achievement motivation. Digit symbol substitution, a maze task, and some anagrams were used as performance measures. Although task difficulty was varied within each type of task, there was no attempt to understand the cognitive processes involved for these tasks. In a later study Revelle, Amaral and Turriff (1976) used practice Graduate Record Examination items because they were convenient and were more challenging for undergraduates than the anagrams used earlier. Revelle, Humphreys, Simon and Gilliland (1980) continued to use GRE items in order to establish the reliability of the Revelle et al. (1976) results but still did not concern themselves with the task parameters.

All of these studies considered the concept of difficulty, but they did not distinguish between difficulty as indexed by error rate, number of problems finished, or number of trials needed to achieve a certain criterion. Nor did any of these studies take into account current models of information processing. In fact, although these studies were meant to be examining the Yerkes-Dodson "Law" (Yerkes & Dodson, 1908), they did not distinguish between rates of learning (i.e., number of trials to criterion in a discrimination task, Yerkes & Dodson, 1908), and speed of retrieval of synonyms and antonyms in a verbal performance task.

Partly in response to criticism of the lack of theoretical meaning of such tasks as the GREs, but mainly in order to explain the Yerkes-Dodson Law, Humphreys and Revelle (1984) tried to organize the motivation and performance literature in terms of several dimensions of information processing.

Learning vs. processing. A primary distinction to make is between those tasks which involve learning to make new associations and those which require processing (reorganization or retrieval) of available material. The study of motivational effects in learning has a long history. The original Yerkes and Dodson (1908) experiment and a subsequent replication of it (Broadhurst, 1959) made use of a discrimination learning task. Spence, Farber and McFann (1956) examined motivational (anxiety induced drive) effects on paired associate learning of easy and difficult lists. Weiner and Schneider (1971) extended the Spence et al. results by showing the importance of feedback rather than item difficulty in determining the error rate when learning paired associate lists.

Recent experiments have looked for motivational effects upon the processing of available information rather than the learning of new information. Several studies have examined the relationship of motivational intensity and GRE performance (Anderson, 1985; Gilliland, 1980; Revelle et al., 1976, 1980). Anderson and Revelle (1982, 1983) tested the effect of caffeine on proofreading and letterscanning. Bowyer, Humphreys and Revelle (1983) showed that caffeine induced arousal interacted with time on task to affect recognition memory. Anderson, Revelle and Lynch (1985) found that caffeine facilitates the intercept but increases the slope in a Sternberg memory search task. Within the processing domain, it is possible to organize the types of information processing resources demanded along three separate dimensions: sustained information transfer, short term memory, and long term memory. (See Humphreys & Revelle, 1984 and Revelle, Anderson & Humphreys, in press, for more extensive reviews of studies examining arousal mediated effects upon information processing.)

Sustained Information Transfer (SIT). The first dimension along which tasks can be ordered measures the extent to which subjects are required to process a stimulus, associate an arbitrary response to the stimulus, and execute a response. We characterize this dimension as measuring information transfer. Examples of low IT requirements include simple and choice reaction time, simple arithmetic, letter scanning, and letter cancellation. In these tasks there is no appreciable retention of information required nor is there an appreciable amount of distraction. Tasks which in addition require subjects to sustain their readiness to respond and which include a temporal or spatial uncertainty in the location of the stimulus we refer to as Sustained Information Transfer tasks. These include standard vigilance tasks, simple letter search tasks, as well as proofreading for non-contextual (e.g., spelling) errors.

Short Term Memory (STM). A second dimension measures the amount of information which must be retained for short periods of time. Tasks with high memory load include traditional experimental measures of STM (e.g., recognition or recall tasks), derived measures such as the speed of memory scanning in a Sternberg paradigm, or simple tasks in which a memory load has been added. Example of the latter include a letter search task in which one is to identify strings of 20 letters that include a memory set of 6 letters (Anderson & Revelle, 1981) or geometric analogies with several transformations from the A to B term (Mulholland, Pellegrino and Glaser, 1980).

Long Term Memory (LTM). A third dimension along which tasks may vary is the amount of retrieval of previously learned material which is necessary. High LTM load would include tasks measuring vocabulary or previously acquired information. Thus a proofreading task would have a higher LTM load than would a letter search task which would in turn have more LTM load than a simple reaction time task.

A typology of tasks. These three dimensions of information processing can be combined to allow for a classification of many different tasks (Figure 6). Sixteen different measures used in recent studies in my lab have been organized in terms of their SIT, STM, and LTM requirements. Although the absolute location in this 3-space is somewhat arbitrary, the relative location is not. Thus, the intercept in a memory scanning task has less STM load than does the slope taken from the same measure. The SIT load in this task is less than that in a recognition or recall task where a subject is required to detect the stimulus as well as retrieve it later. Searching for two letters has less STM load than searching for six letters, just as proofreading for non-contextual errors has less STM load than proofreading for contextual errors. Proofreading, however, has more LTM load than a letter search. Geometric analogies can range from those with few SIT or STM demands (one element and one transformation, to those with greater SIT demands (three elements and one transformation per element), or greater STM demands (one element but three transformations per element) to problems with large STM and SIT demands (three elements and three transformations per element). Finally, the GRE analogies we used in Revelle et al. (1980) were high in SIT, STM, and LTM demands.

The example of analogical reasoning. Perhaps the best way to understand these dimensions is to consider how they relate to a particular task. A recent study of analogical reasoning (Mulholland, Pellegrino & Glaser, 1980) used geometric analogies which differed in the number of elements within each term of the analogy, as well as in the number of transformations applied to the elements. Increases in both elements and transformations led to slower decision times; only increases in transformations increased the error rate. Mulholland et al. proposed that transformations were affecting the short term memory requirements of the task, but elements were not. In our terms, increasing the number of elements increases the SIT demands; increasing the number of transformations increases the STM demands. Geometric analogies have far fewer long term memory demands than than do the verbal analogies found in the Graduate Record Exam or the Scholastic Aptitude Test. Unfortunately, in those exams, the typical problem has only one element per term, and the number of transformations is not as easily determined as it is in geometric analogies.

Inefficiency as an Inappropriate Tradeoff

Atkinson (1974) claimed that the level of performance with which a task is executed depends upon one's ability and efficiency. Implicit in his analysis was the idea that individual differences in ability are not perfectly reflected by individual

FIGURE 6. *A typology of tasks. Tasks are characterized in terms of their relative loading on the dimensions of Sustained Information Transfer, Short Term Memory and Long Term Memory. (Adapted from Revelle, et al., in press).*

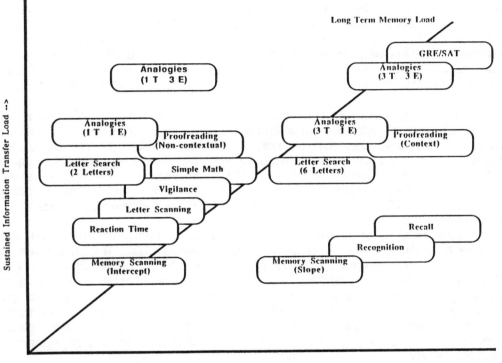

differences in performance. If we take maximum performance as an index of ability, then any level of performance below that can be said to be inefficient. Furthermore, Atkinson (1974) suggested that efficiency depends upon one's strength of motivation and the type of task. Although task variables can be shown to be very important determinants of efficiency (Humphreys & Revelle, 1984), the strength of motivation can lead to less than maximal performance in at least four different ways.

Each of these sources of inefficiency can be expressed as a tradeoff between applying resources to the externally defined reference task versus some other task or task component. Three of these tradeoffs may be analyzed in terms of the directional component of motivation, one in terms of the intensity component. By examining performance on the reference task as a function of performance on other tasks, it is possible to better understand the many meanings of the term "inefficiency."

Time spent between tasks—macro level analysis. Perhaps the simplest tradeoff is merely that between spending time doing something versus doing something else. If one task is considered important by an outside observer (the reference task), but other tasks are considered important by the subject (alternative tasks), then performance on the reference task will be inefficient or less than maximal to the extent that the subject spends time doing the alternative tasks. Graduate students or faculty members who spend time with their family rather than working on a manuscript are being inefficient from the point of view of their academic colleagues, but performing well from the point of view of their families.

It is this sort of tradeoff which is relevant to the broad study of motivation. Individuals with a high need for achievement will spend more time in achieving situations than will those with a lower n-Ach or a higher need for affiliation. Students who spend the weekend studying for exams are using their time more efficiently from the point of view of their achievement oriented professors; students who prefer to spend the weekend at a series of lively parties are spending their time more efficiently from the point of view of their extraverted friends.

Time spent within tasks—micro level analysis. At a much narrower level, it is possible to consider how subjects spend their time within a task. Recent analyses of the effects of anxiety on performance (e.g., Leon & Revelle, 1985; Sarason, 1975; Wine, 1971) have suggested that anxious subjects spend more time worrying or engaging in off task thoughts than do less anxious subjects. Although seemingly inefficient from the point of view of the experimenter, time spent in evaluating one's self esteem, or thinking about what one will do when the test is over can be seen by the subject as a more appropriate use of time than actually engaging in a threatening task.

Leon and Revelle (1985) found that anxious subjects do not do worse because of some differential processing deficit. They found that anxious subjects were slower and less accurate on all types of geometric analogies than were less anxious subjects. The analogies varied in number of elements (SIT load) and number of transformations (STM load). These results supported predictions derived from Sarason and Wine, but contradicted predictions derived from drive theory (Hull,1952; Spence & Spence, 1966), cue utilization theory (Anderson, 1980; Easterbrook, 1959), and working memory theory (Eysenck, 1979).

Strategic allocation of resources. Another reason for inefficient performance that is under the subject's control is the strategic allocation of priorities for different task components. Perhaps the best example of such strategic allocation is found in the tradeoff of speed for accuracy. In even the most basic reaction time task, faster performance can be achieved if there is an increased tolerance for errors. A typical reaction time finding is that RT is linear with log odds (i.e., the logarithm of the probability of correct responses divided by the probability of incorrect responses).

Many tests are scored for the total number correct which is, of course, the product of the number of problems attempted and accuracy on those attempted problems. If accuracy is a negatively accelerated but increasing function of time spent on a problem and the number of problems attempted is a decreasing function of the total time spent per item, then the number of problems correct will be a complex function of task difficulty and error rate. Assume that the probability of passing an item (p) is a logistic function of ability (a), item difficulty (d), and time spent on the item (t):

$$p = e^{(a+t-d)}/(1+e^{(a+t-d)}) \tag{5}$$

and that the number of test items (N) completed in a fixed amount of time (T) is a function of the total time divided by the time spent per item ($N=T/t$). Then the total number of correct items is Np:

$$Np = Te^{(a+t-d)}/(1+e^{(a+t-d)})t. \tag{6}$$

Finding the optimal level of the speed for accuracy tradeoff in terms of total number of problems correct becomes quite difficult, for it depends upon ones's ability (a) and the difficulty of the items (d). If there are individual differences in the tolerance of errors, then even subjects with similar levels of ability will work at different rates (t) and differ in their total number correct (Np). Manipulations which increase accuracy may lead to either increases or decreases in total problems correct, depending upon the subject's ability, the item difficulty, and the initial bias towards speed or accuracy (Figure 7).

Atkinson (1974) reviewed evidence suggesting that anxious subjects are more sensitive to failure than are less anxious subjects. Gray (1981) also has suggested that anxiety is related to a sensitivity to punishment or non-reward. Thus, we would expect anxious subjects to prefer to work slowly in order to minimize errors. Impulsive subjects, however, would be expected to work rapidly, trying to maximize the number of problems attempted with little concern for making errors. An example of the effect of anxiety on speed-accuracy tradeoffs comes from Geen's (1985) comparison of speed versus accuracy in a Stroop color-word naming task. Geen found that when given instructions "to do your best" anxious subjects were slower but more accurate than were non-anxious subjects. However, the two groups did not differ when given instructions to be as accurate as possible or to be as fast as possible.

Automatic allocation of resources. The tradeoff between cognitive resources available for short term memory and sustained information transfer involves the intensity of motivation rather than its direction. Increases in arousal lead to increased resources available for SIT tasks, but to decreased resources available for

FIGURE 7. The effect of speed (number of problems attempted) on performance (number of problems correct) for various levels of problem difficulty. For easy problems maximum performance is achieved by maximizing the number of problems attempted. As problem difficulty is increased, however, the optimal number of problems attempted decreases.

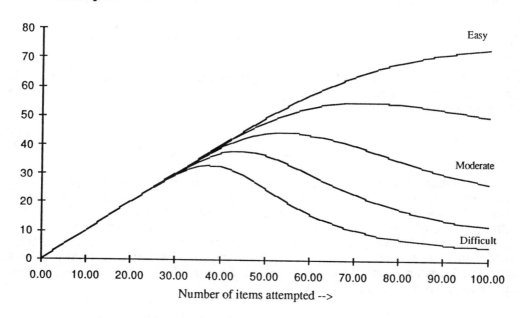

STM tasks (Humphreys & Revelle, 1984; Revelle, Anderson, & Humphreys, in press). Although the construct of arousal is clearly an oversimplification, it is useful as a way of organizing the effects of a variety of seemingly different variables. It should be construed as a conceptual dimension ranging from extreme drowsiness at one end to extreme excitement at the other. It may be manipulated, physiologically indexed, or behaviorally observed. Any particular measure will, however, introduce some irrelevancies. It is the convergence of multiple measures that allows us to use the term arousal. Stimulant drugs (e.g., caffeine and amphetamine), lack of sleep deprivation, time of day (afternoon versus morning), and time on task (early versus late) seem to facilitate performance on SIT tasks but hinder performance on STM tasks. Performance on tasks with low STM loads (tasks on the left side of Figure 6) is facilitated by caffeine while performance on tasks with higher memory loads (tasks on the right side of Figure 6) is hindered by caffeine (Revelle, et al., in press). Performance changes due to arousal can be seen as a tradeoff between resources available for SIT or STM processing.

A clear demonstration that caffeine induced arousal facilitates performance on tasks with low memory load but hinders it on tasks with a high memory load is the recent study by Benzuly (1985) who studied the effects of caffeine and impulsivity on geometric analogies. Benzuly crossed two levels of information transfer load (1 and 3 elements) with two levels of memory load (1 and 3 transformations) to form four types of analogies. She used 0 and 4 mg/kg body weight in a between subjects design. Impulsivity was used as an individual differences variable thought to relate to arousal (low impulsive subjects were expected to be more aroused, Revelle et al., 1980). Caffeine had a main effect effect on performance (improving performance no matter what the SIT load, and interacted with transformations (facilitating those problems with a low STM load, but hindering those with a high STM load). The effect of impulsivity was not significant.

Complex tasks such as geometric analogies or the GREs require large amounts of both SIT and STM resources. Arousal has a positive monotonic effect on resources available for SIT, but a negative monotonic relationship for resources available for STM. The combination of these two functions can lead to an inverted U function. At low levels of arousal (given a placebo, following sleep deprivation, early in the morning, or for less aroused individuals), performance is limited by the availability of SIT resources and increases in arousal will lead to increases in performance. At higher levels of arousal (given a stimulant drug, without sleep deprivation, later in the day, or for more aroused individuals), performance is limited by the availability of memory resources and increases in arousal will lead to decreases in performance (Figure 8).

Anderson (1985) tested these ideas in a within subject design with five levels of caffeine induced arousal. High and low impulsives were given a simple letter scanning and a complex reasoning (GRE verbal items) task. Performance on the letter scanning task (requiring SIT resources) was a positive monotonic function of caffeine dosage for both high and low impulsive subjects. Performance on the GRE (requiring both SIT and STM resources) was an inverted U function of caffeine for the more aroused (low impulsive) subjects, but was an increasing positive function for the less aroused (high impulsive) ones.

A plausible explanation for the automatic effect of arousal on the allocation of resources for SIT, STM, and LTM is that increases in arousal lead to a reduction in the length of the psychological moment. To use an analogy from digital computers, arousal increases the tick rate of the internal clock. The faster tick rate means that information is sampled from the environment more frequently, which leads to faster (and better) performance on SIT tasks such as reaction time, letter scanning, or simple arithmetic. In addition to improving SIT performance, a faster tick rate leads to more samples of the environment for storage in LTM. Increasing the number of samples is roughly equivalent to the effect of increasing study trials in a verbal learning experiment and will improve recognition and recall after long

FIGURE 8. The relationship between arousal, sustained information transfer, and short term memory. Increases in arousal increase resources available for SIT but decrease the availability of resources required for STM. (Adapted from Humphreys and Revelle, 1984).

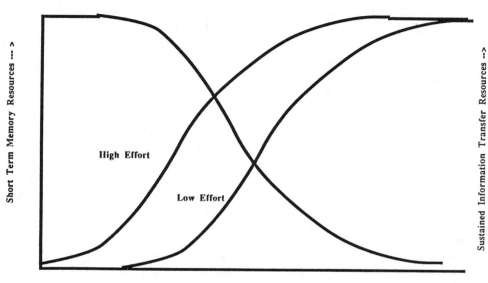

delays. As well as producing the benefit of improving SIT and LTM performance, however, an increased tick rate increases the rate at which information is lost (interfered with) in short term memory. This is a direct consequence of the increased tick rate. For a fixed retention interval, a faster tick rate will lead to more samples from the environment than will a slower tick rate. This is analogous to lengthening the intervening interval or increasing the interference in a short term memory task. Interference from these additional samples will lead to decreased performance in short term memory paradigms.

Summary and Conclusions

Motivational strength affects performance in several different ways. The directional component of motivation determines what tasks are chosen, the latency before starting a task, persistence once started, and the frequency with which a task is chosen. In addition, direction affects tradeoffs of time spent between and within classes of tasks, and strategic tradeoffs between task components. The intensity component of motivation affects efficiency by controlling the tradeoff between the cognitive resources available for sustained information transfer and short term memory.

Both components of motivation need to be considered as dynamic and changing over time. Alternative conceptions of these behavioral dynamics lead to similar conclusions and are useful for understanding how personality traits manifest themselves in everyday behavior. Stable individual differences are seen not in stable behavioral differences, but as consistent differences in the rates of change of behavior. Finally, dynamic models of motivation are compatible with recent developments in distributed models of memory and cognition in that they specify how parallel processing of stimuli and needs can lead to sequential outputs of responses.

Jack Atkinson's contribution to the field of psychology is the result of his high level of performance as well as his dedication to the problem of human motivation. Both the time he spent and his level of performance reflect favorably on his ability and on the strength of his motivation.

REFERENCES

Anderson, K. J. (1980). *The current status of the Easterbrook hypothesis*, unpublished manuscript, Northwestern University.

Anderson, K. J. (1985). *Impulsivity, caffeine and task difficulty: A within subjects test of the Yerkes-Dodson Law*. Unpublished manuscript, Colgate University.

Anderson, K. J., & Revelle, W. (1982). Impulsivity, caffeine, and proofreading: A test of the Easterbrook hypothesis. *Journal of Experimental Psychology: Human Perception and Performance, 8*, 614–624.

Anderson, K. J., & Revelle, W. (1983). The interactive effects of caffeine, impulsivity, and task demands on a visual search task. *Personality and Individual Differences, 4*, 127–134.

Anderson, K. J., Revelle, W., & Lynch, M. J. (1985). *Arousal and memory scanning: A comparison of two explanations for the Yerkes-Dodson effect*. Unpublished manuscript, Colgate University.

Atkinson, J. W. (1957). Motivational determinants of risk-taking behavior. *Psychological Review, 64*, 359–372.

Atkinson, J. W. (1964). *An introduction to motivation*. New York: D. Van Nostrand.

Atkinson, J. W. (1974). Strength of motivation and efficiency of performance. In J.W. Atkinson & J.O. Raynor (Eds.), *Motivation and achievement* (pp. 117–142). New York: V.W. Winston.

Atkinson, J. W., & Birch, D. (1970). *The dynamics of action*. New York: Wiley.

Atkinson, J. W., & Birch, D. (1978). *Introduction to motivation*. New York: D. Van Nostrand.

Atkinson, J. W., & Cartwright, D. (1964). Some neglected variables in contemporary conceptions of decision and performance. *Psychological Reports, 14*, 575–590.

Benzuly, M. (1985). *Caffeine and memory load: Their effect on analogical reasoning*. Unpublished honor's thesis. Northwestern University.

Bolles, R. C. (1980). Some functionalistic thoughts about regulation. In F. M. Toates & T. R. Halliday (Eds.), *Analysis of motivational processes* (pp. 63–75). London, Academic Press.

Broadhurst, P. L. (1959). The interaction of task difficulty and motivation. The

Yerkes-Dodson Law revived. *Acta Psychologica, 16*, 321–338.

Easterbrook, J. A. (1959). The effect of emotion on cue utilization and the organization of behavior. *Psychological Review, 66*, 183–201.

Eysenck, M. W. (1979). Anxiety, learning, and memory: A reconceptualization. *Journal of Research in Personality, 13*, 363–385.

Feather, N. T. (1961). The relationship of persistence at a task to expectation of success and achievement related motives. *Journal of Abnormal and Social Psychology, 63*, 552–561.

Geen, R., & Kaiser, M. (1985). *Test anxiety and performance on the Stroop color word task*. Unpublished manuscript. University of Missouri.

Gray, J. A. (1981). A critique of Eysenck's theory of personality. In H. J. Eysenck (Ed.), *A model for personality* (pp. 246–276). Berlin: Springer.

Halliday, T. R. (1980). Motivational systems and interactions between activities. In F. M. Toates & T. R. Halliday (Eds.), *Analysis of motivational processes* (pp. 205–220). London: Academic Press.

Hamilton, J. O. (1974). Motivation and risk taking behavior: A test of Atkinson's theory. *Journal of Personality and Social Psychology, 29*, 856–864.

Heckhausen, H. (1967). *The anatomy of achievement motivation*. New York: Academic Press.

Hull, C. L. (1952). *A behavior system*. New Haven: Yale University Press.

Humphreys, M. S., & Revelle, W. (1984). Personality, motivation, and performance: A theory of the relationship between individual differences and information processing. *Psychological Review, 91*, 153–184.

Kuhl, J., & Blankenship, V. (1979). The dynamic theory of achievement motivation: From episodic to dynamic thinking. *Psychological Review, 85*, 239–248.

Kuhl, J., & Blankenship, V. (1979). Behavioral change in a constant environment: Shift to more difficult tasks with constant probability of success. *Journal of Personality and Social Psychology, 37*, 551–563.

Leon, M. R., & Revelle, W. (1985). The effects of anxiety on analogical reasoning: A test of three theoretical models. *Journal of Personality and Social Psychology, 49*, 1302–1315.

Locke, E. A. (1968). Toward a theory of task motivation and incentives. *Organizational Behavior and Human Performance, 3*, 157–189.

Ludlow, A. R. (1980). The evolution and simulation of a decision maker. In F. M. Toates & T. R. Halliday (Eds.), *Analysis of motivational processes* (pp. 273–296). London: Academic Press.

McDougall, W. (1903). The nature of inhibitory processes within the nervous system. *Brain, 26,* 153–191.

McFarland, D. J. (1974). *Motivational control systems analysis.* Academic Press: London.

Mulholland, T. M., Pellegrino, J. W., & Glaser, R. (1980). Components of geometric analogy solution. *Cognitive Psychology, 12,* 252–284.

Pachella, R. G. (1974). The interpretation of reaction time in information-processing research. In B. Kantowitz (Ed.), *Human information processing: Tutorials in performance and cognition.* Hillsdale, NJ: Lawrence Erlbaum Associates.

Revelle, W. (1973). *Introversion/extraversion, skin conductance and performance under stress.* Unpublished doctoral dissertation, University of Michigan, Ann Arbor.

Revelle, W., & Michaels, E. J. (1976). The theory of achievement motivation revisited: The implications of inertial tendencies. *Psychological Review, 83,* 394–404.

Revelle, W., Amaral, P., & Turriff, S. (1976). Introversion-extroversion, time stress, and caffeine: The effect on verbal performance. *Science, 192,* 149–150.

Revelle, W., Anderson, K. J., & Humphreys, M. S. (in press). Empirical tests and theoretical extensions of arousal-based theories of personality. In J. Stelau and H. J. Eysenck (Eds.), *Personality dimensions and arousal.* London: Plenum.

Revelle, W., Humphreys, M. S., Simon, L., & Gilliland, K. (1980). The interactive effect of personality, time of day, and caffeine: A test of the arousal model. *Journal of Experimental Psychology: General, 109,* 1–31.

Sarason, I. G. (1975). Anxiety and self-preoccupation. In I. G. Sarason & C. D. Spielberger (Eds.), *Anxiety and stress,* Vol. 2. Washington, DC: Hemisphere.

Schneider, K., & Posse, N. (1982). Risk taking in achievement-oriented situations: Do people really maximize affect of competence information? *Motivation and Emotion, 6,* 259–272.

Spence, J. T., & Spence, K. W. (1966). The motivational components of manifest anxiety: Drive and drive stimuli. In C. D. Spielberger (Ed.), *Anxiety and behavior*. New York: Academic Press.

Spence, K. W., Farber, I. E., & McFann, H. H. (1956). The relation of anxiety (drive) level to performance in competitional and non-competitional paired-associates learning. *Journal of Experimental Psychology, 52*, 296–305.

Toates, F. M., & Halliday, T. R. (Eds.). (1980). *Analysis of motivational processes*. London: Academic Press, 1980.

Weiner, B., & Schneider, K. (1971). Drive versus cognitive theory: A reply to Boor and Harmon. *Journal of Personality and Social Psychology, 18*, 258–262.

Wine, J. (1971). Test anxiety and direction of attention. *Psychological Bulletin, 76*, 92–104.

Yerkes, R. M., & Dodson, J. D. (1908). The relation of strength of stimuli to rapidity of habit-formation. *Journal of Comparative Neurology and Psychology, 18*, 459–482.

Zeigarnik, B. (1938). [On finished and unfinished tasks.] In W. D. Ellis (Ed.), *A source book of Gestalt Psychology*. New York: Harcourt Brace. (Reprinted and translated from Psychological Forschung, 1927, 9, 1–85.)

Chapter Eight

CONTEXTUALISM AND HUMAN MOTIVES

Joseph Veroff

University of Michigan

My commitment to psychology in general and to the study of motivation in particular grew out of an undergraduate thesis that Jack Atkinson helped me design and execute: A study of achievement motivation in high school girls and boys, as measured by a new fangled story-telling device called the Thematic Apperception Test, in which we had subjects tell stories in response to pictures and then coded these stories for motivational content. When I was a senior at Wesleyan, not sure where my main interests would lead and whether this field of psychology was really a legitimate enterprise after all, Jack's enthusiasm for a new approach to motivation and its measurement enabled me to discover the joys of research on human needs. Jack and Dave McClelland, whose slot at Wesleyan Jack had taken over for a year while Dave was on leave, were putting together materials for *The Achievement Motive* with Russ Clark and Ed Lowell (McClelland, Atkinson, Clark & Lowell, 1953). The promise of a new systematic story-telling technique indeed seemed revolutionary at that time. And it still does to this day. In my senior research I wanted to demonstrate that it was a technique that was valid for people other than college males for whom it was originally devised—namely high school students, and especially high school females, who, up to that time had not been studied. The research made me a convert. It was not because the data were that clear-cut. In fact, the results were really very perplexing, as they are today (Sutherland & Veroff, 1985), despite thirty-five years of many related studies. It was because in learning how to code stories for motivational content, I became aware of both the richness of each person's own complicated way of dealing with motivational concerns and the elegant universality of the underlying imaginative processes reflecting motivational thought. Through the TAT you become aware of the contextual and idiosyncratic underpinnings to motivation that each person carries with him/her, as he/she tells a slightly different story. You also become aware of the themes that are common to everyone. Although each person's need for achievement score is assumed to lie somewhere on a single dimensional scale, a researcher who uses the TAT quickly becomes sensitive to each person's unique way of expressing feelings and thoughts about achieving in fantasy.

Over the years it is the complexity of individual differences in the strength of motive as expressed in the TAT that has become especially intriguing to me, and it is that issue upon which I would like to focus in this chapter. While I have continued to be loyal to the simple measure of the achievement motive through fantasy—and later to parallel measures of affiliation and power motives (Veroff, Depner, Kulka, & Douvan, 1980)—I have been absorbed by the ways that situational and developmental contexts affect the nature of these motives (Veroff, 1983), how these motives are expressed in fantasy and how these motives affect human reactions (Veroff & Veroff, 1980). We started out with simple ideas: such as, the higher the achievement motive, the more persistent a person would be at the achievement related task; or, the more a person would choose certain incentives out of an array of preferences. The creativity in Jack's thinking let us see how motives are just one of a *number* of determinants of constantly changing tendencies that are the structure of persistence, or of choice. Jack and his colleague, Dave Birch, posited that situational incentives and expectancies, consummatory tendencies, and forces of inertia all dynamically affect motivational tendencies (Atkinson & Birch, 1970). These concepts are all critical to a complete theory of motivation.

I want to speak of other complex factors that also affect motivation. I want to speak of ways in which contexts affect the nature and strength of the motives in the first place. My undergraduate study of high school girls' achievement motives first alerted me to this (Veroff, 1950). The quality of the achievement motive in women is not exactly like the quality of the achievement motive in men. Further differentiation was required; this is a conclusion about gender differences I will come back to later in this chapter. The general thesis I will attempt to develop is that the dimensions that make up a motive have to be understood in addition to its strength. I will elaborate this point while discussing four assertions about motives: (a) The quality of a motive is different at different points in the life cycle; (b) A motive may be differentiated into sub types which if assessed separately will give the research greater understanding of how motivations affect behavior; (c) Motives interact with each other and hence the quality of a particular motive is contingent on the pattern of other motives operating at the same time in the person's life space; (d) The quality of a motive is dependent on the nature of parallel personal values. Let me discuss each of these issues in turn. I will illustrate some of my points with data from a national survey that a number of us have been analyzing here at Michigan (Veroff, Douvan, and Kulka, 1980).

A Motive is Different at Different Points in the Life-cycle

One of the assumptions often made about a motive is that it is a personal disposition that reflects how important a certain type of incentive is to an individual. A person with a high motive for achievement places high importance on meeting standards of excellence. A person with a low motive for affiliation places little importance on warm relationships with others. As dispositions, motives are relatively stable. They are presumed to be forged in childhood when verbal control is minimal. If this is so, motives are not conscious organizations and they are not easily open to voluntary change. In the early days of our thinking about motives we adopted the prevalent assumption that once a person develops a motive of a given strength, it would remain with him or her for a lifetime. Most of us as personality theorists still harbor that belief (McClelland, 1985).

Furthermore, another assumption we often made is that no new motives of any consequence emerge after childhood for any individual. While there has been some evidence of stability of motive strength over time (Feld, 1967; McClelland, 1985), there is equally compelling evidence for changes in motive strength as well as the emergence of new motives during adulthood (Veroff & Veroff, 1980). Recently, with my colleagues David Reuman and Sheila Feld, I investigated two national surveys (one done in 1957; one done in 1976), both of which used the same thematic apperceptive measure of motives (Veroff, Reuman & Feld, 1984). Thus, for both years we had assessed measures of achievement, affiliation, and power motives. If we looked at a given cohort and examined its mean motive scores in 1957 and again in 1976, we could get a handle on motive stability in cohorts. We could also examine age differences in motive to see whether they were consistent in both years of testing. Overall, we were not impressed with the cohort stability in motives. In most instances we found inconsistencies in the relative motive strengths among cohorts, at least between 1957 and 1976. This set of findings suggest that changes of motives occur as a result of adult socialization, that early childhood socialization itself can not account for the strength of a person's motive over a lifetime.

This is not to say that we found no stability in certain cohort differences. We found some, especially when we controlled for education differences among subjects. Women born between 1927 and 1936 and between 1907 and 1916 were consistently higher in the affiliation motive than the other cohorts. And women born between 1917 and 1926 were consistently higher in the achievement motive. One can speculate about particular historical circumstances in the socialization of these women which may account for the stability indicated in these results. For example, those women born between 1917 and 1926 were consistently high in the achievement motive, in both 1957 when they were in their 40s and in 1976 when they were in their 60s. Most of these women were adolescents during the Great Depression, but young girls during the decade following the passage of women's right to vote. This peculiar combination may have contributed to a high motivational interest in achievement for women, an interest that remained indelible. All of this is mere post facto speculation about this cohort. But to return to the main point I was trying to make, all and all we were less impressed with any stability in motives that could be discerned from cohorts' distinctiveness vis-a-vis each other, and more impressed with the changes in the level of motive scores for different cohorts in different decades.

What does all this mean? It suggests that situational circumstances in adult development, both generally for a cohort and individually for a given person, can strongly affect motives. The most striking set of findings in this regard in the work with Reuman and Feld was a clear diminution of the affiliation motive in women of older ages in both 1957 and 1976. Young adult women start out at a very high level of the affiliation motive, but this seems to diminish gradually over the life cycle. In interpreting these results, we assumed that being uncertain about one's identity is an important basis for people's concern about affiliation. Schachter's classic research (1959) on the topic of affiliation led to a series of studies which demonstrate that seeking out information about one's own uncertainty is critical in evoking the affiliative response. We further assumed that over time women become less uncertain about their identities as women. They marry, or they don't marry. They have children, or they don't. They raise children who are launched and then well out of their domain of influence. In some sense they have integrated the traditional concerns of women by a certain age. Their uncertainties diminish; and, we would argue, their need to seek acceptance from others diminishes, so their fantasy no longer reflects strong affiliation concerns.

If this is so, you may ask, why doesn't the same logic apply to the men's data where we found no changes in the affiliation motive scores over the life cycle? First of all, we assume that compared to women, men's affiliative concerns in early adulthood are lower because they are less engaged by uncertainties about their masculine gender role. The clarity of who men are or who they should be is much better known at an earlier age. Men's major source of uncertainty largely lies in their performance at work. Furthermore, uncertainty about work does not diminish for men over their life cycle, largely because criteria for evaluation about work begin to change over the life cycle. These new criteria about evaluation of men's work keep men's uncertainty at an even plateau across their life course. To back up this speculation we found that men who may have little identification with their work (that is men in low status jobs) show a similar affiliation motive decline to that of women. Furthermore, a small group of women who we can assume have a very strong career identification—professionally employed women—fail to show the decline in the affiliation motive with age. In sum, we interpret the results for women as a reflection of important changes in the adult life cycle of women which allow them to shake off their concerns about identity and the kind of people they are. Hence women develop weaker motives for affiliation as they age. The results for men suggest that changes in men's uncertainties about themselves do not occur over their life cycle. As a result, men show no change in this motive as they age.

Thus, a developmental consideration—greater certainty about yourself over the life cycle—affects the strength of a motive in women—the affiliation motive. One might argue that the quality of the motive in women may change with time—from being largely based on uncertainty to becoming largely based on general conviviality. Unfortunately, we do not have a specific coding of the element of uncertainty as a basis for the affiliation motive to test this hypothesis. It would be an important hypothesis to test in the future.

We can test a similar kind of hypothesis with respect to the achievement motive, since we do have more refined codings of substantive achievement themes that can be used to compare different age groups. Let us also take a look at another result in which age differences emerged in both 1957 and 1976, where we looked for developmental shifts of the achievement motive. We found that older women (60 years and older) have a much lower achievement motive score than younger women. The result was true in both 1957 and 1976. We are able to distinguish three types of achievement imagery, that based on unique accomplishments enacted in stories, on long-term involvement with a career, and on general statements involving the setting of standards of excellence in various tasks. We found that the lower achievement motive for older women was primarily due to their lack of fantasy about long-term involvement with a career. It was not at all apparent in the stories about unique accomplishments or about general concerns about standards of excellence. Thus, the diminishment of the achievement motive in elderly women could be seen as the diminishment of future concerns about status accomplishment, and not a general diminishment of all aspects of the achievement motive.

What are the implications of these developmental results? They suggest that certain motivational concerns may diminish over time if the general support for these concerns shifts in the different context that people enter into and emerge from at different points in their lives. We can thus lose some of our motives or certain aspects of our motives, or at least find their strength faltering, if the circumstances are right. Sudden life transitions can sometimes illustrate these motive shifts quite dramatically. Profound changes in the quality of achievement and affiliation concerns can occur when people have a brush with death, suffer a severe illness, or experience the death of someone very important to their own interpersonal well-being. Profound changes can occur with sudden changes in total life circumstances, such as entering a very different type of job, or in the break up of a long-term family relationship through death or divorce, or filling or emptying the nest.

Over and above important radical life changes across the developmental periods, can we take seriously the possibility that a motive may diminish because of persistent frustration or satiation? Can we lose our achievement motive because we succeed so easily or fail so persistently? The very early experimental studies showed that failure or success conditions did not raise the achievement imagery as much as a so-called ego involved condition where the evaluations about a subject's accomplishment were uncertain (McClelland, Atkinson, Clark & Lowell, 1953). Such anticipatory uncertainty may be required to engage a motive. If this is so, could we suggest that repeated certainties of failure or success may diminish the strength of a motive like achievement? This is an interesting life stage developmental question. We can only get information like this from longitudinal research on the motive measurements. This research also remains to be done.

Indirect evidence relevant to this question comes in McClelland's (1985) report of work done by Diaz (1982). This researcher found a negative correlation between assets plotted over time for competing American and Japanese automobile manufacturers, and the achievement motive assessed from annual letters of the chief executive officers to the stockholders of each company two years later. It was as if failure and success in the auto competition respectively induces lower and higher motives for the company executives or their collective spirits. Indirect evidence granted, and with respect to a short time period in people's lives, but still provocative.

Beyond the effects that success or failure might have on the motive itself, can we consider the possibility that some motives may simply peter out? Can the incentives of the chase pale in the same way that life span developmental psychologists speak of the reduction of libido for most men and women as they age? It is a tempting theory to advance, since whatever results we have about social motives across the life cycle show only decreases in older ages. We have yet to find any increases. In any case, we need a model for thinking about this problem for all motives. Such a model would need to deal with some fundamental assumptions: do we see people as having a limited number of motives that reflect their concerns, or as having an ever expanding number of incentives? If people are limited in their motivational capacities, then as any motive increases in importance or a new motive develops in adulthood, an old one may have to be reduced; it is like the assumption of a closed system. If we assume that motivational capacities can be continually expanding as we mature, then a motive can remain stable in strength as other ones are added. Or, for that matter, we could suggest that as we age, our motivational capacities diminish, and hence some may remain stable but others may diminish with expanding or contracting capacities, we might have a model of a more open system. Which model we follow might help us think about the possibility of changes in motives over the life span. Both the closed and open system approaches would allow us to anticipate changes over the life span, but we can anticipate greater stability with the open system approach.

The logic of the fantasy measure of motives suggests a closed system; it assesses the amount of imaginative thought devoted to given motives. If a subject thinks about one group of motives within a given set of stories, it is difficult for him/her to think simultaneously of another. Using the dynamics of action approach to the fantasy measure, one might suggest that motives that are directing tendencies which are very low in strength will not be easily represented in fantasy.

The closed system approach, toward which I lean, also might suggest that the mere passage of time might diminish a motive because as new incentives become salient in shifting life circumstances, new dispositions or motives may develop and old ones may have to be displaced. Other people's work on aging suggests that there is a shift from instrumental types of motives (like achievement) to more hedonistic ones (like security and physical well-being), as men and women age (Lowenthal, Thurnber, & Chiniboga, 1975). This may be so because as one ages and anticipates mortality, new concerns about physical well-being become more characteristically dominant, become new motives—which may in turn displace other social motives. For example, Lillian Rubin in her book *Women of a Certain Age* (1980) speaks of the anxieties about relationships that successful men experience as their children suddenly grow up and leave home. Their achievement concerns pale, as their sense of loss of family connection becomes more paramount. They feel they never can recapture the joys of parenthood that they had put off while they were younger and more career-minded. Old motives may fade as new ones become prominent. This is closed system thinking and it may be wrong. Much more work needs to be done on this problem.

Sub-types of Motives

Even if people's motives did not diminish in quantity as other important things were happening in their lives, the particular quality of the incentives that define the motives might shift in some way. For example, there may be a greater alignment of incentives that can service two different motives. The particular quality of achievement may become more social as middle-aged men face the disappearance of their children leaving home. Where once men may have been more task-involved with their accomplishments at work, they may now make their efforts more responsive to other people's expectations. Or the quality of achievement may become more directed towards individual pursuits without a keen sense of competition with others, as suggested by Maehr and Kleiber (1981) in their interesting article on the achievement motive in older people.

Thus we can differentiate a motive into sub-types. A motive represents a family of potential concerns united by a common incentive thread—a concern about meeting standards of excellence (achievement), a concern about maintaining close relationships (affiliation), a concern about having impact (power). Although the members of each family are related, they can be meaningfully differentiated as we have explicitly done from time to time with regard to the achievement motive. Earlier in the paper I suggested that we could distinguish the following types of achievement concerns: Unique accomplishment, competing, having long-term career concerns, etc; and we have seen how these distinctions helped clarify developmental changes in women. Elsewhere we (Veroff & Veroff, 1980) have distinguished a number of types of achievement orientations in a different way: Responsibility achievement (accomplishment out of a sense of duty), social comparison achievement (accomplishment through competition with others), and task achievement (accomplishment of a set task). Each of these types is partially assessed with the TAT measure but each can be distinguished with respect to its antecedents and consequences in behavior. Spence and Helmreich (1983) have taken a similar approach in their distinctions about competence, work, and mastery as different types of orientation to achievement. These researchers find that different measures of these dispositions give them different predictions to performance criteria. In our own research we (Veroff, McClelland, & Rubeland, 1975; Veroff, 1977) have noted that women's orientation to achievement may be process-centered rather than impact-centered, and that men have a greater orientation to achievement via power than women do. Again, these qualities in men's and women's motives help clarify how their motivation become enacted in their behaviors. To the extent that we can make these distinctions within motives we will be better observers of human achievement motivation in action.

Some examples are in order of how motives can be better understood by a more complete assessment of their sub-types. In comparing our national surveys of motives and how they related to behavior, one of the most striking changes in how a motive related to reactions to roles in 1957 to 1976 was with regard to job satisfaction. In 1957 men's achievement motive was negatively related to their job satisfaction. In 1976 it was positively related. Since we found that result so intriguing we have been trying out various types of analyses to help us understand it. Why should men who have high achievement motives be less satisfied with their work than those who have low achievement motives in the 1950s but the opposite was true in the 1970s. Some of the analyses that we examined had some payoff. It involved the criteria used to code stories for achievement imagery. We discovered that the imagery coded for unique accomplishment characteristically described the stories of those achievement motivated men who were experiencing job dissatisfaction in 1957 but not those in 1976. One could speculate that the concern for self differentiation and accomplishment, something unique, something which would give some evidence of personal impact was critical to men who had high achievement motives in 1957 and was not being fulfilled in most job settings at that time. One can also argue that between 1957 and 1976 jobs began to change in this respect and began to allow more people to experience personal impact in work than existed earlier. Our analyses of evaluations of jobs held in 1976 contrasted to 1957 in our sample, using the Dictionary of Occupational Titles, shows that there was a significant increase in impact related characteristics of jobs in the 1970s. If this aspect of work has become more common now than it once was it can become less of an issue for the dissatisfactions among men whose orientation to achievement focuses on that issue. In fact, the more individualistic nature of evaluating work may be an explanation of why achievement motivation is positively related to job satisfaction in general in the 1970s. If work changed—from the 1950s to the 1970s—allowing men in 1976 to feel more individuated than men in 1976, then those with concerns of this sort should be particularly gratified in 1976.

Another example. In comparing mean motive scores in our national samples between 1957 and 1976 we have noted an increase in power motives in men and a concomitant decrease in affiliation motive. This pattern sounded ominous to us when we first published the results (Veroff, Depner, Kulka, & Douvan, 1980). It was a pattern that McClelland (1961) had earlier identified in societies that have been particularly susceptible to authoritarianism. A re-analysis of the affiliation motive in terms of positive as opposed to negative imagery (that is whether the motivational content is focused on loss or rejection [negative imagery]) showed that the decline in men's affiliation motives from 1957 to 1976 was only in the negative affiliation imagery. This makes the pattern of decrease less ominous appearing. While men became more oriented toward power over the generation from the 50s to the 70s, they evidently maintained their level of motivation toward positive communion with other people, and lost some of their concern with fearfulness about rejection. This gives us a much more positive view of the motivational drift that has occurred in this country for men in the past generation.

Knowing which sub-type of achievement or affiliation motive is more strongly operative in a person's motivational life can thus alert the researcher to which type of incentive will arouse the person's tendencies to act. We thus will have much better predictions for particular situations. A contextual psychology of motivation is more possible.

If this is all so, why lump the sub-types together as a common motive? Why not differentiate types of motives and let it go at that? Because the same principles of motivation relevant to a general motive are expected to apply to each sub-type. For each type of achievement motive, for example, we assume that feedback, a sense of agency, and understanding of future consequences are all involved. There thus may be some parsimony in considering them all together as one family. For example, to uncover some overall general antecedents to the development of a strong achievement motive, it would perhaps be better to have the general assessment of the family motive that includes all sub-types. The finding that caretakers who appropriately stress independence training regarding childhood mastery tasks have children who have higher achievement motives perhaps depends on the more reliable general measure. For predicting certain behaviors such as moderate risk taking for an ambiguous task—it may not matter which one of the sub-types is engaged, and again the more general measure may be more reliable. For more specific antecedents or consequences it will likely make a difference which one of the sub-types is being measured. Elsewhere I have developed the argument that the emphasis on social comparison for achievement is exactly what sets women and men apart with regard to the achievement motive (Veroff, 1977). Social comparison engages fear of success for women more than it does for men. Social comparison is a more positive orientation to group competition for men than it is for women. Contrariwise, responsibility achievement motivation may be a powerful predictor for women's achievement behaviors, probably because it also engages affiliation concerns, which are more critical in the delineation of the achievement motive for women. Interaction of other motives can thus occur, a topic I wish to discuss next. But by and large I think it will be important to assess separately each of the varieties of achievement, affiliation, and power motives that we can discern and to theorize about these sub-types and their contexts quite separately.

Interaction of Motives: A Typology as a Way to Assess Motives

Ever since Jack Atkinson introduced the idea that one has to account for both the hope of success and the fear of failure motives in order to predict risk-taking behavior, those of us working in the field of motivation were used to considering at least two motives simultaneously in predicting human action. In Jack's model the two motives operated independently but they were jointly used to predict behavior. There have been occasional studies using achievement and affiliation motives simultaneously in the same way. In the dynamics of action thinking Jack also has become intrigued by issues of too much motivation, of there being too many motives aroused. In such thinking about over-motivation, however, the particular motives that are engaged in the setting are not critical. The only important fact is that there are too many motives operating.

A complex treatment of the effects of simultaneous operating motives occurs in McClelland's research (McClelland, 1985) on a typology of personality dispositions involving power and affiliation motives along with a measure of activity inhibition (assessed by the number of negating statements of activities that occur in fantasy). When these measures are considered together, a new entity involving the combined forces of these three dispositions produces an emergent pattern of motives or a motivational typology (McClelland, 1975). Two decisions are needed for this typology: (a) whether or not the power motive is relatively higher than the affiliation motive; (b) whether or not the individual is high or low in activity inhibition. Using these two criteria four types are produced. The first is called an enclave orientation in which power is not high relative to affiliation and activity inhibition is low. In such an orientation people are thought to be oriented toward their own particular group with considerable suspicion about outside groups. This is a very restrictive motivational orientation. The second type is called the bureaucratic orientation. Here power motivation is also not high relative to affiliation motivation but activity inhibition is high. In this motivational type there is a conformist orientation to the group in power. There is a great concern with organizational structure. The third type, the Don-Juan orientation is one in which power motivation is high relative to affiliation but activity inhibition is low. In this kind of motivational type there is a concern for very personal impact without much consideration of the social norms, hence the title Don-Juan. The fourth type seen by McClelland and others to be the most positive social type is the imperialist orientation where power is high relative to affiliation motivation and activity inhibition is high. In this orientation there is a concern for impact but within a socialized or institutionalized context. Therefore, people oriented this way are concerned with doing good for the larger society.

Thus there are emergent new motivational types defined by three dispositions rather than one. McClelland has found these types very useful in distinguishing men's and women's orientation to religion, personal life space, business practice, and interpersonal interaction. In our national surveys we also made these distinctions and have found some exciting results using them. First of all, with regard to the differences between the men's motive scores in 1957 and 1976, the typology analysis suggests that the imperialist syndrome is the one that showed the most remarkable shift from 1957 to 1976. Although we had seen an increase in the power motive and a general decrease in the affiliation motive from 1957 to 1976, when we plotted that within the typology, we found that it was primarily the imperialist syndrome that was shifting upward rather than the Don-Juan syndrome. Hence a more communal or institutional orientation toward power should be on the rise in our culture and not the personal type that we had been concerned about when we first discovered the affiliation and power shifts. This may have very important implications for the build-up of more communal orientation in our society rather than the dissolution of community structure, as so many social observers have predicted. McClelland (1975) has viewed those with the imperialist syndrome to be the movers and shakers in the society, to be motivated to be highly responsible citizens. Perhaps we can look forward to much more constructive social change in the future than we had anticipated.

Another interesting finding using the McClelland typology in the national survey came in our examination of leisure activities. We have been finding it difficult to obtain consistent results using the individual motive scores to understand various aspects of leisure. With the typology we have a very clear finding for both men and women—the Don Juan syndrome is positively related to the number of leisure activities reported by people in response to an open-ended question of what they do when their work is done. Winter and Stewart (1978) have typified the power motive as profligate in men but not in women. If we assume that to be profligate, a person would indulge in many rather than few leisure activities, then our findings suggest that when the more complicated Don Juan assessment is used, the profligate orientation to power emerges for certain women as well.

These are just the beginning use of the more complex motive typology in these national data. We expect many more critical results emerging from more concerted use of the distinctions made.

Quality of Motives and Values Considered Simultaneously

As an advocate of the Thematic Apperception Test assessment of motives, Jack Atkinson has persistently recognized that shortcut assessments through objective testing get at conscious endorsements of incentives—or values—and not the more unconscious highly unverbalizable motives that we have been assessing. The motives and the values are typically unrelated in research findings. McClelland (1985) has also been a strong advocate of this position. Each has assumed that motives are the better predictor of spontaneous motivated behavior and that values may enhance these predictions sometimes, but probably only if motives are also taken into account. Feather (1982) has also differentiated values and motives but has seen them as functionally equivalent. However, most of the evidence suggests that they usually predict different types of responses. What has not often been considered is that the two types of assessment may interact to affect a given reaction. And that is the point of view I would like to propose very briefly.

The fact that motives and values each by themselves have different correlates has been often documented. For instance, in their recent analysis David Smith and I (Veroff & Smith, in press) have shown that while the affiliation motive is not at all related to age in men, a value for belonging—logically similar to a motive for affiliation—is especially high in 50 to 59 year old men, a time when there are considerable self-conscious realignments towards people once men's families have been scattered. At least this is typical in our mobile society. Furthermore, in the elderly the achievement motive seems to predict men's involvement in leisure but not whether they feel leisure is fulfilling. However, values for the sense of accomplishment predict fulfillment through leisure in these elderly men. In our excursion looking at both motives and values, what intrigued us was the possibility that there is something psychologically meaningful about the two being considered together. Smith and I had the idea that as people age their values become more in tune with their unconscious motives. We assume that men and women as they age become more wise about the forces that may guide their lives, forces which they had not been always aware of. We sought evidence for this in the correlations of the motives and certain other values at different points in the lifetime and in general found no clear support for this idea. However, the idea behind the hypothesis still intrigues us. We can generally propose that people in touch with their general motives and who translate them into their expressed values should in effect have a more integrative motivational orientation to their lives. And we have found evidence for this idea. Those who were high in both the achievement motive and value for accomplishment have higher self-confidence then any other group. Furthermore, we found those that were high in need for affiliation and the value for belonging had the highest level of gratification with life roles. Thus we have some evidence that considering both motives and values of a certain incentive together may help predict a different type of motivational orientation, a more integrative one, than considering either the motives or values separately. Biernat

(1986) has also obtained similar results in predicting achievement performance. Values become personal contexts for motives, and vice versa.

Conclusion

What does all this add up to? None of what I have been suggesting advances any fine points of motivational theory. I have only been advocating that we increase the complexity of our thinking about motives. I am pushing for further differentiations about motives in order to evaluate their nature and how they affect human action. In essence I am suggesting that we need to introduce a variety of contexts, some developmental, some intrapsychic, some representative of social settings to get at these qualities that clarify what people are affectively concerned about in their purposeful behaviors. The story-telling procedure we started with still is a good one and certainly the best I know, but we need to refine it by making simultaneous codings of many types of motives and becoming alert to how they interact. Furthermore, we have to account for other motivational forces in people's lives that exist in their more conscious appraisals of their intentions. Such complexity breeds confusion at first but in the long run can give us a more veridical map of what is going on in our motivational lives.

REFERENCES

Atkinson, J. W., & Birch, D. (1970). *The dynamics of action*. New York: Wiley.

Biernat, M. (1986). Achievement motives and values: Different constraints, different effects, unpublished paper.

Diaz, A. J. (1982). *An empirical study of the effect of CEO motives on intra-industry performance with examples drawn from US and Japanese auto manufacturers*. Unpublished Bachelor of Arts thesis, Harvard College, Department of Psychology and Social Relations and Economics.

Feather, N. T. (Ed.) (1982). *Expectations and actions: Expectancy-value models in psychology*. Hillsdale, NJ: Erlbaum.

Feld, S. C. (1967). Longitudinal study of the origins of achievement strivings. *Journal of Personality and Social Psychology*, *1*, 408–414.

Lowenthal, M. F., Thurnber, M. & Chiniboga, D. (1975). *Four stages of life*. San Francisco: Jossey-Bass.

Maehr, M. L. & Kleiber, D. A. (1981). The graying of achievement motivation. *The American Psychologist, 36*, 787–793.

McClelland, D. C. (1961). *The achieving society*. Princeton, NJ: Van Nostrand.

McClelland, D. C. (1975). *Power: The inner experience*. New York: Irvington.

McClelland, D. C. (1985). *Human motivation*. Glenview, IL: Scott, Foresman & Co.

McClelland, D. C., Atkinson, J. W., Clark, R. A. & Lowell, E. L. (1953). *The achievement motive*. New York: Appleton-Century-Crofts.

Rubin, L. (1980). *Women of a certain age*. New York: Basic Books.

Schachter, S. (1959) *The psychology of affiliation*. Stanford, CA: Stanford University Press.

Spence, J. T., & Helmreich, R. L. (1983). Achievement-related motives and behavior. In J. T. Spence (Ed.) *Achievement and achievement motives*. San Francisco: W. H. Freeman & Co.

Sutherland, E., & Veroff, J. (1985). Achievement motivation and sex roles. In V. O'Leary, R. Unger & B. Wallston (Eds.) *Women, gender and social psychology*, Hillsdale, NJ: Lawrence Erlbaum.

Veroff, J. (1950). A projective measure of achievement motivation of adolescent

145

males and females. Unpublished honors thesis. Wesleyan University.

Veroff, J. (1977). Process vs. impact in men's and women's achievement motivation. *Psychology of Women Quarterly, 1*, 228–293.

Veroff, J. (1983). Contextual determinants of personality. *Personality and Social Bulletin, 9*, 331–343.

Veroff, J., & Veroff, J. B. (1980). *Social incentives: A life-span perspective.* New York: Academic Press.

Veroff, J., Douvan, E., & Kulka, R. A. (1981) *The inner American.* New York: Basic Books.

Veroff, J., McClelland, L., & Ruhland, D. (1975) Varieties of achievement motivation. In M. Mednick, L. Hoffman & S. Tangri (Eds.) *Women and achievement.* New York: Holt, Rinehart & Winston.

Veroff, J., Reuman, D, & Feld, S. (1984). Motives in American men and women across the adult life span.. *Developmental Psychology, 20*, 1142–1158.

Veroff, J., Depner, C., Kulka, R., & Douvan, E. (1980). Comparison of American motives: 1957 versus 1976. *Journal of Personality and Social Psychology, 39*, 1249–1262.

Winter, D. G., & Stewart, A. J. (1978). Power motivation. In H. London & J. Exner (Eds.), *Dimensions of personality.* New York: Wiley.

Chapter Nine

HUMAN VALUES, VALENCES, EXPECTATIONS AND AFFECT:

THEORETICAL ISSUES EMERGING FROM RECENT

APPLICATIONS OF THE EXPECTANCY-VALUE MODEL

N.T. Feather

The Flinders University of South Australia

More than 25 years have passed since I first came to the University of Michigan to work with Jack Atkinson and to develop ideas about the analysis of persistence in achievement situations (Feather, 1961, 1962). My memories of those early years are very positive ones. To a young Australian on study leave from a small, recently established University in the New England region of New South Wales, the shift to Michigan in the late 1950s was a major turning point. Though at Michigan for only a short time as a graduate student, I formed friendships that have stayed with me throughout my life. The lively and stimulating academic environment provided intellectual experiences that helped to shape my ideas, even though my interest in expectancy-value models was already well-established before I arrived but ready to be more finely tuned. It has been a source of satisfaction to me that the analysis of persistence developed in those graduate years turned out to be a watershed, triggering the development of a new conceptual approach to motivation, the dynamics of action (Atkinson & Birch, 1970).

After my return to Australia, I continued to conduct research on persistence as part of a program of studies that tested implications from Atkinson's theory of achievement motivation (Atkinson & Feather, 1966), but my interest in the topic waned and I turned to other things. Parenthetically, it seems to me that persistence continues to be an important dependent variable in current research as evidenced, for example, by some of the studies that have appeared in recent years in the areas of learned helplessness, intrinsic motivation, attribution theory, self-esteem processes, and control theory. The time is ripe for a review and integration of these newer developments, linking them to ideas that emerged from my earlier analysis and to subsequent modifications contained in the dynamics of action. That is not a task that I intend to attempt now, but I hope that someone might undertake it in the near future, given the fact that persistence in a given activity (and its obverse, change in activity) are central problems for theories of motivation.

My early persistence studies were the products of a continuing commitment to exploring the implications of the expectancy-value approach to the analysis of motivated action (Feather, 1982a).[1] As I have noted previously (Feather, 1982e), the distinctive characteristic of this approach is the attempt:

> to relate action to the perceived attractiveness or aversiveness of expected consequences. What a person does is seen to bear some relation to the expectations that the person holds and the subjective value of the consequences that might occur following the action. We are dealing with a basic question in psychology, the relationship of actions to expectations, where these expectations encompass beliefs about the implications of behavior, and where an important set of these implications consists of consequences that have positive or negative perceived value. (p. 1)

My commitment to studying this approach over a number of years reflects a belief that it provides an important theoretical means of bridging the gap between cognition and action. Much of recent cognitive psychology has been restricted to constructing concepts and models that deal with cognitive representations and cognitive processes. The need to link knowing and doing remains a central problem, however, and the expectancy-value approach is a major contribution from the psychology of motivation that offers a possible solution to this question.

The analysis of behavior in relation to expected consequences has had wide application in psychology. I noted many years ago that it had been used by psychologists working in such diverse areas as level of aspiration, the rat's performance at a bar-pressing task, social learning and clinical psychology, achievement motivation, SEU decision theory, and the study of object preference (Feather, 1959). My recent book, *Expectations and Actions*, examined the current status of expectancy-value models in relation to a number of different contexts, using contributions from some of the theorists who were involved in the development of this approach and from others who were familiar with it because of its relevance to their own research interests (Feather, 1982c). These contributions clearly indicated that the conceptual approach has continued to have wide application and that it has been extended and become more sophisticated over the years, the extension and liberalization of the approach being most evident in recent work in human motivation and the dynamics of action. Table 1 lists some of the theorists who have been associated with the approach and the concepts they have employed. The list could be expanded so as to take account of more recent developments but it does cover a fairly wide time span from the 1940s through to the present day.

In this chapter I do not intend to cover the sort of ground I dealt with in detail in my recent book (Feather, 1982c). The last chapter of that book contains discussion of the present status of the expectancy-value approach and includes suggestions about future directions that might be taken (Feather, 1982b). There is little more that I can add at this stage to the points that were made in that chapter. I believe that it will be more fruitful for present purposes to describe two current

TABLE 1

Examples of Expectancy-Value Models

Theorist	Determinants Involved in Resultant Tendency to Act
Tolman	Expectation, need–push, valence
Lewin et al.	Subjective probability × valence
Atkinson	Expectancy × (motive × incentive value)
Feather	Success probability, attainment attractiveness
Edwards	Subjective probability × utility
Rotter	Expectancy, reinforcement value
Peak	Instrumentality × attitude (affect)
Rosenberg	Instrumentality × importance
Vroom	Expectancy × valence; where valence is instrumentality × valence
Dulany	Hypothesis of the distribution of the reinforcement × value of the reinforcement
Fishbein	Probability × attitude

Note. Adapted from Feather (1959b) and Mitchell (1974). Table 3.1 presents the models in simplified form and focuses on the expectancy and valence concepts.

applications of expectancy-value theory in which I have been involved. The first application deals with the relationship between values and actions; the second is more concerned with accounting for negative affective reactions that frequently follow the experience of unemployment. Both applications raise theoretical issues of a general kind that continue to demand attention and they broaden the scope of contexts to which the expectancy-value approach has been applied. Separately, the applications also contribute to our understanding about two important issues that respectively concern the psychology of values and the psychological impact of unemployment.

Values and Actions

How can values be incorporated into a theory of motivation? Let me begin by commenting briefly on two approaches, the first by Milton Rokeach and the second by David McClelland.

Rokeach (1973, 1979a, 1979b) has persistently advocated the need for psychologists to study the role of values in thought and action. He deplores the fact that social psychologists have generally ignored the importance of values in their research, though the empirical investigation of values has been given considerable attention in the disciplines of anthropology, sociology, and philosophy. His seminal contributions represent an important step in the direction of redressing this neglect. Rokeach (1979a) conceives of values as:

cognitive representations of human needs on the one hand and of societal demands on the other. They take the psychological form of prescriptive or proscriptive beliefs about the desirable means and ends of action. They are organized hierarchically to serve as standards or criteria . . . that the socialized self—a self born with biological needs continuously shaped by societal demands—employs to judge the efficacy of itself not only as a competent self . . . but also as a moral self. (p. 295)

Values are seen as standards of "oughts" and "shoulds", as central aspects of the self-concept, as transcending objects and situations, as relatively stable but not unchanging across the life-span, as determinants of attitudes and behaviors, as limited in their number when compared with the many specific beliefs and attitudes that people possess, as inculcated and transmitted by different social institutions, as organized into hierarchies of importance, and as serving as standards and criteria in many different ways. Values are not regarded as affectively neutral. People feel strongly when their important values are challenged or frustrated, when they experience moral dilemmas, when they become involved in intergroup conflict, and when their values are satisfied or fulfilled.

Rokeach's research program has focused upon the effects of creating a sense of self-dissatisfaction about competence or morality on subsequent cognitive and behavioral change (e.g., Ball-Rokeach, Rokeach, & Grube, 1984). He achieves this in experimental studies by creating discrepancies between self-cognitions implicating values on the one hand and cognitions about attitudes and behaviors on the other. These discrepancies are assumed to threaten self-maintenance and self-enhancement. He views the phenomenal experience of self-dissatisfaction as "the most crucial variable initiating a process of enduring change in cognitions and behavior—in the experimental social psychologist's laboratory, in the clinic, and in everyday life" (Rokeach, 1979a, p. 297).

I feel uneasy about Rokeach's view that self-dissatisfaction has the crucial motivating role. I have the same reservation about Bandura's use of self-dissatisfaction as a motivator of enhanced effort when standards are not met in the course of task performance (e.g., Bandura & Cervone, 1983). Both approaches accentuate the negative. People are represented as acting to reduce negative states that are products of comparisons where self-standards are central and where the subjective reality represented by knowledge about one's attitudes, beliefs, or performance falls short of those standards. That view of behavior seems to me to be too negative and conservative; it reminds me of earlier theoretical approaches in which the organism was seen as a tension-reducing or equilibrium-maintaining system, acting so as to reduce negative discrepancies that give rise to negative affective states. This way of thinking ignores the positive side of human action, the fact that much of a person's behavior can be seen as directed toward immediate and long-term goals that arouse anticipations of positive affect. People not only seek to reduce discrepancies and avoid negative states; they also strive for positive goals that maintain or enhance feelings of satisfaction when compared with present conditions.

Let us now turn to McClelland's (1985) recent statements about the importance of distinguishing values from motives. He defines a motive as "a recurrent concern for a goal state based on a natural incentive—a concern that energizes, orients, and selects behavior" (p. 590). A person with a strong achievement motive, for example, would be one who frequently thinks about doing things well even when there is no stimulus to do so. The goal states involved in motivational concerns are assumed to have a biological basis involving natural incentives which McClelland analyzes in terms of three components: a sign stimulus, a state of central affective arousal, and a consummatory act. The achievement motive, for example, is assumed to be a derivative of the variety incentive which is conceived in terms of a sign stimulus (small variations from expectancy), a consummatory experience (mild variety), an emotion (interest-surprise), and consummatory acts (exploratory behavior).

The logic of this analysis reminds me of William McDougall's attempts earlier this century to relate more complex sentiments to instinctual springs of action (e.g., McDougall, 1932). McClelland makes a similar assumptive leap even though he draws upon current knowledge from ethology, emotional experience and expression, learning theory, psychophysiology and from other areas. Basing motives on a limited number of incentives such as variety, impact, contact, and consistency is justified by McClelland on the grounds that "it explains why there should be relatively few major motive systems, why they have such a pervasive effect on behavior, and why motives are so intimately connected with emotional states" (p. 591).

McClelland believes that motives are best measured by coding motivational concerns in associative thought or fantasy. Motives are not necessarily conscious and they may therefore not be identified by persons as part of their self-image. The conscious value placed on achievement, affiliation, and power is essentially uncorrelated with projective measures of the achievement, power, and affiliation motives. Hence, McClelland argues that it is important to separate motives and values. Values "represent the usually conscious conceptions in terms of which people organize their experience and preferences" (McClelland, 1985, p. 536). They are assumed to be much more affected by social norms and by societal and institutional demands, though some may also have a link to natural incentives. They are measured by asking people what things are important to them and they are intimately tied in with a person's conscious view of self. They are associated with affect, as when values are either fulfilled or thwarted. Values, in combination with motives, opportunities, and skills, are assumed to determine action tendencies. However, motives are assumed to play a greater role with respect to operant behaviors whereas values are better predictors of cognitive choices. Thus, "motives are more important for predicting what people *will spontaneously do*, whereas values are more important for determining what they will cognitively decide should be done" (McClelland, 1985, p. 536).

My approach to the analysis of values owes a lot to the contributions of Rokeach and it also finds many of McClelland's ideas congenial. I am not, however, persuaded by McClelland that motives and values should be completely separated. Clearly the two variables have some distinctive characteristics but there is also a degree of functional and conceptual overlap between them. A detailed exposition of my views on the concept of value is contained in earlier publications (Feather, 1975, 1982d). I prefer to treat values and value systems as abstract structures or schemata, that is, as:

> organized summaries of experience that capture the focal, abstracted qualities of past encounters, that have a normative or oughtness quality about them, and that function as criteria or frameworks against which present experience can be tested . . . . But they are not affectively neutral abstract structures. They are tied to our feelings and can function as general motives (Feather, 1982d, p. 275).

As motives, they influence a person's subjective definition of the situation so that certain objects, activities, and states of affairs within the immediate situation acquire positive valence (become attractive) or negative valence (become aversive) to use Lewin's terminology (Lewin, 1936). Like needs and wants, a person's values may selectively sensitize the individual to certain objects and activities within a situation. Just as food and ways of getting food will become salient and acquire demand characteristics when a person is hungry, so too will a person's values sensitize the person "to perceive some potential events and activities as desirable and worth approaching or continuing with, and other aspects as undesirable, to be avoided or terminated" (Feather, 1982d, p. 277).

Note that I am not saying that motives and values are the only influences on valences. There are plenty of other factors that influence the extent to which particular objects or events are seen as attractive or aversive. Some foods, for example, may be seen as more attractive by a hungry person than are others depending on their objective characteristics; some possible outcomes of action may be seen as more attractive to a person in relation to a dominant value (e.g., equality) than are others because they are better instances of that dominant value. I believe that the links between particular valences and more general personal motives, values, and other variables require a lot more conceptual analysis and investigation within the psychology of motivation. We can list various factors that influence the subjective attractiveness and aversiveness of objects and events but we are still some considerable distance from having an adequate, comprehensive theory of the processes that determine valences or demand characteristics in particular situations. I will return to this point subsequently.

The assumption that values can induce valences provides a means of linking values with action within the framework of the expectancy-value analysis of motivated action. Assume, for example, that a person's freedom of action is blocked or threatened. One would expect that certain possible outcomes that relate to the restoration of freedom may become more or less valent depending in part on how important freedom is as a general value within a person's value system. The person's way of coping with the loss of freedom would be related to the perceived attractiveness or aversiveness of those different possible solutions. What the person does would also be related to the means or ways of behaving that are available. Some of the alternative courses of action may be perceived as more positively valent or attractive than others; other actions may be perceived as negatively valent or aversive. For example, individuals who assign being courageous a key place in their value system will be attracted to courses of action that involve standing up for one's beliefs; individuals for whom being honest is an important value will tend to avoid actions that involve deceit and falsehood. The final action taken, however, would also depend upon the person's expectations about the likely success of various possible ways of behaving. Some courses of action may be seen as likely to restore freedom, others as likely to be ineffective. These valences and expectancies that relate to possible outcomes and courses of action are assumed to be key variables that combine to influence which course of action is taken (Feather, 1982d, pp. 277–280).

James Newton and I applied the preceding analysis to the prediction of a person's willingness to participate in social movement organizations (Feather & Newton, 1982). In one of the studies in the research program, we presented subjects with descriptions of two social movement organizations and asked them to check specific actions that they would be willing to volunteer to undertake in support of each respective organization, assuming they had 10 hours of free time per week. The list included such actions as signing a petition to be sent to the proper authorities, handing out pamphlets on street corners, and participating in peaceful rallies and marches. The number of actions they checked was the first measure of willingness to assist the organization. A second measure was the number of hours they would be prepared to contribute to the organization each week, assuming that they had 10 hours of uncommitted time available.

We also obtained from our subjects rankings of the importance for self of 18 terminal and 18 instrumental values using Form D of the Rokeach Value Survey (Rokeach, 1973). The terminal values in Rokeach's (1978) lists concern general goals such as equality, freedom, family security, and salvation; the instrumental values concern modes of conduct such as being ambitious, honest, logical, and self-controlled. In addition, we obtained a measure of attitude toward the organization ("To what extent do you personally agree or disagree with the views expressed in the pamphlet published by this organization?"), and a measure of expectancy of success ("How helpful do you think your own personal efforts will be as a contribution to the organization's success?").

Newton and I assumed that aspects of the description of the social movement organization would have positive or negative valence depending upon the values that the person holds. For example, descriptions in a pamphlet that represented an organization as supporting "hard work and investment", "respect for legitimate authority", and "decent standards of morality" would be expected to be attractive or have positive valence for respondents who assigned high relative importance to such values as ambitious, obedient, and salvation from Rokeach's (1973) lists of terminal and instrumental values. Other aspects of the pamphlet that criticized "progressive intellectuals" and deplored a "misguided obsession with civil liberties" would be expected to have negative valence for people who ranked such values as freedom and being broadminded and intellectual as high in relative importance within their own value priorities. We did not measure the actual pattern of valences that was assumed to be elicited by a pamphlet. Instead we assumed that respondents performed some cognitive integration of the positive and negative valences that applied to aspects of the description of the social movement organization and that this cognitive integration was reflected in their current overall attitude toward the organization referred to in the description. This assumption needs to be checked in future research. Certainly, however, there was evidence that the values from Rokeach's lists related to the attitude measures in the direction that one would predict, thus providing indirect support for the values-valences-attitude link.

Table 2 presents the results for the study under discussion. Two fictional social movement organizations were involved. The first organization was called the "Movement to Promote Community Standards" and the second was called the "Campaign to Safeguard Individual Rights." The two organizations were contrasted in the values that they were said to promote, the Movement being a more traditional, conservative organization and the Campaign much more liberal in its stance toward issues. These value orientations were specified in the respective pamphlets that described the organizations. Subjects read the pamphlet for each organization before indicating their attitude toward the organization and their willingness to assist it.

Table 2 Multiple Correlations (Rs) and Proportions of Variance Explained (R^2s) from Stepwise Multiple Regression Analyses Predicting Action Measures from Attitude and Expectancy[d]

	Action measures					
	Number of volunteer actions for Movement or Campaign			Number of volunteer hours for Movement or Campaign		
Independent variables	R	R^2	R^2 change	R	R^2	R^2 change
Study 1						
Movement						
Step 1 Attitude	.616	.380	—	.495	.245	—
2 Expectancy	.672	.451	.071[c]	.554	.307	.062[c]
3 Attitude × expectancy	.689	.474	.023[a]	.583	.340	.032[a]
Campaign						
Step 1 Attitude	.466	.217	—	.369	.136	—
2 Expectancy	.521	.271	.054[b]	.429	.184	.048[b]
3 Attitude × expectancy	.525	.275	.004	.432	.186	.003

[a]$p < .05$.
[b]$p < .01$.
[c]$p < .001$.
[d]Significant increments in R^2 as tested by the F test are identified by superscripts.

The results in Table 2 support the theoretical analysis. Adding expectancy to attitude led to a statistically significant increase in the amount of variance in the action measures that could be accounted for. Thus, the additive combination of attitude and expectancy provided a better prediction to each of the behavioral variables than either attitude or expectancy considered alone. The further addition of the attitude x expectancy product, however, did not lead to statistically significant increments in the variance for the Campaign measures but only for the Movement measures.

The results of this study, together with a follow-up investigation that increased the degree of commitment to action, encourage the view that the expectancy-value approach may turn out to be very useful in the analysis of the conditions under which values relate to overt action. In another context I have argued that relationships between sex-role characteristics and behavior might also be analyzed using the expectancy-value approach on the assumption that definitions of masculinity and femininity imply a value base (Feather, 1984).

These applications show that one can extend the scope of expectancy-value theory to encompass the effects of values as well as the effects of motive dispositions. This extension opens up new areas of inquiry such as those already noted. It also brings the approach into contact with research into attitude-behavior relationships (e.g., Feather & Newton, 1982; Fishbein & Ajzen, 1975).

A crucial aspect of this theoretical extension is the assumption that there is a link between a person's general values and the valences that are attached to outcomes and actions in specific situations. How might this link occur? We have already seen that both motives and values are commonly conceived as linked to the affective system by structured networks of association (Feather, 1975, 1982d; McClelland, 1985). If one conceives of valences as involving anticipated positive or negative affect associated with performing actions and experiencing outcomes, then one can make the connection between the specific and the general, between anticipated affect in a particular situation and the underlying general motives and values that people hold. The content of a defined situation becomes linked to the affective system via a person's dominant motives and values and the anticipated positive and negative affect that is aroused within a means-end structure functions as a basic motivational source for the particular action that is taken. Specific features of a situation key into a person's motive and value structures. Once the connection is made the affective system is recruited in such a way as to provide an added dimension to cognitive appraisal, one that involves anticipations of positive and negative affect associated with the different actions and outcomes that are available within the defined situation. The processing probably first occurs in a "bottom-up" direction, moving from the particular to the general and then back again to the specific.

The assumption that valences may be conceived in terms of anticipated positive and negative affect is compatible with the further assumption made by Feather and Newton (1982) that attitudes can be regarded as cognitive integrations of valences. Attitudes are commonly defined as positive or negative affective reactions toward objects and situations (e.g., Fishbein & Ajzen, 1975; Thurstone, 1931). An integration of various anticipated affects that refer to specific components of actions and outcomes would produce a resultant affective reaction that defines a person's overall attitude. In this way one can forge further links between concepts from the psychology of motivation and the general area of attitudes and interests.

Unemployment and Depressive Affect

I now turn to my second recent application of the expectancy-value approach in which I have used the approach to make predictions about the depressive affect that can follow unemployment. The question of how people react to unemployment is one of great social significance. A number of studies of this question appeared during the 1930s stimulated by the devastating effects of the Great Depression. These investigations described the adverse effects of prolonged unemployment on the psychological well-being of those who suffered it—effects such as the development of apathy, depression, self-doubt, resignation, diminished self-esteem, and fatalistic beliefs. Many of these early studies were reviewed by Eisenberg and Lazarsfeld (1938). In recent years new studies of the psychological impact of unemployment have appeared in the literature, prompted no doubt by the current relatively high levels of unemployment in many countries. I initiated research into unemployment in the late 1970s and the research program has continued since then with the involvement of a number of students and colleagues (Feather, 1985c).

I will focus on two studies from the program which relate to the expectancy-value approach. It can be assumed that a person's failure to obtain an attractive or positively valent goal will lead to more disappointment than would be the case for a goal that is less attractive. Failure to attain a goal means loss of the benefits that attainment would confer and disappointment should increase the higher the goal is in its net attractiveness, that is, the greater the perceived loss that is sustained (Feather, 1982a, Table 3.7, p.70). It might also be assumed that disappointment about failure will be greater when expectations of success are initially high than when they are low. Failure tends to be more aversive when the subjective probability of success is high than when it is low; one feels worse about failing at a task that is seen to be very easy than one that is perceived to be very difficult (Feather, 1969, 1982a). Taken together, these two assumptions imply that disappointment about failure will be higher the more strongly motivated a person is to achieve a goal, given the assumption that expectations and valences combine multiplicatively to determine the strength of a person's tendency to approach a goal. Thus, disappointment about failure should be greater when a person has high expectations and perceives a goal as attractive than when a person has low expectations and perceives a goal to be less attractive. In terms of the expectancy-value approach the former person would have a stronger tendency to pursue the goal than the latter. This analysis suggests the general prediction that:

the negative or depressive affect that follows failure to obtain employment will be greater among those individuals who perceive work as attractive, who have high expectations of obtaining a job, and who are more strongly motivated to seek work, when compared with those with lower levels of valence, expectation, and motivation. This prediction applies to all stages of job seeking, early as well as late, even though expectations of success and motivation to seek work may be relatively low after consistent failure to find employment. (Feather & Davenport, 1981, p. 424)

Philip Davenport and I tested these predictions in a study that involved a large sample of just over 200 unemployed young people (Feather & Davenport, 1981).[2] Our subjects completed a questionnaire that contained a wide variety of items spanning expectations of success, the attractiveness or positive valence of employment, motivation to seek employment as indexed by effort and need, causal attributions or reasons for unemployment, and amount of depressive affect associated with being unemployed. In our data analysis we split subjects into four groups depending upon their ratings of depressive affect and examined changes in our major variables across the four levels of depressive affect. Table 3 presents these results.

Table 3
Mean Ratings of Major Variables in Relation to Four Categories of Affect

Variable	Range	Affect category				Main effect of depressive affect, $F(3, 201)$
		Glad ($n = 30$)	Neutral ($n = 68$)	Depressed ($n = 58$)	Very depressed ($n = 55$)	
Expectation of success						
Initial confidence	1–5	3.07	4.01	4.26	4.30	7.38***
Present chances	1–5	2.53	3.15	2.93	2.85	3.02*
Present confidence	1–5	3.03	3.18	3.14	3.09	.03
Employment valence	3–15	9.77	11.03	11.19	11.76	3.47*
Motivation to work						
Initial effort	1–5	3.47	3.93	4.02	4.31	2.32
Present effort	1–5	2.47	3.21	3.24	3.62	5.06**
Initial need	1–5	3.27	4.09	4.42	4.46	7.17***
Present need	1–5	2.20	3.32	4.07	4.15	25.17***
Causal attribution						
Internal attribution	1–5	3.40	2.51	2.19	2.22	7.05***
Competence deficiency	4–20	13.67	12.40	14.17	13.00	2.44
External difficulty	4–20	12.27	13.53	14.60	14.45	2.80*

Note. There were minor variations in *n*s due to missing data in some analyses (1–3 cases).
* $p < .05$. ** $p < .01$. *** $p < .001$.

Table 3 shows that subjects with higher levels of depressive affect were those who indicated that they were initially more confident about getting a job (higher expectations), who reported that they were more in need of a job when first leaving school, who viewed employment as an attractive goal, and who provided higher ratings of present effort and present need. These findings were consistent with our major predictions. The results also showed that those subjects with higher levels of depressive affect were more likely to blame their unemployed status not on themselves but on relatively stable external difficulties. Thus, increasing depressive affect was associated with more attention to external barriers as a cause of unemployment.

Finally, the results indicated that ratings of confidence, effort, and need tended to be lower for the present situation when compared with the situation when the unemployed person first left school. Thus, there was evidence that the experience of unemployment had led to reduced expectations and had also affected levels of effort and motivation. Such changes would be predicted from an expectancy-value model, assuming that the causes of failure to get a job were seen to be relatively stable and unchanging. Note, however, that these differences were between judgments of present confidence, effort, and need and judgments of these variables as they were retrospectively recalled for the situation when the young unemployed person left school. Clearly, a proper causal analysis would require collecting data on these variables at different points in time in a longitudinal study that followed subjects as they left school and found or did not find jobs.

There are two further qualifications of the findings of the Feather and Davenport (1981) study that should also be made. In the first place, the frustrated positive motivation to find work would be expected to lead to other affective reactions as well as depressive affect. The affect associated with frustration may be complex in nature. Unemployed people who want jobs may not only feel depressed about the lack of employment but also hostile and resentful, especially where the cause of the frustration is seen to lie in the external situation and not in themselves (Weiner & Litman-Adizes, 1980). Second, it would be a mistake to equate situation-specific depressive affect with depressive symptomatolgy in the clinical sense. Depressive affect is a normal part of everyday living as a not infrequent reaction to stressful situations. It is often transient and situation bound, whereas more general forms of depression are more enduring and color many parts of a person's life.

Can the expectancy-value approach also be applied to more severe forms of depression that might follow prolonged unemployment? One can use the basic concepts in the model along with assumptions about changes in causal attributions and the self-concept to make some predictions. More severe and enduring forms of depression may develop when aversive events continue despite a person's efforts to prevent them (helplessness) and where, over time, a person's expectations of achieving desired goals or avoiding negative outcomes shift to very low levels that signal a state of hopelessness. In some people one might observe a shift from transient, situation-specific affective states to more general forms of depression following prolonged and/or repeated periods of unemployment. This shift may be accompanied by diminished self-esteem, by a strengthening belief that one's unemployment will continue despite one's efforts to get a job (helplessness), by very low expectations of finding a job (hopelessness) and by increasing attribution of negative events to internal, stable, and global causes. The unemployed person with a more severe depression may also display greater evidence of motivational deficits such as passivity and apathy when compared with an unemployed person who, for whatever reason (e.g., support from others, internal and external resources), is better able to cope with the situation. These various ideas are consistent with cognitive and attributional analyses of depression that involve concepts of helplessness, hopelessness, attributional styles, negative cognitive sets, and faulty information processing (e.g., Abramson, Seligman, & Teasdale, 1978; Beck, 1967, 1976; Feather & Tiggemann, 1984; Peterson, Schwartz, & Seligman, 1981; Weiner, 1980).

Some of these ideas were tested in a second study that I conducted in collaboration with James Barber (Feather & Barber, 1983). We used the same measure of depressive affect as was used in the Feather and Davenport (1981) study ("When you think about being unemployed how does it make you feel?") and we also included measures of internal and external attribution for unemployment, items concerned with initial and present expectancies of getting a job, and an item designed to measure the importance of having employment. In addition, however, we added a general measure of depression—the short form of the Beck Depression Inventory (BDI; Beck & Beck, 1972), a modified version of the Rosenberg (1965) Self-Esteem Scale (Bachman, O'Malley, & Johnston, 1978), and an item designed to measure perceived uncontrollability or the extent to which subjects felt that the cause of their unemployment could be changed, whether by themselves or by anyone else. So as to obtain some information about unemployment history, we also asked our subjects how long they had been without a job and how many jobs they had applied for.

The study involved over 100 unemployed young people and they completed a questionnaire containing the items and the scales. Table 4 shows the main results. These results are interesting in that they reveal different patterns of correlates for situation-specific depressive affect and for the general measure of depressive symptoms. Those subjects who provided higher ratings of depressive affect about unemployment also tended to report that not having a job was an important concern (and hence, by inference, that employment was important to them) and they were more likely to endorse external causes as reasons for their unemployment. These findings are consistent with those of the previous study (Feather & Davenport, 1981). The BDI depression scores, however, were linked to a different set of variables. These scores were positively related to the perceived uncontrollability of the cause of unemployment, positively related to endorsement of internal causes, and negatively related to self-esteem. So those who were more depressed reported that they were more helpless about the causes of unemployment; they were more likely to blame themselves for being unemployed; and their evaluations of self were lower. These results were as predicted. The results also suggested that the job history variables (weeks out of work, number of unsuccessful job applications) were having some effect. Thus, perceived uncontrollability and attributions to internal causes were both positively correlated with number of weeks out of work; internal attributions and BDI depression scores were both positively related to number of unsuccessful job applications. Note, however, that because data from our subjects were obtained from the same point in time, we cannot establish whether these relationships were causal. One needs detailed longitudinal studies to resolve questions about causality (see Feather & O'Brien, in press).

The hierarchical multiple regression analyses in Table 5 add to the picture and support the conclusion that situation-specific depressive affect and BDI depression have different sets of correlates. The two kinds of depression were minimally correlated ($r = .13$, *ns*). Note also that the two attribution measures added only a small amount to the variance accounted for (about 5% in the case of depressive affect and about 7% in the case of BDI depression). The addition of all variables to the regression equation enabled one to account for only 31% and 40%

Table 4

Means and Standard Deviations of Major Variables and Correlations With Depressive Affect, BDI Depression, Number of Weeks Out of Work, and Number of Unsuccessful Job Applications

				r with			
Variable	Range	M	SD	Depressive affect	BDI depression	Weeks out of work	No. of unsuccessful job applications
Expectation of success							
Initial confidence	1–7	4.73	1.95	−.12	−.17	−.08	.08
Present confidence	1–7	3.12	1.92	−.07	−.08	−.03	.04
Employment importance	1–7	5.68	1.84	.44***	.19	−.02	.17
Perceived uncontrollability	1–7	3.37	1.79	−.12	.31***	.23*	−.01
Attribution measures							
Internal causes	4–28	13.02	5.13	.05	.28**	.32***	.20*
External causes	4–28	17.53	4.46	.19*	.03	.12	−.07
Self-esteem score	10–50	39.23	6.38	−.13	−.46***	−.12	−.11
Depressive affect	1–7	5.26	1.57	—	.13	−.05	−.01
BDI depression	0–39	6.06	5.65	.13	—	.11	.26*

Note. BDI = Beck Depression Inventory. N = 116. There were some variations from this N due to a small number of missing cases for some variables. Ns for correlations involving weeks out of work ranged from 95 to 110 due to some missing cases. Ns for the correlations involving number of unsuccessful job applications ranged from 91 to 99 due to some missing cases. Two-tailed tests are reported for the correlations. For weeks out of work, M = 57.51, SD = 67.86; for number of unsuccessful job applications, M = 62.39, SD = 98.72. Weeks out of work and number of unsuccessful job applications were positively correlated, $r(93)$ = .40, $p < .001$.
* $p < .05$. ** $p < .01$. *** $p < .001$.

of the variance in depressive affect and BDI depression respectively. Some of the variables were measured by single item scales, however, of unknown reliability and there are obviously many other variables, such as the personal economic and social costs of not having a job, the degree of social support, and the different ways in which people learn to cope with negative outcomes that were not part of the study but that would be expected to affect the psychological damage that unemployment might cause.

Table 5

Multiple Correlations and Proportions of Variance Explained From Hierarchical Multiple-Regression Analyses

		Dependent variables					
		Depressive affect			BDI depression		
Step	Independent variable	R	R^2	R^2 change	R	R^2	R^2 change
1	Weeks unemployed + unsuccessful job applications	.046	.002	.002	.256	.066	.066*
2	Age + sex	.118	.014	.012	.335	.112	.047
3	Internal causes	.135	.018	.004	.424	.180	.067**
4	External causes	.245	.060	.042*	.424	.180	.000
5	Perceived uncontrollability	.289	.083	.023	.519	.270	.090**
6	Employment importance	.499	.249	.166***	.557	.310	.040*
7	Initial confidence + present confidence	.525	.276	.027	.578	.334	.024
8	Self-esteem	.553	.306	.030	.631	.398	.064**

* $p < .05$. ** $p < .01$. *** $p < .001$.

One finding from the Feather and Davenport (1981) study that was not replicated was the positive correlation between expectancy of getting a job and depressive affect about unemployment. Even in the earlier study, however, this relationship was found only for the retrospective measure of initial confidence when a person first left school and not for the other two expectation measures. This failure to replicate indicates that the expectancy-affect relationship is not as simple as one might assume. If high expectations reflect perceived competence and self-esteem, then these self-perceptions may act as a buffer against feelings of disappointment. Conversely, if low expectations reflect perceived inadequacy and low self-esteem, then failure confirms these beliefs and low expectations may link up with depressive reactions. In fact, Barber and I did find that initial confidence scores were positively correlated with global self-esteem and negatively correlated with depressive symptoms (Feather & Barber, 1983). I have confirmed these relationships in subsequent research with secondary school students (Feather, 1983).

In a recent factor-analytic inquiry I have also shown that a dimension labeled employment importance can be distinguished from a dimension labeled helplessness-pessimism (Feather, 1986). These two factors respectively relate to the valence and expectation components of the general expectancy-value model and their identification opens up new avenues of research into the psychological impact of unemployment that can draw upon that theoretical approach. For example, one can proceed to specify the variables that predict to employment importance (valence) and to helplessness-pessimism (expectation). Figure 1 presents the results of a path analysis based upon data obtained from students who answered a questionnaire concerning work and unemployment in their penultimate year of secondary school in the study that yielded the two factors (Feather, 1986). The path analysis shows that higher social class predicted to more internal attribution in the way the students explained current youth unemployment, to higher school grades, and to an employed rather than an unemployed father or guardian. Higher internal attribution for youth unemployment predicted more school guidance received by the students about their employment prospects and higher school grades obtained by the students predicted staying at school longer. Less guidance about employment obtained at school, less internal attribution for youth unemployment, and lower school grades predicted helplessness-pessimism about employment prospects among the secondary school students who were sampled in the study. The seven variables presented in Figure 1 were together able to predict only 17.9% of the variance in the helplessness-pessimism scores. When the same structural analysis was applied to the employment importance scores, there were no statistically significant path coefficients for any of the paths linking variables to employment importance. It was possible to account for only 4.6% of the variance in the employment importance factor scores when all seven predictor variables in

Figure 1 were included in the regression equation.

FIGURE 1. *Path diagram linking social class and other variables to helplessness-pessimism. The numbers on the lines are standardized beta coefficients.*

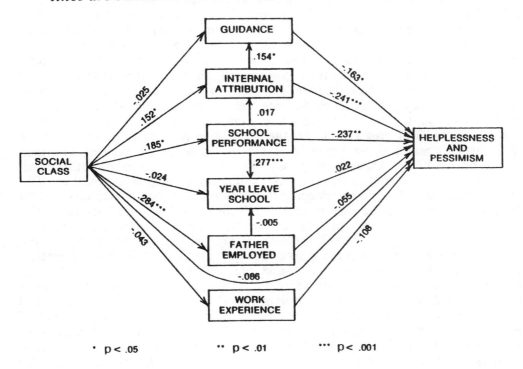

* p < .05   ** p < .01   *** p < .001

Currently I am exploring how well derived measures of job valence and control-optimism (the helplessness-pessimism dimension in reverse), defined on the basis of a factor analysis, predict to job-seeking behavior among young unemployed people. The results so far suggest that job valence, measured in terms of items concerned with each person's stated need for a job and disappointment/depression about being unemployed, reliably predicts to job-seeking behavior but the control-optimism variable does not predict to job-seeking behavior. Control-optimism was measured in terms of each person's stated optimism about job prospects, a low level of feelings of helplessness about being unemployed, and beliefs that the present cause of unemployment will not persist and can be changed. The reasons for the latter unanticipated result are being explored. This research opens up new areas of inquiry concerned with the variables that underlie job-seeking behavior among the unemployed and further extends the expectancy-value (valence) framework to real-life settings.

I have moved somewhat beyond the earlier point of my discussion concerned with expectation-affect linkages. To return to that point, it is evident that we need more research into expectation-affect relationships that take account of different types of expectation and different types of affect. In expectancy-value theory the expectations are expectations about the possible outcomes of alternative actions. They may be based upon a number of different sources of information such as the perceived difficulty of a task, information about the performance of others and knowledge of one's own past performance at the same task or at similar tasks. Affective reactions to success or failure will differ depending upon the source of the expectation (e.g., consistency versus consensus information) and the causal interpretation that is likely following the outcome. For example, when one's expectation of success at a task is based upon consensus information such as norms (e.g., 90 % of students pass the test), reactions to failure would be expected to take a different form from those reactions that occur when the expectation is primarily related to consistency information deriving from a person's reliable pattern of past performance on the task. Where an outcome disconfirms a long established expectation based on past experience, the expectation is likely to be preserved and the outcome treated as an unreliable event or "noise in the system" (Feather, 1982a, pp. 82–83; Heckhausen, in press). When a task is obviously skill-related, affective reactions linked to expectations and outcomes would be expected to differ when compared with the corresponding reactions for a chance-related task. These examples indicate that the nature of the affective reactions may vary depending upon a person's cognitive appraisal of the situation, the source of a person's expectations, the extent to which expectations are well-established or overlearned, the causal attributions for performance, the way success or failure is interpreted, and so on. As further examples, situations where failure implies a lack of competence (as when a person unexpectedly fails despite a lot of effort) would be especially likely to be associated with negative affects such as disappointment and depression; those situations where unexpected failure can be attributed to lack of effort would more likely give rise to feelings of guilt and shame, especially when there is evidence of high ability; where the attribution for failure is to external barriers seen to be interposed by others the affect may involve anger and aggression when expectations of success were high to begin with.

One could multiply these examples. The general point to be made is that affective reactions to situations may take different forms depending on expectations, outcomes, and cognitive appraisals. This point, of course, is not a novel one. The idea has been around for many years and, in recent times, various authors have again directed our attention to cognition-affect linkages (e.g., Feather, 1985a; Lazarus & Folkman, 1984; Smith & Ellsworth, 1985; Weiner, 1982). It is an important point to remember, however, when investigating relations between expectations and affective reactions to outcomes. In the case of unemployment studies it implies that the affect associated with unemployment will be closely tied to a person's cognitive appraisal of self, situation, and outcome.

The Role of Affect

The two recent applications of expectancy-value theory that I have described raise fresh issues and demonstrate the heuristic value of persisting with a general model and exploring its various implications over a long time frame. This strategy enables one to revise and augment the model in the light of new evidence and in relation to other relevant theoretical developments and to test its range of application in both experimental and applied contexts. The possibility of further refinements to a theoretical approach are often multiplied when one attempts to apply the approach to real-life events such as, in the present case, the analysis of willingness to assist social movement organizations and the psychological impact of unemployment. An exclusive commitment to laboratory studies can sometimes lead to a neglect of other important variables that are also part of the causal texture and that only become apparent when one attempts to analyze ongoing behavior in realistic settings.

I want to conclude by making some further observations on two issues that I see as important in the further development of the expectancy-value approach and that were foreshadowed in my discussion of the research findings that I presented. The first issue concerns the role of affect, the second concerns the nature of expectations.

It should be obvious that I see affect as a basic component of the expectancy-value model. Motives and values are assumed to be linked to the affective system; positive and negative valences are assumed to involve anticipations of positive and negative affect respectively; and actions, positive goals, and aversive events are associated with affective reactions. How does all of this proceed?

In terms of temporal priority the arousal of a motive or value comes first. Specific cues engage underlying motives or values that function as generalized structures incorporating the focal, abstracted aspects of an individual's experience within a cognitive-affective network. Whether these structures incorporate prototypical content (e.g., Rosch, 1975) or abstractions of elements that are universally present remains to be resolved. Once these structures have been accessed, however, they influence the way the particular situation is structured or appraised. Some objects and events then are perceived as attractive or desirable; other objects and events become aversive or undesirable; and still others remain neutral because they are unrelated to the underlying motive or value structures. The positive and negative valences are charged with anticipated positive and negative affect, i.e., the appraisal of the situation is a cognitive-affective appraisal.

I have already given an example of how this process might operate in discussing how descriptions of social movement organizations might connect with dominant value systems and give rise to patterns of valences (Feather, 1982d; Feather & Newton, 1982). The same process is involved when a general motive such as the achievement motive is aroused by task instructions such as "You must do well" and success at the task is seen as attractive, when the hunger motive is elicited by internal or external cues and food acquires positive valence, or when a possible activity is seen as attractive in relation to some underlying motive or value.

In each of these cases anticipations of positive affect occur. In other cases, the anticipated affect would be negative as would occur, for example, when a person with strong egalitarian values sees an authoritarian course of action in a negative light or when negative affect about possible failure is aroused in a person with a strong avoidance motive. Thus, the engagement of a motive or value has a basic effect on the way the individual appraises a situation in relation to means and ends. Actions and their possible consequences then become invested with positive or negative affect within the constructed map of a person's anticipations.

This process of motive and value engagement requires more analysis and investigation than it has had in the past. We have tended to neglect the detailed explication of how motives and values come to be aroused. The recent renewed interest in affect and cognition should help to redirect our attention to this problem (e.g., Clark & Fiske, 1983). Models that deal with affective networks (e.g., Bower, 1981), with processing in terms of underlying cognitive structures (e.g., Feather, 1971; Mandler, 1983; Rosch, 1975), and with attitude accessibility (e.g., Fazio, Powell, & Herr, 1983) are all relevant to this question. We should draw from these recent contributions to cognitive psychology and social psychology and build models that enable us better to understand the conditions under which motives and values are accessed or aroused and their effects on a person's definition of the situation. These questions are especially relevant to our understanding of the conditions leading to the initiation of new sequences of behavior.

The other side of the coin is the analysis of affect once a behavior sequence has run its course. This topic seems to have received rather more attention in recent years than the question of motive or value arousal that I have just discussed. For example, how affect relates to outcomes and to causal attributions has been a focal interest in the program of research by Weiner and his colleagues (Weiner, 1982; Weiner, Russell, & Lerman, 1979), and in the studies of the psychological impact of unemployment that I have described (Feather & Davenport, 1981; Feather & Barber, 1983). Here also the process of cognitive appraisal is important, although Weiner (1982) points out that there are outcome-dependent effects that appear to be independent of the attributions made. A further point to remember is that there are reciprocal influences between causal attributions and affects. Positive and negative affects (e.g., happiness, depression) and motives and values can influence the sorts of attributions people provide as explanations for outcomes and events (e.g., Feather, 1985a; Izard, 1983) and the attributions themselves can determine particular kinds of affect as Weiner (1982) has shown. Both kinds of influence need to be considered.

In most cases the affect that is experienced following an outcome would be closely related to the anticipated positive and negative affect that occurs prior to the outcome, though there would be exceptions (see Feather, 1982a, pp. 70–71; 1982b, p. 413). Note that valences and the anticipated affect associated with them would depend not only on the nature and strength of underlying motives and values, but on other determinants as well, such as the degree to which an outcome is perceived as instrumental to attaining other consequences that are positively or negatively valued and the extent to which a person's past experience with a particular outcome has been accompanied by positive or negative affect. As noted previously we need to give more attention to the determinants of valence (and anticipated affect). Here is an aspect of the expectancy-value approach that is crying out for more detailed conceptual analysis and investigation.

The Nature of Expectations

I now turn to the nature of expectations. In discussing our failure in the Feather and Barber (1983) study to replicate the predicted relationship between high expectations and disappointment or depressive affect about unemployment, I noted that there is scope for more research that looks at expectations based upon different sources (e.g., one's own past performance versus information about the performance of others). Information about the source and strength of an expectation becomes especially important when one is predicting the type of causal attribution that will be provided and the affective reaction that might occur when the expectation is either confirmed or disconfirmed by the outcome. My recent book, *Expectations and Actions*, contains further discussion of the importance of being able to specify the basis on which prior expectations are constructed when predicting subjects' attributions for subsequent outcomes (Feather, 1982a, pp. 82–83; Feather, 1985b, pp. 188–190). In that book I also discuss the determinants of expectations, the ways in which expectations can be measured, and the question of different types of expectations, referring in particular to distinctions made by Heckhausen (1977) and Bandura (1977, 1982). Heckhausen (1977) has incorporated his distinctions, along with elaborations of the valence concept, into his version of expectancy-value theory. There is a need to investigate whether the different types of expectation discussed by Heckhausen have different implications for behavior.

Implications of the distinction made by Bandura (1977) between outcome expectations and efficacy expectations also remain to be developed, at least as they relate to the expectancy-value approach. Expectancy-value models have focussed upon outcome expectancies defined in the single case by a person's subjective estimate of the likelihood that a given action will lead to a specified outcome. Efficacy expectations refer to the "conviction that one can successfully execute the behavior required to produce the outcomes" (Bandura, 1977, p. 193). An efficacy expectation, therefore, belongs to the same family of concepts as perceived competence, person as "origin", perceived control, mastery, the concept of "can," and self-concept of ability. Most investigators who apply the expectancy-value approach assume that subjects are able to execute the response that is required and they focus upon the implication relations involved in outcome expectancies. It should be noted, however, that the distinction between outcome and efficacy expectations is by no means clearcut. One's subjective estimate that a given response will lead to a particular outcome (e.g., an outcome expectancy that working hard at an examination will result in a good grade) will be influenced by one's perceived self-efficacy. The correlations obtained in the Feather and Barber (1983) study between subjects' ratings of initial confidence of getting a job and their levels of self-esteem would reflect in some degree beliefs about self-efficacy or perceived competence.

The definition of outcome also needs more conceptual clarification. In the case of extrinsic outcomes like getting a good grade in an examination or winning social approval from an audience, it is easy to point to a clear outcome. In other cases, however, the outcome may be intertwined with task performance, as it is, for example, in much of the research in achievement motivation. One's perceived self-efficacy at a task may then relate to implicit standards or criteria that signpost successful or unsuccessful outcomes and subsequent feelings of success or failure. Thus, a belief that one can successfully execute an action may be difficult to dissociate from a belief that the action will lead to subjectively perceived task-based outcomes that define success or failure. Similar observations have been made recently by Eastman and Marzilier (1984). They also point out that different outcomes (e.g., handling a poisonous versus a non-poisonous snake) may have a significant effect on one's assessment of self-efficacy. For these reasons, I believe that there is some conceptual fuzziness in the distinction between outcome expectations and efficacy expectations.

Yet it is important in future developments of the expectancy-value approach to sort out different possible meanings of the concept of expectation and, where clear conceptual distinctions can be made, to explore the implications of these distinctions for the general theoretical approach. Other questions that require more analysis include the implications of specifying expectations along dimensions such as strength, magnitude, and generality; the process by which outcome expectations become chained together and refined; their relationship to other concepts in the literature such as schemata, scripts, and plans; the extent to which expectations involve conscious experience and cognitive content; and how expectations might be measured (see Feather, 1982b, for further discussion of these issues).

Let me now conclude. It should be clear that my recent applications of expectancy-value theory raise some basic issues that concern the nature of motives, values, valences, and expectations and the role of affect in sequences of motivated behavior. I am confident that attention to these issues will lead to a further strengthening of what has been a central approach to the psychology of motivation over many years. This approach enables us to go some way toward bridging the gap between cognition and action. It takes both person and situation variables into account and, in its focus on expected consequences and subjective evaluation, it provides a powerful lever for capturing much of the cognition and purpose that is inherent in the ongoing stream of human behavior.

FOOTNOTES

[1]The "value" aspect of the expectancy-value approach refers to incentive values and not to the values that people hold. The relationship between human values and subjectively perceived incentive values is discussed later in this article. To avoid confusion, I refer in some of my recent publications to the expectancy-valence model to bring out the point that the model involves both expectations about the consequences of actions and beliefs about the perceived attractiveness (positive valence) and aversiveness (negative valence) of those consequences. Note also that actions themselves can have positive or negative valence (be attractive or aversive). Because the term "expectancy-value" has wider currency, I use it in the present article but it is synonymous with "expectancy-valence."

[2]Note that the variables that we investigated in relation to depressive affect involved only a subset of possible variables. Clearly, depressive affect about unemployment and more global depressive symptoms would also be related to other features of an unemployed person's situation such as the extent to which the person is suffering economic deprivation (poverty) and social costs.

REFERENCES

Abramson, L. Y., Seligman, M. E. P., & Teasdale, J. D. (1978). Learned helplessness in humans: Critique and reformulation. *Journal of Abnormal Psychology, 87*, 49–74.

Atkinson, J. W., & Birch, D. (1970). *The dynamics of action*. New York: Wiley.

Atkinson, J. W., & Feather, N. T. (Eds.) (1966). *A theory of achievement motivation*. New York: Wiley.

Bachman, J. G., O'Malley, P. M., & Johnston, J. (1978). *Adolescence to adulthood*. Ann Arbor, MI: Institute for Social Research.

Ball-Rokeach, S. J., Rokeach, M., & Grube, J. W. (1984). *The great American values test: Influencing behavior and belief through television*. New York: Free Press.

Bandura, A. (1977). Self-efficacy: Toward a unifying theory of behavioral change. *Psychological Review, 84*, 191–215.

Bandura, A. (1982). Self-efficacy mechanism in human agency. *American Psychologist, 37*, 122–147.

Bandura, A., & Cervone, D. (1983). Self-evaluative and self-efficacy mechanisms governing the motivational effects of goal systems. *Journal of Personality and Social Psychology, 45*, 1017–1028.

Beck, A. T. (1967). *Depression: Clinical, experimental, and theoretical aspects*. New York: Harper & Row.

Beck, A. T. (1976). *Cognitive therapy and the emotional disorders*. New York: International Universities Press.

Beck, A. T., & Beck, R. W. (1972). Screening depressed patients in family practice: A rapid technic. *Postgraduate Medicine, 52*, 81–85.

Bower, G. H. (1981). Mood and memory. *American Psychologist, 36*, 129–148.

Clark, M. S., & Fiske, S. T. (Eds.) (1982). *Affect and cognition: The seventeenth annual Carnegie symposium on cognition*. Hillsdale, NJ: Erlbaum, 1982.

Eastman, C., & Marzillier, J. S. (1984). Theoretical and methodological difficulties in Bandura's self-efficacy theory. *Cognitive Therapy and Research, 8*, 213–229.

Eisenberg, P., & Lazarsfeld, P. F. (1938). The psychological effects of unemployment. *Psychological Bulletin, 35,* 358–390.

Fazio, R. H., Powell, M. C., & Herr, P. M. (1983). Toward a process model of the attitude-behavior relation: Accessing one's attitude upon mere observation of the attitude object. *Journal of Personality and Social Psychology, 44,* 723–735.

Feather, N. T. (1959). Subjective probability and decision under uncertainty. *Psychological Review, 66,* 150–164.

Feather, N. T. (1961). The relationship of persistence at a task to expectation of success and achievement related motives. *Journal of Abnormal and Social Psychology, 63,* 552–561.

Feather, N. T. (1962). The study of persistence. *Psychological Bulletin, 59,* 94–115.

Feather, N. T. (1969). Attribution of responsibility and valence of success and failure in relation to initial confidence and task performance. *Journal of Personality and Social Psychology, 13,* 129–144.

Feather, N. T. (1971). Organization and discrepancy in cognitive structures. *Psychological Review, 78,* 355–379.

Feather, N. T. (1975). *Values in education and society,* New York: Free Press.

Feather, N. T. (1982a). Actions in relation to expected consequences: An overview of a research program. In N. T. Feather (Ed.), *Expectations and actions: Expectancy-value models in psychology* (pp. 53–95). Hillsdale, NJ: Erlbaum.

Feather, N. T. (1982b). Expectancy-value approaches: Present status and future directions. In N. T. Feather (Ed.), *Expectations and actions: Expectancy-value models in psychology* (pp. 395–420). Hillsdale, NJ: Erlbaum.

Feather, N. T. (1982c). *Expectations and actions: Expectancy-value models in psychology.* Hillsdale, NJ: Erlbaum.

Feather, N. T. (1982d). Human values and the prediction of action: An expectancy-valence analysis. In N. T. Feather (Ed.), *Expectations and actions: Expectancy-value models in psychology* (pp. 263–289). Hillsdale, NJ: Erlbaum.

Feather, N. T. (1982e). Introduction and overview. In N. T. Feather (Ed.), *Expectations and actions: Expectancy-value models in psychology* (pp. 1–14). Hillsdale, NJ: Erlbaum.

Feather, N. T. (1983). Causal attributions and beliefs about work and unemployment among adolescents in state and independent secondary schools. *Australian Journal of Psychology, 35*, 211–232.

Feather, N. T. (1984). Masculinity, femininity, psychological androgyny, and the structure of values. *Journal of Personality and Social Psychology, 47*, 604–620.

Feather, N. T. (1985a). Attitudes, values, and attributions: Explanations of unemployment. *Journal of Personality and Social Psychology, 48*, 876–889.

Feather, N. T. (1985b). Beliefs, attitudes, and values: Trends in Australian research. In N. T. Feather (Ed.), *Australian psychology: Review of research* (pp. 187–217). Sydney: George Allen & Unwin.

Feather, N. T. (1985c). The psychological impact of unemployment: Empirical findings and theoretical approaches. In N. T. Feather (Ed.), *Australian psychology: Review of research* (pp. 265–296). Sydney: George Allen & Unwin.

Feather, N. T. (1986). Employment importance and helplessness about potential unemployment among students in secondary schools. *Australian Journal of Psychology, 38*, 33–44.

Feather, N. T., & Barber, J. G. (1983). Depressive reactions and unemployment. *Journal of Abnormal Psychology, 92*, 185–195.

Feather, N. T., & Davenport, P. R. (1981). Unemployment and depressive affect: A motivational and attributional analysis. *Journal of Personality and Social Psychology, 41*, 422–436.

Feather, N. T., & Newton, J. W. (1982). Values, expectations, and the prediction of social action: An expectancy-valence analysis. *Motivation and Emotion, 6*, 217–244.

Feather, N. T., & O'Brien, G. E. (in press). A longitudinal study of the effects of employment and unemployment on school-leavers. *Journal of Occupational Psychology*.

Feather, N. T., & Tiggemann, M. (1984). A balanced measure of attributional style. *Australian Journal of Psychology, 36*, 267–283.

Fishbein, M., & Ajzen, I. (1975). Belief, attitude, intention, and behavior: An introduction to theory and research. Reading, MA: Addison-Wesley.

Heckhausen, H. (1977). Achievement motivation and its constructs: A cognitive model. *Motivation and Emotion, 4*, 283–329.

Heckhausen, H. (in press). Why some time out might benefit achievement motivation research. In J. H. L. van den Bercken, T. C. M. Bergen, & E. E. J. de Bruyn (Eds.), *Achievement and task motivation*. Berwyn, PA: Swets, North America.

Izard, C. (1982). Comments on emotion and cognition: Can there be a working relationship? In M. S. Clark & S. T. Fiske (Eds.), *Affect and cognition: The seventeenth annual Carnegie symposium on cognition* (pp. 229–240). Hillsdale, NJ: Erlbaum.

Lazarus, R. S., & Folkman, S. (1984). *Stress, appraisal, and coping*. New York: Springer.

Lewin, K. (1936). *Principles of topological psychology*. New York: McGraw-Hill.

Mandler, G. (1982). The structure of value: Accounting for taste. In M. S. Clark & S. T. Fiske (Eds.), *Affect and cognition: The seventeenth annual Carnegie symposium on cognition* (pp. 3–36). Hillsdale, NJ: Erlbaum.

McClelland, D. C. (1985). *Human motivation*. Glenview, IL: Scott, Foresman & Co.

McDougall, W. (1932). *The energies of man: A study of the fundamentals of dynamic psychology*. London: Methuen.

Peterson, C., Schwartz, S. M., & Seligman, M. E. P. (1981). Self-blame and depressive symptoms. *Journal of Personality and Social Psychology, 41,* 253–259.

Rokeach, M. (1973). *The nature of human values*. New York: Free Press.

Rokeach, M. (1979a). Some unresolved issues in theories of beliefs, attitudes, and values. *Nebraska symposium on motivation* (pp. 261–304). Lincoln, NE: University of Nebraska Press.

Rokeach, M. (Ed.) (1979b). *Understanding human values: Individual and societal*. New York: Free Press.

Rosch, E. (1975). Universals and cultural specifics in human categorization. In R. W. Brislin, S. Bochner, & W. J. Lonner (Eds.), *Cross-cultural perspectives on learning* (pp. 177–206). New York: Wiley.

Rosenberg, M. (1965). *Society and the adolescent self-image*. Princeton, NJ: Princeton University Press.

Smith, C. A., & Ellsworth, P. (1985). Patterns of cognitive appraisal in emotion. *Journal of Personality and Social Psychology, 48,* 813–838.

Thurstone, L. L. (1931). The measurement of attitudes. *Journal of Abnormal and Social Psychology, 26,* 249–269.

Weiner, B. (1980). *Human motivation.* New York: Holt, Rinehart, & Winston.

Weiner, B. (1982). An attributionally based theory of motivation and emotion: Focus, range and issues. In N. T. Feather (Ed.), *Expectations and actions: Expectancy-value models in psychology.* Hillsdale, NJ: Erlbaum.

Weiner, B., & Litman-Adizes, T. (1980). An attributional expectancy-value analysis of learned helplessness and depression. In J. Garber & M. E. P. Seligman (Eds.), *Human helplessness: Theory and applications* (pp. 35–57). New York: Academic Press.

Weiner, B., Russell, D., & Lerman, D. (1979). The cognition-emotion process in achievement-related contexts. *Journal of Personality and Social Psychology, 37,* 1211–1220.

Chapter Ten

FUTURE TIME PERSPECTIVE: A

COGNITIVE-MOTIVATIONAL CONCEPT

Willy Lens

University of Leuven (Belgium)

Theoretical Definitions

Frank (1939) is one of the first to stress the importance of time perspective in the study of human behavior. Future time perspective (FTP) was for him a cognitive-dynamic orientation towards future goals. Children learn progressively to react no longer in an impulsive way to internal and external stimuli, but to take anticipated behavioral outcomes into account. Those anticipations help to define the present situation.

Frank's conceptualization of time perspective is strongly influenced by Lewin's topological psychology. Lewin (1931) discusses the effect of the past and especially of the future on present behavior and explains how the past and the future are progressively integrated by the child in its *life space:*

> The child no longer strives solely for present things, not only has wishes that must be realized at once, but his purposes grasp toward a tomorrow. The goals which determine the child's behavior are thrown continually further into the future. A decisive extension of the psychologically present life-space of the child is based upon this temporal displacement of goals. (Lewin, 1931; English translation, 1935, p. 173)

Lewin conceives of psychological future as part of what Frank (1939) called *time perspective:*

> The psychological future is part of what L. K. Frank has called 'time perspective.' The life-space of an individual, far from being limited to what he considers the present situation, includes the future, the present, and also the past. Actions, emotions and certainly the morale of an individual at any instant depend upon his total time perspective. (Lewin, 1948, p. 104)

Referring to Frank (1939), Lewin (1942a) defines time perspective as: "the totality of the individual's views of his psychological future and his psychological past existing at a given time" (pp. 215–242), and future time perspective as the present anticipation of future goals: "The setting of goals is closely related to time perspective. The goal of the individual includes his expectations for the future, his wishes, and his day-dreams" (Lewin, 1942b).

Also Lersch (1938; tenth edition 1966) stresses the fact that, at each moment in time, the past and the future are part of an individual's psychological situation and that the orientation toward the future is due to motivational aspirations:

> Wie die Vergangenheit, so ist andererseits auch die Zukunft in der Gegenwart des Erlebens enthalten. Jede erlebte Gegenwart is Vorgriff in die Zukunft. Das gilt in dem Masse, als jeder Augenblick des seelischen Lebens durchwirkt ist von der Thematik und Dynamik seelischer Strebungen, die auf die Verwirklichung eines noch nicht bestehenden Zustandes gehen. (Lersch, 1966, p. 47)

Bergius (1957) makes an interesting distinction between a conative and a cognitive component in future orientation. The conative component represents the propulsivity or motivational, dynamic orientation towards future goals. The cognitive component has to do with the subjective expectation that the anticipated goals will be realized.

Fraisse's (1963) conceptualization of time perspective and its behavioral effects is very similar to Lewin's:

> We live in the present; in other words, our behavior is a function of everything which determines it *here and now*. But these present activations are constantly referring us to what has already passed away or to what has not yet come to be . . . our actions at any given moment do not only depend on the situation in which we find ourselves at that instant, but also on everything we have already experienced and on all our future expectations, . . . each of our actions takes place in a temporal perspective, it depends on our temporal horizon at the precise moment of its occurrence. (p. 151)

For Fraisse (1963) the future results from imagining realistic motivational goals: "The future only unfolds in so far as we imagine a future which seems to be *realizable*" (p. 172). "There is no future without at the same time a desire for something else and awareness of the possibility of realizing it" (Fraisse, 1963, p. 174). Fraisse (1963) quotes Guyau (1902, p. 33) to underline how the psychological future originates in motivational strivings: "We must desire, we must want, we must stretch out our hands and walk to create the future. The future is not what is coming to us but what we are going to" (p. 173).

Also for Nuttin (1964; 1980; Nuttin & Lens, 1985), the psychological future is essentially related to motivation: "the future is the time quality of the goal object: the future is our primary motivational space" (Nuttin, 1964, p. 63). Being oriented toward the future is for Nuttin a new and original phenomenon that originates in a state of motivation or need. A need or motive implies a dynamic relationship toward something that is not yet present, but anticipated or expected. Needs as such create, however, only a rather vague orientation toward the future. But, due to their higher cognitive functions, human beings elaborate their originally vague and general cravings into more or less specific motivational goals, means-end structure or behavioral plans and projects (Nuttin, 1984). These motivational realizations on the cognitive, representational level have a more or less elaborated temporal structure. The presently anticipated goals are situated somewhere in the future. Even the maintaining type of motivation (Raynor, 1982) is by definition future oriented. The temporal distance of motivational goals can vary from very short (e.g., to visit my mother this afternoon) to very long (e.g., to go to heaven). Some life periods or some time periods may contain many goals and others much less. A long FTP hence means to have relatively many goals that are situated in a rather distant future. Individuals with a short FTP, on the other hand, strive for goals that are predominantly situated in a rather near future. For Nuttin "future time perspective is formed by the more or less distant goal objects that are processed by an individual" (Nuttin & Lens, 1985, p. 22). But he also claims "that future time perspective is a prerequisite for the elaboration of long term projects" (Nuttin & Lens, 1985, p. 22). These two assumptions are, however, not contradictory, if one accepts—as Nuttin does—reciprocal influences within developmental processes. The perception of a long chronological future is necessary, but not sufficient, to develop a long motivational future time perspective by formulating long distance goals or behavioral plans or projects. Many of our motivational goals, subgoals, and instrumental acts, intended to lead to those goals, have a more or less well defined temporal localization. We plan in advance the time period *when* we want to achieve a goal or *when* we will perform the necessary instrumental acts. In order not to forget when we want to do something, we may even write it down in our calendar. Our daily behavior, and certainly our activities over weeks and months or even years, is to a large extent regulated and planned in advance. We use a time sharing mechanism while working at the realization of several different motivational goals or behavioral projects. Nuttin (1985) argues that a behavioral change in the stream of behavior, may not only be determined by the hierarchy or relative strength of underlying behavioral tendencies (Atkinson & Birch, 1970), but also by the temporal signs of behavioral projects and motivational goals.

Operationalizations of Future Time Perspective

Notwithstanding this rather high agreement among the original and well known theoretical conceptualizations of future time perspective (FTP) as a cognitive-dynamic variable, the concept became a very ambiguous one in the literature. Numerous correlational or differential studies created a great terminological and methodological confusion. A large discrepancy developed between the FTP-concept in its strict sense as a motivational variable, and the very heterogeneous studies relating (the extension of) FTP to variables such as age, sex, social class, intelligence, need for achievement, delinquency, psychopathology, etc.

We do not intend to give a complete review of all techniques used to measure FTP. Such reviews can be found in Wallace and Rabin (1960) and Nuttin, Lens, Van Calster, and De Volder (1979). Rather we limit ourselves to the most frequently used operational definitions of FTP. The large discrepancy between the theoretical conceptualizations described in the previous section, and these operational definitions will become evident.

A first type of instruments (Tell me a story-technique) measure the extension of FTP by the duration of an action sequence that is described in a story (Leshan, 1952). If the subjects do not explicitly mention the time span of the action sequence, they are asked to do so afterwards. The total duration of the action is usually taken as an index of FTP-extension. Others (Wohlford, 1966; Black & Gregson, 1973) distinguish between the time span of that part of the story that is situated in the past (retrospective time span or retrotension) and the one that is situated in the future (prospective time span or protension).

Barndt and Johnson (1955) intended to improve this method by giving a story beginning to the subjects (Story Completion Technique). The story beginning may have a certain temporal structure (e.g., Ten o'clock one morning. Al met his friend Jerry near the center of town . . .) or it may be unstructured temporally (Joe is having a cup of coffee in a restaurant. He's thinking of the time to come when . . .). It is evident that the temporal situation in the story beginning strongly affects the time span covered in the action sequence: the first type of story beginnings typically arouse action sequences of a much shorter duration than the second type of beginnings. Others (Teahan, 1958; Epley & Ricks, 1963) use TAT pictures or similar pictures to elicit stories.

The spontaneous Future Events Test or the Personal Future Events Test are more direct or personal techniques to measure the extension of FTP. Subjects are first asked to list a number of events that they expect to experience in the future. In a second step they are asked to indicate for each of those events how old they will be at the moment that the event will happen. The mean or median of those ages, or of the differences between the present age of the subject and those ages, are used as indices of FTP-extension (Wallace, 1956). Lamm, Schmidt and Trommsdorff (1976) use the maximal difference score, rather than the mean or median.

This technique becomes less interesting when a list of events is presented to the subjects (Stein & Craik, 1965). Although the listed events are selected in such a way that they may happen in everybody's life, it is still possible that the subjects would never spontaneously think about them because they are not part of their psychological world. For both types of events, there is no guarantee that they are objects of a positive or negative motivational concern. They may be purely cognitive anticipations of things that are expected for the future but neither hoped for nor feared.

Rizzo (1967) and Cantril (1965)—among others—do measure future time perspective in personal motivational orientations. They induce a certain moment in the future (e.g., ten years from now) and then ask the subjects to list their motivational concerns for that future moment. It is not unreasonable to assume that some subjects, who spontaneously would never think that far in the future, do give some answers anyway, to comply with the request. Brim and Forer (1956) do not impose a certain temporal distance, but ask subjects for the temporal span of their motivational orientations in general. Such a question seems to be too abstract for many subjects.

Unlike these briefly described measures of FTP, Nuttin's Motivational Induction Method (MIM) is closely related to the theoretical conceptualization of FTP as a cognitive-motivational variable. The MIM (Nuttin & Lens, 1985) is a direct first person sentence completion technique to collect from differential or experimental groups of subjects a representative sample of their individual conscious goals, aspirations or motivational plans and projects. Subjects are asked to complete 40 (30 or 20 in the shortened versions) positively and 20 (15 or 10 in the shortened versions) negatively formulated first-person sentence beginnings (e.g., I strive to . . . ; I work for . . . ; I fear that . . . ; I would not hesitate . . . ; I would not like it if . . .). They are instructed to do so by formulating a personal goal or desire that comes to their minds when reading each sentence beginning. The sentence beginnings induce only a general motivational orientation, but not a specific motivational category. As such, they orient the subjects toward the future but not toward a particular moment or interval in the future. The expressed goal objects may apply to the present moment or to a still very distant future moment (Lens & Gailly, 1980). Two scoring techniques were developed to analyze the data: one to identify the motivational content of the expressed goal objects in terms of an empirically developed list of motivational main- and subcategories, and another to localize those motivational goals on a temporal scale in order to measure the extension and the density of the FTP that is involved (Nuttin & Lens, 1985). The mean or median of the temporal distances (in years) between the temporal localizations of the goal objects in the future and the present moment is a first measure of FTP extension. The proportion of the number of motivational objects in the near future (within a two-year period) to the number of motivational objects in the distant future is used as a second measure of the FTP extension.

Future time perspective became the object of predominantly differential research that was much less concerned with the behavioral effects of FTP than with how it relates to other personality characteristics. A large number of very heterogeneous studies using very different measurement instruments are all grouped under the same denominator of future time perspective. The value and certainly the comparability of their results are of course highly questionable. The concept of FTP lost the core of its original meaning in most of its operational definitions. It has mostly been studied in its own right and not as a cognitive-motivational variable affecting behavior.

Future Time Perspective in Experimental Psychology

In comparison with the behavioral effects of the past (through learning and memory) the role of the future has been strongly neglected in the mainstream of experimental psychology with its mechanistic models of behavior. Those who advocated, however, the study of molar behavior, rather than molecular S-R associations, have always taken into account the behavioral effects of the future through the process of expecting a goal or behavioral end result. For McDougall (1923) and Woodworth (1921) molar behavior was motivated and goal oriented or purposive. McDougall (1923) describes purposive action as "action that seems to be governed or directed in some degree by *prevision of its effects*, by prevision of that which still lies in the future, of events which have not yet happened, but which are likely to happen and to the happening of which the action itself may contribute" [italics added] (p. 48). Woodworth (1921) defines a motive as "tendency towards a certain *end-result or end-reaction*" [italics added] (p. 84).

Also, Tolman (1932) stressed that psychology should study the molar, global behavior of a total organism in interaction with its environment. Such behavior is for Tolman *goal-oriented* or purposive (purposive behaviorism). But Tolman does not explain purposiveness by referring to hypothetical, neurological mechanisms or to mental contents such as conscious goals, plans or intentions. He defines purpose as the *persistence until* character and the docility of behavior. Molar behavior is also cognitive. It implies knowledge about the situation, expectancies about which stimuli should be present when the reaction will lead to the goal, and when it will do so.

Hull published in the thirties a series of theoretical articles in which he made a distinction between motivation (to strive for goals) and learning (reinforcing connections). He explained the effect of a behavioral goal or end term on present behavior not in terms of mental contents such as knowledge or expectancy, but in terms of the hypothetical conditioned fractional anticipatory goal reaction. In his elaborated theory of the determinants of a behavioral reaction, Hull (1943) did not follow up this idea. The frequency, the amount, the quality and the delayed or immediate character of the goal or reward were assumed to affect the conditioned habit-strength (sHr). This theory could, however, not explain the *immediate* behavioral effects of a change in the reward, because the strength of S-R connections or of the habit changes only gradually and not immediately. Especially Crespi's (1944) findings on the elation and depression effects brought Hull (1952) and Spence (1956) to revise the Hullian theory of the excitatory reaction potential. Both introduced the concept of incentive motivation. For Hull (1952) this second type of motivation is determined by the quantity and the quality of the goal object or reward. The temporal lag between a reaction and the reward is considered by Hull to be a determinant of habit-strength but by Spence (1956) as a determinant of incentive motivation. Hull explains the behavioral effect of the "anticipated" goal object in terms of the conditioned fractional antedating goal response, as he did in the thirties. This reaction (r_g) produces the goal stimulus (s_g) which, together with the drive stimulus and external stimuli, arouses the reactions that lead to the goal object. It is a pure stimulus-act: $r_g - s_g$ (Hull, 1952, p. 151). Hull and Spence translated cognitive concepts such as expectation and purpose in S-R terms or pure stimulus acts:

The fact that the fractional goal reaction (r_g) occurs in an antedating manner at the beginning of the behavior chain or sequence *constitutes on the part of the organism a molar foresight or knowledge of the not-here and the not-now*. It is probably roughly equivalent to what Tolman has called "cognition." (Hull, 1952, p. 151)

Indeed, the r_g - s_g mechanism leads in a strictly logical manner into what was formally regarded as the very heart of the psychic: interest, planning, foresight, foreknowledge, expectancy, purpose and so on. (Hull, 1952, p. 350)

The behavioral effects of delayed gratification have mostly been studied in learning experiments with animals. In these experiments the delay-interval was usually very short. See Renner (1964) for a review.

In most of the experimental studies, the delay of gratification or reinforcement was caused by introducing a waiting time between some final instrumental reaction and the obtainment of the reward. Hull (1952) and Spence (1956), however, make a most interesting distinction between the *non-chaining* and the *within-chain* case of delayed reinforcement. In the non-chaining type of delayed reinforcement, time intervals of different lengths are introduced between a series of responses and the obtainment of the reward. The within-chain case of delayed reinforcement, on the other hand, refers to different lengths of instrumental response chains leading to the goal. The temporal distance between the start of a series of instrumental reactions and the moment of reinforcement or the goal reaction varies because of a different number of required instrumental reactions. In this case, there is no time interval or waiting period after the final instrumental reaction. Hull (1952) explains the debilitating effect of delay of reinforcement in terms of habit-strength. Spence (1956) assumes that the incentive motivation decreases with increasing delay of gratification.

Future time perspective in the sense of being oriented towards motivational goals in the immediate, the more distant, or the far distant future is conceptually strongly related to delay of reinforcement or delay of gratification. A long FTP means to strive for relatively more goals in the distant future and a short FTP means that the individual strives mostly for goal objects that can be realized or achieved in the immediate or near future. Individuals with a long FTP delay their gratification relatively more than individuals with a short FTP. The temporal delay that is involved in goal setting and motivational planning can be of the non-chaining type or of the within-chain type of delayed reinforcement, or even a combination of both. Mischel's (1981) research on the self-imposed delay of gratification is an example of the non-chaining type of delay. In his first paradigm Mischel studies the correlates or determinants of children's preference for an immediate smaller reward or for a delayed larger reward. After helping the experimenter with a task, the children can choose between an immediate but objectively smaller reward and *waiting* for a delayed but objectively larger reward. The time lag between the instrumental act (performing a task) and receiving a reward for the act differs. The children do not have to perform additional instrumental actions during the delay time. Also Mischel's second paradigm on the variables (more specifically different types of cognitions) that affect how long a child waits for a preferred but delayed reward (or stops waiting and gets the non-preferred alternative reward), is an example of the non-chaining type of delay of gratification. The child only has to wait long enough to get the larger reward. No instrumental actions are required during the delay or waiting time. However, the self imposed delay of gratification that is implied in goal setting or motivational planning is quite often of the within-chain type. When individuals formulate motivational goals for the near or for the distant future, they cannot just wait for the reward to happen but have to perform a series of instrumental actions to realize or to achieve their goal. For example, a high school graduate who wants to become a high school teacher must study four more years at the university in order to achieve his goal. That goal cannot be achieved by just waiting. Her friend wants to become a surgeon. She delays an important gratification much longer than four years. But also here, just waiting many more years will not bring her that important reward. She must also study successfully during all those years. In planned research we test if the different types of cognitions during the delay time have the same effect on the delay capacity when instrumental acts must be performed during the delay interval as Mischel (1981) found for a waiting interval.

Whatever type of delay of gratification is involved in motivational goal setting, individuals characterized by a long future time perspective perceive a given time interval between the present and the future moment at which the goal can be achieved subjectively as being shorter than subjects with a short FTP. Further, it is the psychological or perceived temporal distance that affects the subjective value of the anticipated goal object. A given delayed goal will lose less subjective value because of the delay time for individuals with a long FTP than for individuals with a short FTP. This brings us to the expectancy-instrumentality-value theories of motivation as another important line of research that is highly relevant when studying the motivational role of future time perspective.

FTP and Cognitive Theories of (Achievement) Motivation

Based on Tolman's purposive behaviorism (Tolman, 1932), Lewin's force model (Lewin, 1938) and the economic decision theories (Edwards, 1954), cognitive theories of human motivation (e.g., Atkinson, 1964; Atkinson & Feather, 1966; Feather, 1982; Heckhausen, 1977; Rotter, 1954; Vroom, 1964) explain motivational processes from their functional relationship with interacting cognitive (expectancy, instrumentality) and affective variables (valences, incentive values). The role of the future is explicitly recognized in these theories, but FTP as a personality trait is not. The motivational effect of anticipated goal objects in the future on present behavior is explained in terms of expectancy, instrumentality and anticipated value. Although Heckhausen (1977) makes a distinction between immediate and delayed behavioral consequences, most of these cognitive theories do not explicitly discuss the temporal distance as such in relation to the goal objects. For Rotter "time, in and by itself, is not the crucial variable" (Rotter, Chance, &

Phares, 1972, p. 23). He explains choice between immediate versus delayed gratification in terms of expected reinforcement value and/or in terms of expectancy or trust.

In Atkinson's theory of achievement motivation or risk-taking model, the future is explicitly not taken into consideration. The strength of the resultant tendency to strive for success in an achievement task is only determined by the achievement motive and test anxiety as personality dispositions and by the subjective probability or expectancy of success in that achievement task. Future implications of present success or failure are not considered. However, the future is present in the definition and in the Thematic Apperception Test-measure of the need for achievement. McClelland, Atkinson, Clark and Lowell (1953) define a motive as "the reintegration by a cue of a change in an affective situation" (p. 28). The learned anticipation of a change in affective states motivates present behavior. Involvement in the attainment of a long-term achievement goal is one of the three criteria to score a TAT-story for Achievement Imagery (McClelland et al., 1953). For McClelland (1958, p. 542) future orientation might well be a corollary of the need for achievement. Heckhausen (1967, pp. 41–45) summarizes empirical evidence for the relationship between the need for achievement and future time perspective or future orientation.

Based on the differential effects of the perceived instrumentality of present success for future successes on the immediate level of performance in an achievement task (Atkinson, 1966; Raynor, Atkinson, & Brown, 1974; Raynor, 1970), Raynor (1969, 1974) elaborated the original theory of achievement motivation. His cognitive elaboration is the first mathematical formalization of the motivational role of the future in present achievement oriented behavior. Raynor (1969) conceives of FTP not as a personality trait but as a perceived situational or task characteristic. Originally Raynor defined the degree of future orientation as the number of anticipated tasks or steps in a contingent path of achievement tasks. A series of consecutive achievement tasks is called a contingent path if success in a previous task is a necessary and sufficient condition to perform the next task. Within a given path the temporal distance toward the final task or goal will, of course, decrease as the number of steps or tasks still to be performed decreases. However, a contingent path of two steps may cover a much longer time span than a contingent path of four steps (Gjesme, 1974). More recently Raynor (1981; Raynor & Entin, 1982), therefore, makes a distinction between this first meaning of FTP, now called *task hierarchy*, and a second meaning or the *time hierarchy* of a contingent path. Time hierarchy refers to the temporal duration of a contingent path. The motivational effects of time and task hierarchy are opposite. Task hierarchy is positively related to the strength of the resultant positive or negative achievement motivation, and time hierarchy is negatively related. The closer (in space or time) the individual comes to the goal, the stronger the motivation for it. (See Miller's goal gradient hypothesis in Miller, 1944.) Success-oriented individuals (need for achievement stronger than fear of failure) will be more motivated for an immediate achievement task if it constitutes the next step in a contingent path of still many steps which can be taken in a relatively shorter time interval. Failure-threatened individuals (fear of failure stronger than the need for achievement) will be more anxious, more inhibited, hence less motivated to the extent that the contingent path has more steps and can be finished in a shorter time interval. In real life most contingent paths are only partially contingent. A *partial contingent* path is defined by Raynor (1982) as "a path . . . where an immediate positive outcome guarantees the opportunity to continue, but an immediate negative outcome has no bearing on future striving" (p. 311). The motivating characteristics of partial contingent paths are assumed to be somewhere between those of a non-contingent path (Atkinson's theory of achievement motivation) and those of a contingent path (Raynor's more general theory of achievement motivation). In a first approach of partial contingent paths, Lens and Cassiman (1984) studied the motivational effect of anticipating a second chance to strive for success in an achievement task after failure in the first trial. They hypothesized that the anticipation of a second trial undermines the achievement motivation. Success-oriented subjects will be more motivated in the first trial when there is only one chance than they are when knowing that an initial failure can be overcome in a second trial. Failure-threatened individuals will be less anxious and hence more motivated in the first trial when they do expect a second chance. As predicted by Atkinson's theory of achievement motivation, success oriented subjects perform significantly higher ($p < .001$) than failure-threatened subjects when there is only one chance or trial to be successful. This difference in the first trial disappears when a second opportunity is promised for those who fail in that first trial. For both motive groups the difference in level of performance between the two conditions is in the expected direction but statistically not significant.

As noted by Gjesme (1975, 1981) and De Volder and Lens (1982) not the chronological time that is involved in a contingent path, but the subjectively perceived temporal length or duration is motivationally relevant. People with a long FTP as a personality trait experience a given time interval into the future as much shorter than people with a short FTP do. Gjesme (1975) found indeed that the motivational effect of time hierarchy is mediated by individual differences in what he calls the degree of future orientation. The opposite motivational effects of time hierarchy for success- and for failure-oriented subjects are less strong for individuals with a long FTP than for individuals with a short FTP. Gjesme applies the temporal goal-gradient hypothesis (Miller, 1944) to the resultant tendency to strive for success. If we do this, however, to the two component tendencies separately (the positive tendency to strive for success and the negative tendency to avoid failure), then his data can only be explained if we assume that for success-oriented individuals the approach-gradient is steeper than the avoidance-gradient, and that the opposite holds for failure-threatened individuals.

In our more recent research of the motivational significance or behavioral effects of FTP, we try to conceptualize FTP in terms of the broadly applied expectancy-instrumentality-value models of human motivation (e.g., Feather, 1982). We (De Volder & Lens, 1982) make a distinction between a more cognitive and a more dynamic aspect. The *cognitive aspect* is conceived of as a disposition to perceive and to take into account the long-term consequences of present behavior. It is the perceived instrumentality of a present behavioral act or outcome to reach not only goals in the near future but also in the more distant future. It is assumed that individuals with a long FTP see more easily the implications of their present actions (instrumentality) for the distant future. The *dynamic* aspect is conceived of as a disposition to ascribe a high valence to goals, even if they can only be reached in a more distant future. The anticipated incentive value of a motivational goal generally decreases with increasing temporal distance to that goal, everything else assumed to be constant. But this decrease will be stronger for people with a short FTP than for those with a long FTP. A given delay-time is experienced as shorter by individuals with a long FTP than by individuals with a short FTP. The motivational significance of perceived instrumentality and of anticipated incentive value are, of course, well known. This conceptualization of FTP explains the often found positive correlation between the extension or depth of FTP and school results.

De Volder and Lens (1982) asked 251 11th and 12th grade boys to rate the valence of 23 rather generally formulated goals and the subjective probability of reaching each goal if they would study hard and if they would not study hard. The difference between these two subjective probabilities defines the instrumental value of studying hard for each goal (Heckhausen, 1977). The goals can be localized in one of three time zones: the near future (within two years), the distant future (more than two years from now) and the open-present (now and forever). Mean ratings of anticipated incentive value and of perceived instrumentality were related to grade point average (above or below the median). We found that high and low achievers do not differ regarding the value that they attach to the goals that can be reached in the near future nor regarding the perceived instrumentality of studying hard for reaching those goals. But for the motivational goals in the distant future, the two differences are significant ($p < .01$) and in the predicted direction. High achieving students do attach more value to goals in the distant future and their present school work is more instrumental to reach those goals than is the case for low achieving students.

Perceiving the instrumentality of present study activities not only for more or less immediate goals but also for goals in the distant future, and to be able to attach a high valence to goals even if they can only be reached after a long time interval, increases the strength of motivation for the present instrumental actions.

In a replication of this study we now measure also individual differences in the extension of FTP to correlate them with perceived instrumentality and anticipated incentive value. We hypothesize that the motivational effect of differences in FTP is mediated by these two variables.

Affective Attitude Toward the Future

In the previous section we discussed the motivational meaning of FTP in its proper sense, as it is characterized by its extension, density, structure and degree of realism. Time orientation and time attitude are two other aspects of psychological time. Time orientation (De Volder, 1979) refers to the dominant or preferential direction of an individual's thoughts and actions towards the past, the present or the future. Time attitude means the more or less positive or negative attitude towards one's personal past, present, or future life period. The positive, neutral, or negative characteristics of past, present, and future events or experiences constitute the affective attitude toward the personal past, present, and future (Nuttin & Lens, 1985, p. 91). An individual's affective or emotional outlook on his or her future in general constitutes his or her affective attitude towards the future.

As for future time perspective, the affective attitude towards the future is also conceived of as a personality trait and related to other personality variables such as age, sex, social class, to success and failure experiences and to psychopathological disorders such as depression and suicidal ideation.

We have recently tried to study the motivational significance of the affective attitude towards the future, or its effects on study motivation and school performance among 12th grade high school boys (Van Calster, Lens, & Nuttin, 1986). To do so we translate this concept also into the language of the expectancy-instrumentality-value models in cognitive motivational psychology. In general, these models calculate the strength of motivation for an action as a multiplicative function of the subjective probability of an action outcome and the valence of the outcome (Vroom, 1964). The valence of an action-outcome is given by the algebraic sum of the products of the perceived instrumentality of the outcome for different consequences, and the valences of these consequences. More simply, the strength of motivation is measured by the algebraic sum of the products of the instrumental value of an action for reaching motivational goals and the anticipated value of those goals.

Studying and performing well in high school can be instrumental for very many goals in the near and in the distant future. Many of these goals may not be very specific yet for 12th grade boys. Therefore, Van Calster, Lens and Nuttin (1986) did not ask the students to generate their own goals, nor did they present them with such a list. We measured their affective attitude towards their personal future in general with the Time Attitude Scale (Lens, 1975; Nuttin & Lens, 1985). This score was then used as a substitute for the algebraic sum of the valences of all more or less important and personally relevant future goals. Secondly, we measured the instrumental value of studying or performing well in high school, not for a series of future goals, but for the personal future in general. The data confirmed the predicted interaction of perceived instrumentality (high versus low) and the affective attitude towards the future (low, medium, high). Students with a high positive attitude towards their future and high perceived instrumentality are significantly more motivated and obtain significantly higher exam scores than when they have a low (negative) attitude towards their future, or than when they have a high positive attitude but a low perceived instrumentality.

Summary and Conclusion

Although the behavioral role of the future was not completely denied in experimental psychology, it was at least strongly neglected for a long time. Theoretical concepts such as fractional antedating goal response, expectancy and anticipated incentive value were used to account for the present behavioral effects of goal objects in the immediate future.

The concept of future time perspective, as one aspect of the psychological future, was introduced in general psychology by Frank, Lewin, and others. Those early theoretical publications all stressed very much the motivational meaning or behavioral role of future time perspective as a personality trait. The anticipated future goal objects are integrated in the present life space and as such do effect present goal oriented behavior.

In spite of these original and well known theoretical conceptualizations of future time perspective as a cognitive-motivational variable, most empirical research used operationalizations or measures of FTP in which its motivational origin is lacking. Secondly, most of the research on FTP as a personality trait are correlational, differential studies in which FTP is seen as the criterion rather than as a predictor of an overt behavioral criterion.

In our own research and that of Rand and Gjesme in Oslo on the behavioral effects of FTP, more speculative theoretical considerations about the motivational role of FTP are replaced by the conceptual framework of the expectancy-instrumentality-value models in which the motivational effects of expectations for the future and of the anticipated values of motivational goals are formalized. This approach of FTP finds its origin in the original work of Atkinson, Raynor and Brown on the motivational significance of perceived instrumentality or importance of present success for future successes and Raynor's conceptualization of FTP in terms of task hierarchy and time hierarchy. We do, however, for the time being, still consider FTP and its aspects such as extension and affective attitude towards the future as a personality trait. Ongoing and future research is planned to find out if the motivational or behavioral effects of FTP can be accounted for via subjective expectancy and the anticipated incentive value of the goal object and the perceived instrumentality of present actions for future goals.

REFERENCES

Atkinson, J. W. (1964). *An introduction to motivation*. New York: Van Nostrand Reinhold Company.

Atkinson, J. W. (1966). An approach to the study of subjective aspects of achievement motivation. In Symposium 13, Motives and consciousness in man. *Proceedings of the 18th Int. Congress of Psychology*, Moscow.

Atkinson, J. W., & Birch, D. (1970). *The dynamics of action*. New York: Wiley.

Atkinson, J. W., & Feather, N. T. (Eds.). (1966). *A theory of achievement motivation*. New York: Wiley.

Barndt, R. J., & Johnson, D. M. (1955). Time orientation in delinquents. *Journal of Abnormal and Social Psychology, 51*, 343–345.

Bergius, R. (1957). *Formen des Zukunftserlebens*. München: Johann Ambrosius Barth.

Black, W. A., & Gregson, R. A. (1973). Time perspective, purpose in life, extraversion and neuroticism in New Zealand prisoners. *British Journal of Social and Clinical Psychology, 12*, 50–60.

Brim, O. G., & Forer, R. (1956). A note on the relation of values and social structure to the life planning. *Sociometry, 19*, 54–60.

Cantril, H. (1965). *The pattern of human concerns*. New Brunswick, NJ: Rutgers University Press.

Crespi, L. P. (1944). Amount of reinforcement and level of performance. *Psychological Review, 51*, 341–357.

De Volder, M. (1979). Time orientation: A review. *Psychologica Belgica, 19*, 61–79.

De Volder, M., & Lens W. (1982). Academic achievement and future time perspective as a cognitive-motivational concept. *Journal of Personality and Social Psychology, 42*, 566–571.

Edwards, W. (1954). The theory of decision making. *Psychological Bulletin, 51*, 380–417.

Epley, D., & Ricks, D. R. (1963). Foresight and hindsight in the TAT. *Journal of Projective Techniques, 27*, 51–59.

Feather, N. T. (Ed.). (1982). *Expectations and actions: Expectancy-value models in psychology*. Hillsdale, NJ: Erlbaum.

Fraisse, P. (1963). *The psychology of time*. Wesport, CT: Greenwood Press.

Frank, L. K. (1939). Time perspectives.. *Journal of Social Philosophy, 4*, 293–312.

Gjesme, T. (1974). Goal distance in time and its effect on the relations between achievement motives and performance. *Journal of Research in Personality, 8*, 161–171.

Gjesme, T. (1975). Slope of gradients for performance as a function of achievement motive, goal distance in time and future time orientation. *Journal of Psychology, 91*, 143–160.

Gjesme, T. (1981). Is there any future in achievement motivation? *Motivation and Emotion, 5*, 115–138.

Guyau, J. M. (1902). *La genèse de l'idée de temps*. Paris: Alcan.

Heckhausen, H. (1967). *The anatomy of achievement motivation*. New York: Academic Press.

Heckhausen, H. (1977). Achievement motivation and its constructs: A cognitive model. *Motivation and Emotion, 1*, 283–329.

Hull, C. L. (1943). *Principles of behavior*. New York: Appleton-Century-Crofts.

Hull, C. L. (1952). *A behavior system*. New Haven: Yale University Press.

Lamm, H., Schmidt, R. W., & Trommsdorff, G. (1976). Sex and social class as determinants of future orientation in adolescents. *Journal of Personality and Social Psychology, 34*, 317–326.

Lens, W. (1975). Sex differences in attitude towards the personal past, present, and future. *Psychologica Belgica, 15*, 29–33.

Lens, W, & Cassiman, B. (1984). *The motivational significance of anticipating a second chance to strive for success*. Unpublished manuscript, University of Leuven/Louvain, Research Center for Motivation and Time Perspective.

Lens, W., & Gailly, A. (1980). Extension of future time perspective in motivational goals of different age groups. *International Journal of Behavioral Development, 3*, 1–17.

Lersch, Ph. (1938). *Aufbau der Person*. München: Johann Ambrosius Barth.

Leshan, L. L. (1952). Time orientation and social class. *Journal of Abnormal and Social Psychology, 47,* 589–592.

Lewin, K. (1931). An address given in February 1931 at a convention on problems of the Montessori Method. *Die Neue Erziehung, 2,* 99–103.

Lewin, K. (1935). *A dynamic theory of personality: Selected papers.* New York: McGraw-Hill.

Lewin, K. (1938). *The conceptual representation and the measurement of psychological forces.* Durham, NC: Duke University Press.

Lewin, K. (1942a). Field theory of learning. *Yearbook of the National Society for the Study of Education, 41,* part 2, 215–242.

Lewin, K. (1942b). Time perspective and morale. In G. Watson (Ed.), *Civilian morale. Second yearbook of the S.P.S.S.L.* Boston: Houghton Mifflin.

Lewin, K. (1948). *Resolving social conflicts. Selected papers on group dynamics.* (Edited by G. W. Lewin). New York: Harper & Brothers.

McClelland, D. C. (1958). The use of measures of human motivation in the study of society. In J. W. Atkinson (Ed.) *Motives in fantasy, action and society* (pp. 518–552). Princeton, NJ: Van Nostrand.

McClelland, D. C., Atkinson, J. W., Clark, R. A., & Lowell, E. L. (1953). *The achievement motive.* New York: Appleton-Century-Crofts.

McDougall, W. (1923). *Outline of psychology.* New York: Scribner.

Miller, N. A. (1944). Experimental studies of conflict. In J. McV. Hunt (Ed.), *Personality and the behavior disorders, Vol. 1.* New York: Ronald Press.

Mischel, W. (1981). Objective and subjective rules for delay of gratification. In G. d'Ydewalle & W. Lens (Eds.), *Cognition in human motivation and learning* (pp. 33–58). Leuven & Hillsdale, NJ: Leuven University Press & Erlbaum.

Nuttin, J. (1964). The future time perspective in human motivation and learning. *Acta Psychologica, 23,* 60–82.

Nuttin, J. (1980). *Motivation et perspectives d'avenir.* Leuven: Presses Universitaires de Louvain/Leuven.

Nuttin, J. (1984). *Motivation, planning, and action: A relational theory of behavior dynamics.* Leuven & Hillsdale, NJ: Leuven University Press & Erlbaum.

Nuttin, J. (in press). *The respective role of cognition and motivation in behavior dynamics, intention, and volition.*

Nuttin, J. & Lens, W. (1985). *Future time perspective and motivation: Theory and research method.* Leuven & Hillsdale, NJ: Leuven University Press & Erlbaum.

Nuttin, J., Lens, W., Van Calster, K., & De Volder, M. (1979). La perspective temporelle dans le comportement humain. In P. Fraisse et al. (Eds.), *Du temps biologique au temps psychologique* (pp. 307–363). Paris: Presses Universitaires de France.

Raynor, J. O. (1969). Future orientation and motivation of immediate activity: An elaboration of the theory of achievement motivation. *Psychological Review, 76,* 606–610.

Raynor, J. O. (1970). Relationships between achievement-related motives, future orientation, and academic performance. *Journal of Personality and Social Psychology, 15,* 28–33.

Raynor, J. O. (1974). Future orientation in the study of achievement motivation. In J. W. Atkinson & J. O. Raynor, *Motivation and achievement* (pp. 121–154). Washington, DC: Winston & Sons.

Raynor, J. O. (1981). Future orientation and achievement motivation: Toward a theory of personality functioning and change. In G. d'Ydewalle & W. Lens (Eds.), *Cognition in human motivation and learning* (pp. 199–231). Leuven & Hillsdale, NJ: Leuven University Press & Erlbaum.

Raynor, J. O. (1982). Motivational determinants of music-related behavior: Psychological careers of student, teacher, performer, and listener. In J. O. Raynor & E. E. Elliot, *Motivation, career striving, and aging* (pp. 309–329). Washington, DC: Hemisphere.

Raynor, J. O., & Entin, E. E. (1982). *Motivation, career striving, and aging.* Washington, DC: Hemisphere.

Raynor, J. O., Atkinson, J. W., & Brown, M. (1974). Subjective aspects of achievement motivation immediately before an examination. In J. W. Atkinson & J. O. Raynor, *Motivation and achievement* (pp. 155–171). Washington, DC: Winston & Sons.

Renner, K. E. (1964). Delay of reinforcement: A historical review. *Psychological Bulletin, 61,* 341–361.

Rizzo, A. E. (1967). The time moratorium. *Adolescence, 2,* 429–480.

Rotter, J. B. (1954). *Social learning and clinical psychology.* New York: Prentice-Hall.

Rotter, J. B., Chance, J. E. & Phares, E. J. (1972). *Applications of social learning theory of personality*. New York: Holt, Rinehart & Winston.

Spence, K. W. (1956). *Behavior theory and conditioning*. New Haven: Yale University Press.

Stein, K. B. & Craik, K. H. (1965). Relationship between motoric and ideational activity preference and time perspective in neurotics and schizophrenics. *Journal of Consulting Psychology, 29*, 460–467.

Teahan, J. E. (1958). Future time perspective, optimism and academic achievement. *Journal of Abnormal and Social Psychology, 57*, 379–380.

Tolman, E. C. (1932). *Purposive behavior in animals and men*. New York: The Century Co.

Van Calster, K., Lens, W., & Nuttin, J. (1986). The affective attitude toward the personal future and its impact on motivation in high school boys. *American Journal of Psychology*.

Vroom, V. (1964). *Work and motivation*. New York: Wiley.

Wallace, M. (1956). Future time perspective in schizophrenia. *Journal of Abnormal and Social Psychology, 52*, 240–245.

Wallace, M., & Rabin, A. I. (1960). Temporal experience. *Psychological Bulletin, 57*, 213–236.

Wohlford, P. (1966). Extension of personal time, affective states and expectations of personal death. *Journal of Personality and Social Psychology, 3*, 559–566.

Woodworth, R. S. (1921). *Psychology: A study of mental life*. New York: Holt, Rinehart and Winston.

Epilogue

David C. McClelland

Harvard University

It was an impressive and moving experience to listen to the papers presented in this volume, to observe the interest and enthusiasm of the audience, and to chat with those who had been associated with Jack Atkinson at different stages in his career. The papers are solid contributions to knowledge about human motivation and reflect the way in which Atkinson fired several generations of students at the University of Michigan with enthusiasm for motivation research of very high quality. What is striking about the papers is their diversity: Clearly Jack fostered no orthodoxy but encouraged people to pursue a topic that had come up in the development of motivation theory and to think for themselves about it. And they have. So there are important new contributions here to topics that have long concerned him, to topics such as the dynamics of action, the relation of the situation and the person to action, of the role of a computer model in building a theory of motivation in action. This collection of papers is a testimony both to his ability to define important problems in the field of motivation that need resolution and to his energy and skill in encouraging others to work zealously to think through ways of resolving them. Figuring out the dynamics of action will be an enterprise that engages the attention of scholars as long as there are psychologists and people around for them to study, and I simply cannot imagine how anyone ever can attempt to deal with the problem without starting with the important theoretical and empirical contributions Atkinson and his associates have made of it.

But it is not my purpose to review the contributions to the study of motivation that Jack and those associated with him have made, to sift and sort them and evaluate their true worth. That is a task which I am neither objective nor competent enough to carry out well. And it can safely be left to history. It has seemed more appropriate for me to look back 40 years and reflect a little on how the whole creative enterprise got started and on the role that Jack played in it. For research studies of human motivation, particularly achievement motivation, using methods Jack and I had employed, grew in number from 1 to 2 a year in the early 1950s to 160 or so a year in the late 1970s (Heckhausen, Schmalt and Schneider, 1985). Interest in this type of research grew rapidly and spread to several centers in the United States, in Germany, India and other countries. Many books on the subject were published. One might almost speak of this development as a "movement" and think of the University of Michigan as the center of the movement because Jack Atkinson was there, and also Joe Veroff, guiding research in motivation.

So questions naturally arise such as how did this movement get started? Why did it develop so rapidly? What role did Jack play in it? These questions are particularly poignant today when the movement appears to be slowing down, as interest shifts away from motivation to cognition, and away from unconscious motives to self-reported values and attitudes, as chapters in this book testify. How did it all get started? And how did it happen to assume the shape it took? Since I was in at the beginning perhaps I am in the best position to shed some light on such questions.

It started in 1946 at Wesleyan University, a small liberal arts college in Middletown, Connecticut, which had a strong research tradition in psychology. I had just returned to teach there as a very junior assistant professor after spending the war years in Philadelphia at Bryn Mawr College. Jack had also returned from the war, which he had spent as a flight instructor, to finish his bachelor's degree. We had organized a symposium to celebrate the 50th anniversary of the founding of the psychological laboratory at Wesleyan; all the teaching staff were young and new; and many of the students were veterans who were highly motivated to get going and make up for the time they had lost in the war. More than that I felt strongly at the time that many of them had been through really horrifying experiences in the war which they seldom spoke about, at least to me, but which had developed in the most sensitive ones an intense interest in the darker side of human nature. They had seen their friends killed, were trained to kill others and perhaps succeeded, worked under conditions of intense boredom or intense vigilance for long hours, had been separated from loved ones never knowing for sure whether they would see them again. They had experienced emotions and motivational states that are very remote for the average undergraduate who has usually only read about them and experienced them vicariously. I felt then, and still feel that living intensely emotionally turns certain people's interest to inner states, to psychology, and particularly to the psychology of motivation, to trying to understand the basic springs of action and emotion. By way of contrast, in good times, when we seem pretty much in control of what we are experiencing, we tend to get more interested in cognitive factors that determine what we do. At such times life seems more like a game of chess in which you just have to figure out what to do to get a particular result and then do it. Perhaps that is why there is less interest in motivation today in a time of relative prosperity in which things are pretty much going our way, except of course for oppressed minorities at home and abroad. At any rate it is hard for people who have been kicked around by a war or as a persecuted minority to have all that much interest in rational calculations. They know that the feelings of others have often outweighed their own rational calculations.

One might ask, if this is so, why there wasn't an interest in motivation, particularly unconscious motivations, after the Vietnam War as I am claiming there was after World War II. The answer is that we won World War II and lost the Vietnam War. You not only have to be interested in unconscious motives, you have to have faith if you are to do scientific research on them, that you can win out in such an endeavor. So in 1946 I believe there was not only an intense interest in the darker forces in human psychology but also a belief that we could learn to understand them scientifically and ultimately to conquer them as we had conquered Hitler and the forces of darkness in World War II. After all it was not long after this that the Ford Foundation was set up with a charter written in part by psychologists which essentially argued that through the behavioral sciences we could learn enough about human nature to introduce peace, democracy and economic development throughout the world. The country in general felt this way in 1946. So did the Department of Psychology at Wesleyan which was young and had rededicated itself to the empirical study of human behavior. So did a significant number of veterans who were returning to normal life wanting to understand better the kinds of experiences they had undergone in the war. All that was required was a spark that would set in motion a movement to investigate human motivation scientifically.

Jack Atkinson was the spark. He arrived on campus ready to go, ready to return to the normal world of study, career, and baseball, having closed the book on his war experiences. His interests were primarily philosophical: He wanted to figure out even then what the ultimate springs of human behavior were and how they got translated into action. At Wesleyan the best students in psychology were encouraged to write a senior thesis as candidates for a degree with distinction. There were five such senior projects that year being carried out by very able students, all but one of them veterans. Jack's was the most philosophical. My recollection is that I persuaded him to gather some empirical evidence on the issues that interested him. His thesis title was "The Relationship Between an Individual's Needs and Values." Even then Jack was asking the important questions. We have been working on the answer to that one ever since and still have a ways to go before finding it although neither Jack nor I would be happy with the suggestions in this volume that the resolution to the issue involves ignoring or glossing over the differences between needs and values. For the whole starting point of the inquiry was the common observation that what people said they valued was not a good index of what they would do. And on the other hand vital needs not well-represented in consciousness often did seem to determine what people would do. War experiences demonstrated that. And Freud's notions about the importance of unconscious motives were just then beginning to affect thinking in academic psychology. If one were to understand the role of conscious values and unconscious motives in influencing behavior, the very first step would appear to be finding ways of measuring each of these variables and then studying how they related to each other and to action. That was to be the agenda for years to come.

But it required another historical accident to get the ball rolling. Jack was graduating in the middle of the 1946–47 academic year and while he had been admitted to graduate school at the University of Michigan the following September because of his brilliant record, he had to have some way to make a living until then. At the 50th anniversary celebration for the Wesleyan Psychological Laboratory, a Navy captain from the submarine base in New London, Connecticut had mentioned that the Office of Naval Research (ONR) was interested in supporting research in psychology. We had thought their interest would be in applied problems such as in the visibility of flares of different colors at sea, but to our surprise they provided financial support for Jack's interest in studying the effects of arousing a need like hunger on behavior. They were impressed by him, by the kinds of questions he asked, and they were also interested at that time in establishing the fact that they supported basic as opposed to simply applied research. Once we had received money for research of this kind, it seemed only natural that we would continue that kind of research in order to keep the money flowing in. So we moved on to arousing other motives like what we called the "need for Mastery" (later called the need for Achievement) to see what their effects would be on all kinds of behavior from performance to perception and apperception. In this way the movement to study human motivation gradually gained momentum.

But there is a key point in this little bit of history that should not be overlooked: In a very real sense I was Jack's first student in the psychology of motivation. He came to me with an interest in motivation, as other students did with other interests, at that time and since. He engaged me in thinking about motivation in order to help him plan his thesis and his subsequent work on ONR funds. There is no reason to think had he not been there that I would have gone into the field of human motivation. I was curious about lots of things at the time and felt that it was difficult and even a little boring to work in just one area which all my advisers had been saying I should do in order to become a real expert. Jack with the help of ONR funding changed all that. He has the gift of asking the right questions and of continuing to ask them over and over in different ways until you can't help but get involved in trying to answer them to clarify your understanding of what moves behavior. So I got started in the field of motivation by Jack just as his later students did.

As I think back over the origins of the movement of the scientific study of human motivation, I am reminded of Thomas Edison's statement that invention is one-tenth inspiration and nine-tenths perspiration, except that I would say it is nine-tenths motivation in the sense that someone has to keep fixated on a goal. The perspiration is the result of the fixation. And Jack has been a master of keeping fixated on a goal: He wants to figure out the springs of human action and he has persisted endlessly in pursuing that goal in such a way that it engaged not only himself in the quest for that knowledge but others like me and those represented in this book. We can all take heart from his example and renew our faith that a science of human behavior is really possible if we only persist as he has.

REFERENCE

Heckhausen, H., Schmalt, H. D., & Schneider, K. (1985). *Achievement motivation in perspective*. Orlando, FL: Academic Press.